HEALING LOVE THROUGH THE TAO

CULTIVATING FEMALE
SEXUAL ENERGY

*I have come upon Master Chia's Taoist prac-
tice in my old age and find it the most satisfying and enriching practice of all those I have
encountered in a long life of seeking and
practicing.*

Felix Morrow

HEALING LOVE THROUGH THE TAO
CULTIVATING FEMALE SEXUAL ENERGY

MANTAK CHIA & MANEEWAN CHIA

AWAKEN HEALING ENERGY

HEALING TAO BOOKS/Huntington, New York

PUBLISHER AND EDITOR: Felix Morrow

DESIGN AND PRODUCTION: David Miller

EDITOR: Valerie Meszaros

EDITORIAL CONTRIBUTORS: Helen Stites, Michael Winn, Juan Li

ILLUSTRATOR: Juan Li

First Published in 1986 by

Healing Tao Books

P.O. Box 1194

Huntington, NY 11743

ISBN: Cloth Edition 0-935621-04-0

Paperback Edition 0-935621-05-9

Library of Congress Card Number: 86-81049

Manufactured in the United States of America

01 02 03 04 05 / 20 19 18 17

CONTENTS

5. Cultivating Ovarian Power   68

8. Dual Cultivation

The Goal of the Taoist Practice
International Healing Tao Course Offerings
Outline of the Complete System of the Healing Tao
Course Descriptions:
    Introductory Level I: Awaken Healing Light
    Introductory Level II: Development of Internal Power
    Introductory Level III: The Way of Radiant Health
    Intermediate Level: Foundations of Spiritual Practice
    Advance Level: The Realm of Soul and Spirit

ACKNOWLEDGMENTS

I thank foremost those Taoist Masters who were kind enough to share their knowledge with me, never imagining it would eventually be taught to Westerners. I acknowledge special thanks to Marcia Kerwit for her written contributions, sharing her experiences and candid opinions concerning the practice of Healing Love.

I thank the artist, Juan Li, for his illustrations throughout the book. I also thank Suzanne Gage, illustrator of the book *A New View of a Woman's Body,* for her groundbreaking work in illustrating women's anatomy which provided inspiration for some of the drawings in this book.

I thank the many contributors essential to the book's final form: Gunther Weil, Ph.D., Rylin Malone, and many of my students for their feedback, particularly Michael Winn and Juan Li for their recommendations; Valerie Meszaros for editing the book, copyediting, and proofreading; Helen Stites for proofreading, and editing and copyediting assistance; and John-Robert Zielinski and Adam Sacks, our computer consultants. Special thanks are extended to David Miller for overseeing design and production and to Felix Morrow for his valuable advice and help in editing and producing this book, and for his work as publisher of Healing Tao Books.

Without my mother, my wife, Maneewan, and my son, Max, the book would have been academic—for their gifts, my gratitude and love.

A WORD OF CAUTION

The book does not give any diagnoses or suggestions for medication. It does provide a means to improve your health in order to overcome imbalances in your system and to provide a richly rewarding sexual experience. People who have high blood pressure, heart disease, or a generally weak condition, should proceed slowly in the practice, particularly Ovarian Breathing. If there is a medical condition, a medical doctor should be consulted.

ABOUT MASTER MANTAK CHIA
AND MANEEWAN CHIA

MASTER CHIA

Master Mantak Chia is the creator of the system known as The Healing Tao and is the Founder and Director of the Healing Tao Center in New York. Since childhood he has been studying the Tao way of life as well as other disciplines. The result of Master Chia's thorough knowledge of Taoism, enhanced by his knowledge of various other systems, is his development of the Healing Tao System, which is now being taught in many cities in the United States, Canada and Europe.

Master Chia was born in Thailand to Chinese parents in 1944, and when he was six years old he learned to "sit and still the mind"—i.e., meditation—from Buddhist monks. While he was a grammar school student, he first learned traditional Thai boxing and then was taught Tai Chi Chuan by Master Lu, who soon introduced him to Aikido, Yoga and more Tai Chi.

Later, when he was a student in Hong Kong excelling in track and field events, a senior classmate, Cheng Sue-Sue, presented him to his first esoteric teacher and most important Taoist Master, Master Yi Eng, and he began his studies of the Taoist way of life. He learned how to pass life-force power from his hands, how to circulate energy through the Microcosmic Orbit, how to open the Six Special Channels, Fusion of the Five Elements, Inner Alchemy, Enlightenment of the Kan and Li, Sealing of the Five Sense Organs, Congress of Heaven and Earth, and Reunion of Man and Heaven. It was Master Yi Eng who authorized Master Chia to teach and heal.

In his early twenties, Mantak Chia studied in Singapore with Master Meugi, who taught him Kundalini and Taoist Yoga and the Bud-

Mantak and Maneewan Chia

dhist Palm, and he was soon able to get rid of blockages of the flow of life-force energy in his own body as well as in the patients of his Master.

In his later twenties, he studied with Master Pan Yu, whose system combined Taoist, Buddhist and Zen teachings, and with Master Cheng Yao-Lun, whose system combined Thai boxing and Kung Fu. From Master Pan Yu he learned about the exchange of the Yin and Yang power between men and women and also the "Steel Body," a technique that keeps the body from decaying. Master Cheng Yao-Lun taught him the secret Shao-Lin Method of Internal Power and the even more secret Iron Shirt methods called "Cleansing the Marrow" and "Renewal of the Tendons."

Then, to better understand the mechanisms behind the healing energy, Master Chia studied Western medical science and anatomy for two years. While pursuing his studies, he managed the Gestetner Company, a manufacturer of office equipment, and became well acquainted with the technology of offset printing and copying machines.

Using his knowledge of the complete system of Taoism as the foundation, and building onto that with what he learned from his other studies, he developed the Healing Tao System and began teaching it to others. He then trained teachers to assist him, and later established the Natural Healing Center in Thailand. Five years later he decided to move to New York to introduce his system to the West, and in 1979 he opened the Healing Tao Center there. Since then, centers are have been established in many other locations, including Boston, Philadelphia, Denver, Seattle, San Francisco, Los Angeles, San Diego, Tucson and Toronto, and groups are forming in Europe, England, Germany, the Netherlands and Switzerland.

Master Chia leads a peaceful life with his wife, Maneewan, who teaches Taoist Five Element Nutrition at the New York Center, and their young son. He is a warm, friendly and helpful man, who views himself primarily as a teacher. He uses a word processor when writing his books and is equally at ease with the latest computer technology as he is with esoteric philosophies.

To date he has written and published five Healing Tao Books: in 1983, *Awaken Healing Energy Through the Tao;* in 1984, *Taoist Secrets of Love: Cultivating Male Sexual Energy;* in 1985, *Taoist Ways To Transform Stress Into Vitality;* and in 1986, *Chi Self-Massage: The Tao Way of Rejuvenation* and *Iron Shirt Chi Kung I. Healing Love through the Tao: Cultivating Female Sexual Energy* is his sixth book.

MANEEWAN CHIA

Born and raised through her early years in Hong Kong, Maneewan Chia subsequently moved with her parents to Thailand, where she grew up to attend the University and earn a B.S. degree in Medical Technology. Since childhood Mrs. Chia has been very interested in nutrition, which she learned by assisting her mother in Chinese health food cooking. Since her marriage to Mantak Chia, she has studied the Healing Tao System and presently assists him in teaching classes and running the Healing Tao Center.

AUTHOR'S NOTE

In the last pages of this book, the reader will find descriptions of the courses and workshops offered by our Healing Tao Centers. This material is also in effect a comprehensive description of the whole Taoist System. All of my books together will be a composite of this Taoist world view. Each of my books is thus an exposition of one important part of this system. Each sets forth a method of healing and life-enhancement which can be studied and practiced by itself, if the reader so chooses. However, each of these methods implies the others and is best practiced in combination with the others.

The foundation of all practices in the Taoist System, the Microcosmic Orbit Meditation, is the way to circulate CHI energy throughout the body and is described in my book *Awaken Healing Energy Through the Tao*. This practice is followed by the meditations of the Inner Smile and the Six Healing Sounds, set forth in my book *Taoist Ways To Transform Stress Into Vitality*. All three meditations are emphasized throughout the Taoist System, and their mastery is essential to your successful practice of Healing Love.

As you read the information provided in this book and become aware of concepts not contained in Western thought, you will deepen your understanding of the relevancy of these practices to your physical, emotional and spiritual advancement.

Mantak Chia

1. THE TAOIST VIEW OF WOMEN'S CHI ENERGY

A. How Energy is Used

The Taoist sages looked at their own energy as a total unit. In one day, for instance, a young and healthy person earns 100 percent of his required energy from eating, resting, and exercise, and spends approximately 60 to 70 percent maintaining his daily life: working, eating, digesting, breathing, walking, etc. One might consider 100 percent energy as 100 energy credits, similar to bank credit. But, as he ages, he gradually earns less and less, even though his body requires the same expenditures, and he starts to overdraw his account by drawing energy from the vital organs—the kidneys, liver, spleen, lungs, heart, and pancreas—and glands and, finally, from the brain.

Taoism explains that the major way men lose energy is through ejaculation, while women's major loss of energy occurs through menstruation, and not through sexual intercourse. For a young, healthy woman, this means an additional energy expenditure as she carries on her daily business. Assuming that a woman starts having periods at age twelve and continues through menopause in her fifties, she could have as many as 300 to 500 menstrual periods in her lifetime. Each month the ovaries produce an egg that contains highly perfected creative energy. A great deal of energy also goes into creating necessary hormones as well as the uterine lining, which provides a nest for a fertilized egg. If we consider our tremendous population today, we cannot afford many children, but we can afford one or two. This means we use only one or two eggs. The remaining 300 to 500 highly charged eggs are eliminated. This expenditure accounts for 30 to 40 percent of a woman's daily energy allotment. If this sexual energy is continually permitted to pour outward, she loses 30 to 40 percent of

27

her life-force energy. However, there is a way to transform this energy into vital energy for the organs, glands, brain, bone marrow and into spiritual energy.

B. The Principal Energy—"Jing"

We are all born with an abundance of energy that the Taoists call the principal energy, or "Jing." In women it is Jing, the generative or creative energy, that is necessary to make the eggs, create the uterine lining and hormones, and keep a woman sexually active. The Jing energy, supplemented with the energy of the air we breathe and the food we eat, permits the woman's body to endow her eggs with the life-force energy that will be carried into the next generation.

The Jing energy also converts into life-force energy for the organs, which energy is called "CHI." The ancient Taoists, after identifying this type of energy, observed that conserving or restoring Jing energy could promote a longer and healthier life.*

Sexual energy (creative energy) is the only energy that can be doubled, tripled or increased even more. Therefore, if we want to conserve or restore lost principal energy, sexual energy provides the means to create that extra power, if we conserve, recycle, and transform it back into principal energy. We then will have more energy available to transform into CHI, which in turn becomes transformed into another type of energy called "Shen." The word "Shen" means spiritual energy. (Figure 1-1)

Jing: Generative or creative energy. Jing is the most refined substance a person is born with. It is also referred to as the "Principal Energy" as it is essential for carrying out the functions of the body. All other energies in the body are dependent on Jing. Jing is transformed into Chi or life force as it interacts with the vital organs. The conservation and nurturing of Jing energy is the basis for the Taoist Internal practices. Jing is stored in all living tissue, especially the kidneys, sperm and ova.

Ching: Essential Energy. Ching is the energy produced by the sexual organs. In women it is the energy of the ovaries, in men, that of the sperm. Ching energy is denser than Chi and therefore moves slower when circulated in the body. As Ching energy circulates inside the body the organs are revitalized and nourished.

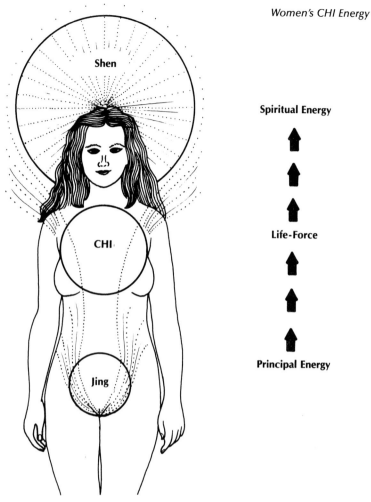

FIGURE 1-1
The Transformation of Principal Energy into
Life-Force and Spiritual Energy

C. Emotional Expense

When we are young and healthy we expend this principal energy, or Jing, freely, which serves us well until we reach the age of approximately 24 years. Although in the Tao System it is believed that each person is born with the good virtues of gentleness, kindness, respect, honesty, fairness and righteousness, when he or she grows up all kinds of cultural and social influences gradually change all the good virtues. The person begins to live under constant stress, feeling the pressures of hastiness, anger, fear, worry and other negative emotions. These gradually eat up the principal life-force, lessening the sexual creative energy. By the age of 24 too much of life's stress has developed and accumulated, accompanied by emotional disturbances or problems, and overstimulated sexual activity. The principal energy, spent so freely in younger years, begins to be transformed into a negative energy, stimulating and forcing more emotional energy and increasing sexual activity.

As the negative emotions drain the life-force from us, robbing us of our sexual energy, they can account for a loss of anywhere from 10 to 60 percent of our life-force energy. Too much negative emotional energy leaves us with less life-force energy to work with, and therefore less energy to build hormones and replace the lost sexual energy. There will not be enough energy left with which to build and feed the soul and spirit.

1. "Dumping" Negative Emotions

People regard negative emotions as "garbage energy" which must be disposed of in some way. Since negative emotional energy and sexual energy still constitute our life-force energy, if we dispose of or dump out this "garbage energy," we are also dumping out our life-force. Now, to supply the needs of our bodies, we continue to draw from our principal energy, and by the time we are 40, we have spent 50 to 60 percent of it. By the age of 65 most of us are living from a dwindling amount of this vital energy until, finally, we run out of it.

The law of energy is that energy cannot be destroyed, it can only be transformed. When you dispose of this negative or "garbage energy" by "dumping" it out, someone else has to pick it up. When you dump your anger on someone, that person also has to dump it, and if he or she cannot dump it on you, it will be dumped onto someone else. This anger will eventually come back to you again with extra force, bringing with it fear, sadness, haste and all kinds of stress. This is also impossible to bear, so you again find a way to dump it. There will be no end to the dumping, and the negative emotions will continue to multiply. This will greatly reduce sexual, creative, and generative energy.

D. Life-Force Energy (CHI)

1. Transforming Negative Energy into Life-Force Energy (CHI)

You need to know how to transform negative energy into positive energy and good feelings. In this book you will learn how to gradually restore lost sexual, creative and generative energy by opening a certain channel that runs through your body. Once you have your channel open through techniques such as Ovarian Breathing, you can circulate both the negative energy and the sexual energy through this channel. As these two energies are combined and circulated, a natural process of combustion changes the negative energy to life-force energy. This creates a positive energy cycle, giving you more vital energy to cope with your negative emotions.

There is another way to deal with negative emotional energy: by directly transforming it back into positive CHI. Later in the Healing Tao practice, by learning the Fusion of the Five Elements, the second part of the Taoist meditation, we will learn how to harmonize the different types of emotional energy with the organs that have come to be associated with them. We differentiate these associations (hot/heart/impatient/hasty, cold/kidney/fearful, warm/liver/angry, mild/warm/spleen/worry, and cool/dry/lung/sad/grief), becoming aware of their presence or appearance, as well as the different kinds of negative energy that remain trapped in our organs where they may later turn into illnesses. By using Fusion of the Five Elements, we can counteract, harmonize and transform the negative energy into positive life-force.

2. Gaining Additional CHI through Lovemaking

The only way to gain additional CHI is to transform sexual energy that would normally be released in lovemaking by recycling it back into CHI, thereby providing us with an extra 30 to 40 percent of life-force. In this book you will learn the Taoist methods of Healing Love to accomplish this: namely, Ovarian Breathing and the Orgasmic Upward Draw. Both methods will help to recycle and transform a part of the sexual energy into CHI.

3. CHI—the Key to Attaining Good Health

The Taoist masters view CHI as the key to attaining good health and realize that good health enables us to condense and transfer more CHI to a higher grade of energy. This enables us to have even more CHI available to build up the energy body, or soul body, and create and nourish the most important thing in each of our lives: our immortal spirit, or spirit body. With our present rate of energy expenditure, we have no extra energy to accomplish this.

In the health field today there are many methods available to help us increase life-force (CHI), such as massage, acupressure, shiatsu, jin shin do, jin shin jyutsu, tai chi chuan, chi kung, health food, herbs, meditation, yoga, etc. However, it is the Taoist Masters' view that the most abundant and easiest energy that can be transformed into CHI and a higher grade of energy is sexual energy. In the Healing Love practice we show very clearly a way to recycle sexual energy and store it, but it is most important to transform it first into CHI and then spiritual energy. Otherwise you will gradually build up too much CHI, which can lead to serious imbalances.

Young people, for example, have a lot of life-force energy available, but they do not know how to channel it properly. Their answer is to burn up excess energy in the fastest way: by using drugs, consuming alcohol, smoking, or other stimulants. These methods of stimulation initially give the user ten or twenty times as much energy, but they draw all the energy out from wherever it is available, namely, the organs, glands, and brain. Afterwards the user is left with low-key energy. When he or she wants to return to the same high level of energy, it means a return to the stimulants, but this time the user has less energy to draw from, and the high will not be the same. The result is a higher dosage, or changing to a more powerful stimulant. A person who is in a low-key CHI energy state will not be as affected by the drug because the drug does not have much life-force energy to draw from. For this reason young people become much more easily dependent upon drugs, sex, or other addictions. Transforming the abundant CHI properly will eliminate the need to burn the energy up with stimulants or participate in excessive sexual activity.

E. Creative Force—Sexual Energy

The basic function of sex is reproduction. Beyond that, each time we are sexually active we generate a lot of life-force energy. When we have a normal orgasm, the life-force pours out of us into the universe. If we can learn to redirect the orgasmic energy inward and upward instead of outward, the energy will reach a higher center of the body, and we will experience the even greater orgasmic experience known as total body orgasm, or organs' and glands' orgasm, an experience never felt as a result of normal sex. Thus, we can create more energy, store it, and transform it into life-force energy, thereby increasing our total energy.

1. Positive Energy Will Increase Sexual Creative Energy

Thus far, in keeping with the teachings of the Taoist Masters, we have been classifying our body energy into many different types of energy: positive and negative, sexual, life-force, etc. All of these energies have very different properties. If we identify them, we can start to control them, transforming everything negative into positive, and cultivating the good energies that please us.

Just as negative emotions deplete our life-force, thereby reducing sexual creative energy, cultivating good virtue increases sexual creative energy. By using the Orgasmic Upward Draw method taught in this book, instead of losing sexual energy through outward-leaking orgasms, we bring the highly charged sexual creative energy up to wrap, pack and energize the organs and glands. In the Tao System it is within the organs that our emotions, or virtues, are stored. Once an organ is restored to its original healthy condition, good virtue will emerge and can be cultivated to produce more positive energy to nurture each of the other organs and the glands. As weak, sick organs begin to produce good energy, they will gradually affect other organs, making them healthy as well.

2. Good Virtue—the Heart of the Healing Tao

Practicing good virtue is the heart of the Healing Tao. The entire system depends upon the energy of love, joy, kindness, gentleness, respect, and honesty. In the Healing Tao we believe that good nature is basic to humans, not because we are afraid of going to hell and burning eternally, of returning as a lower animal form, or of suffering in our next life, but because we believe that doing good for others is equally and immediately beneficial to ourselves. It is a simple concept. When you are kind to others, you are kind to your liver, the organ associated with kindness. Your liver becomes stronger as you give it more life-force. The idea is that you do good to others as you do good to yourself, but not out of fear of being punished.

In the Healing Love practice we return the flow of our sexual creative energy into our organs and glands to strengthen the weakened body and increase the life-force. The development of more good life-force helps in the transformation of all anger, fear, sadness and depression.

3. Losing-Energy Pleasure and Gaining-Energy Pleasure

If a woman is not interested in having a baby, her sexual activity is for pleasure only. The Taoists identify two kinds of pleasure: "losing-energy pleasure" and "gaining-energy pleasure." Most of us are well experienced in losing-energy pleasure.

We have described the brief, intense pleasure that drugs, such as marijuana, heroin, cocaine, or amphetamines, introduce into the system as they quickly draw and burn up life-force from a person's organs, brain, and glands. This is like a bonfire started with gasoline—it burns very intensely and is very gratifying, but the fuel is gone and the fire becomes extinguished all too soon. The increased desire to experience that intense excitement, followed by the increased use of drugs, draws out the vital energy from the organs as well as from the brain and bone marrow.

Some of the entertainment we seek is also losing-energy pleasure. When we are entertained in excess with activities such as watching television, energy from our organs is required to pay attention, and so our life-force energy is drawn out toward the event we are watching and hearing. We imagine ourselves to feel good because we perceive ourselves as relaxing, thereby decreasing our stress. We do feel the release, but our vital organs are being drained of their life-force by this excessive energy expenditure. This stress to our organs creates a negative energy, and if we do not have the means to transform it back into positive energy, we will accumulate too much and eventually our negative emotions will burst out.

Even though something such as quiet music can help us relax and create a sense of harmony in the body, too much attention to it will make our eyes, ears and nervous system lose energy to the outside. Afterwards, we continually seek new songs, movies and shows because these things are never satisfying our needs, but are further arousing and increasing our need for stimulation. The more we try to satisfy one or two of the senses by an outside means, the greater the need for satisfaction we create for all the senses. When you try to satisfy the mouth and tongue, the eyes, ears and nose need something to stimulate them. It is a never-ending, increasing requirement of the senses. Multibillion-dollar businesses have arisen to satisfy our senses. They make tremendous profits because ultimately they do not really satisfy us or bring us true joy and true happiness. If these companies created entertainment that would satisfy us for a long time, they would go out of business.

The Taoists regard our organs as the body's parents and the senses as the children. When they separate there is no harmony, but rather disharmony and need. People try to search for happiness, satisfaction and love outside of themselves rather than within. They listen to the desires of their bodies rather than their minds and spirits. The more they search, the more they create a need and will never really find what they are looking for. Instead they create a deterioration within themselves. True happiness, true joy and true satisfaction come with inner peace.

By turning inward we will not lose the energy outward, and so can gain energy for ourselves. For example, if we eat a tasty food but do not have an inner harmony in our organs and senses, our eyes will want more, like children in a toy store. We might decide to see a movie, and then the ears want to be stimulated as well. We then might decide to go to a nightclub or a bar. In the end we might feel the need to get drunk, to smoke, or take drugs. Turning sexual energy and the resultant orgasm inward is the first step to gaining-energy pleasure and to a control of the senses. Once you have more sexual energy inside, the organs will become stronger and will then be able to control, satisfy, and balance the senses.

35

4. "Beyond Orgasm"

The normal outward-pouring orgasm is a form of losing-energy pleasure, i.e., we release life-force energy out and we experience pleasure. In the Taoist view of arousal, however, it is the fusion of all the energy contributed by the organs and glands with the highly refined sexual energy that creates orgasmic energy. Rather than releasing orgasms outward, as in the normal sexual act, we learn to turn this energy inward to recycle, increase and highly refine it. Through the practice of the life-force meditation known as the Microcosmic Orbit meditation, we begin to learn how to recycle the ovaries' energy. In the beginning it is difficult and you must practice to retain the energy within yourself, but once you feel and gain control of your own energy, you will experience new pleasures which are indescribable. This sensation is called "Beyond Orgasm" or "Valley Orgasm."

The concept of an orgasm that is "Beyond Orgasm" is difficult to explain because we do not have a word in Western languages or a cultural concept to express it. It is a new idea to us. Remember, however, that when the automobile was invented, few people thought it could replace the horse. Later, people realized the benefits of the horseless carriage.

Cultivation of "Beyond Orgasm" can be compared to climbing a 10,000-foot mountain. In normal orgasm we run up 1,000 feet and run back down and try again tomorrow to get past 1,000 feet. Most people climb the mountain this way, perhaps reaching 2,000 feet on a good day. The sensations may be limited to the genitals or rhythmic pulsations, and relaxation may be experienced throughout the entire body, but the energy itself is lost to the universe and can no longer be developed inside the body. "Beyond Orgasm" goes further and further each time. When you climb this 10,000-foot mountain, you climb to 1,000 feet, rest, set up camp and spend the night. The next day you climb further, rest and camp, and you continue in this manner until you reach the peak. There you enter another realm of pleasure.

F. What is Ovarian Kung Fu?

Originally the Taoist sexual exercises were called "Ovarian Kung Fu." Some students feel this sounds too violent or too much like martial arts. The term "kung fu," however, means discipline or intensive work, referring to one who puts time into practice. Ovarian Kung Fu implies an expression of power and control, of the ability to take command of one's body and sexual life.

In the Healing Tao System's Ovarian Kung Fu training, we practice to gain, increase, collect and transform ovarian (sexual) energy. It is important to remember that building up energy in your body without knowing what to do with it is dangerous. Some systems advocate releasing the energy from time to time in some way, like releasing a pressure valve. They will recommend occasional outward-pouring orgasms for this purpose. The Healing Tao System, however, stresses the importance of learning the Microcosmic Orbit, the means by which the energy can be circulated in the body, ultimately to be stored in a safe area (the navel) for later use and transformation into a higher form of energy. If you consider a computer analogy, learning how to push a button will not teach you how to operate a computer. Although pushing the button will give you a result, until you know and understand the system, you will not be able to control that result. To insure proper training in the art of Healing Love, the concepts, the steps involved, and an idea of the pleasure that lies ahead will be explained in detail.

G. Women's Sexual Energy

1. The Ovaries Contain Life-Force Energy

As previously stated, the Jing (principal) energy of a woman provides her with life-force energy. This life-force energy is contained to a large extent in the ovaries. It is here that the hormones are produced that determine a woman's breasts, voice, etc. The ovaries constantly produce sexual energy. The Ovarian Breathing Process to be taught in this book releases the energy produced by the ovaries, and makes it possible to store this energy, which has a Yang (active) quality, in the woman's body. After ovulation and before menstruation the energy is milder, as the properties of the energy change from Yang to Yin (passive). Also, during this part of the cycle the energy is at its highest stage of development for absorption and transformation.

Ovarian Breathing, if practiced every day, can start the absorption process and conserve the life-force energy that otherwise would be lost through menstruation. This is the process by which the sexual energy is transformed to CHI. As a result of this practice, women often notice a distinct shortening of the duration of the menstrual flow, or a decrease of cramps or other problems associated with their periods. With continued practice menstruation may cease, because all the sexual energy is being transformed into a higher life-force energy.

Under ordinary circumstances menstruation can stop for a variety of reasons, such as poor diet, depression, emotional stress, childbirth or menopause. Since a functioning body draws its energy from every resource it has, a body requiring additional energy makes compensations to supply that energy where it is needed. A nursing mother, for example, will not experience menstruation, because the blood normally involved in the menstrual cycle would be drawn to the breast and converted into milk. Menstruation resumes only when nursing stops. Women athletes, when under strict training, will cease menstruating because all the energy has been transferred into physical fitness. Similarly, it should be noted that many women, after menopause, lead very active, healthy lives, and usually do well in pursuing their careers, because their bodies now have the benefit of energy formerly required to maintain their monthly cycles.

It is beneficial to understand that menstruation is for the purpose of the next generation. Energy not used for this purpose but conserved through Ovarian Breathing becomes part of the vital energy of the body, thereby prolonging youth and providing ample energy for transformation into a higher form of energy. The transformed energy is a creative and healing energy which can raise a woman's life-force potential and ultimately increase her spiritual energy. Also, the cessation of menstruation can be reversed at any time and restored to normal flow after a few months of stopping the practice.

2. Ovarian Energy Develops a Higher Consciousness

Ovarian energy is the energy used for the development of one's higher consciousness. These practices that transform the sexual energy into CHI provide the foundation for the spiritual exercises that transform sexual and CHI energy into Shen, a sheer spiritual energy. The process of cleansing the internal organs of negative emotions described previously is called "inner alchemy" by the Taoists, and it is this inner alchemy that restores to the organs their birthright of love, joy, gentleness, kindness, respect, honesty, fairness, and righteousness. Once the organs are cleansed and healthy, and you have developed the ability to transfer and transform sexual energy into life-force energy, the spiritual development can begin. It is at this level that the generative energy of the ovaries is used in what the Taoists call "giving birth to yourself," which means developing the spirit body from which you will attain enlightenment.

3. Ovary Energy—the Best Cosmetic

The ovaries contribute most of their energy during sexual arousal. Many other organs are contributors—the liver, spleen, kidneys, heart, lungs, and brain, as well as glands—the pineal, pituitary, thymus, thyroid and adrenal. All of these energies blend together to form sexual energy, a highly charged force that brings us to the point of orgasm. It is at this point that our habit of losing-energy pleasure must be overcome. By doing Ovarian Kung Fu exercises, we can transfer this energy to a higher quality energy by moving it up the spine to the brain. Because the properties of sexual energy during arousal is Yang (or active) in nature, you can revitalize the nervous system, increase brain power and memory, and stay healthy and youthful. As a great secret taught by the Taoist sages to empresses and concubines, these methods enabled the women in an emperor's court to maintain their sexual activity, beauty, and health for a long time. Many Taoist women consider the results of these exercises to be the best cosmetic in existence.

4. Duration of a Woman's Sexual Life

In ancient Chinese history very little was written about the sexual experiences of women, although there does exist the documentation of Su Nu, the medical and spiritual guide to the Yellow Emperor, who in almost endless lists detailed the voluptuous responses of women to their capable lovers. We also have read that nuns in Buddhist convents could learn exercises that would eliminate their menstrual cycles forever. (The exercises were called "Slaying the Red Dragon.") Therefore, what knowledge we now have of the duration of a Taoist woman's sexual life passed down to us verbally from the Taoist sages varies greatly with the outlook and lineage of the Master. Some Taoist Masters advise women to stop having sex after 40, due to the supposed worn out state of the body caused by childbirth. With the Ovarian Kung Fu method as it is now taught by The Healing Tao, a woman can continue sexual activity for as long as she desires because no energy is lost; in fact, energy is gained through the transformation of her sexual energy.

5. Organs' Orgasm—the True Orgasm

A. THE OUTWARD ORGASM

Generally the orgasmic feeling is a pulsation of the vagina, the ovaries and the cervix. In the Tao System we say that a lower center, or genital, orgasm happens only in the genital region and pours outward; we call this an "outward orgasm." It takes a short time to occur, but it takes a long time to bring the woman to this kind of orgasm.

B. THE INWARD ORGASM

The "inward orgasm," or the "organs' and glands' orgasm," is extended for the woman. Her partner must stimulate her to bring the orgasm inward and upward, stage by stage, and organ by organ. The orgasmic feeling can be amplified intensely in this way, but how much it intensifies depends upon how much she practices. By moving the pulsation into the organs, a new field of orgasm is opened up that she has never felt before.

In usual sexual practices muscles are tense and the fluids of the glands pour out, losing in this outward flow the sexual energy of these glands as well. This kind of orgasm is temporary, short and not continuous. In Taoism it is said that when all the energy pours out, that is the end of the journey.

In an inward orgasm, or organs' orgasm, the orgasm actually travels through all the organs, glands and nervous system, thrilling and revitalizing them with the life-force of sexual, creative and generative energy.

6. Who is Responsible for your Orgasm?

Many women have sexual experiences but are unable to experience an orgasm. Often a woman will blame her male partner, saying that he does not know how to bring her to orgasm, and that he ejaculates too soon. Sex is a two-person happening. The energies of both people must bring their hormones into harmony.

H. A Good Sexual Relationship—the Three Levels of Sexual Energy

To establish and maintain a good sexual relationship, the energies of both partners must be on the same level: they both must be healthy physically and emotionally, and their spiritual levels must be the same. Then, when the two people are together, their energies—physical, emotional, and, finally, spiritual—unite as one.

1. Physical Level

Tuning yourself before making love is very important. How much differs from woman to woman, depending upon her level of energy. The practices of Ovarian Breathing and the Orgasmic Upward Draw strengthen a woman's vagina and direct the CHI flow to her sexual organs. Many women who do not exercise the lower region—the ovaries, cervix and vagina—lack CHI flow and lose muscle tone. Eventually the energy leaks out, turning the sexual region cold. Their menstrual periods might come at the wrong time. They might have pre-menstrual syndrome, headaches, lower abdominal aches, or adverse emotional reactions, any of which can affect their energy levels, lowering their sexual energy as well as their general energy. It takes a much longer time for a woman to be aroused to her "boiling point," or point of orgasm, than it takes a man to become aroused. It takes more heat and energy to bring ice water to a boil, just as it takes longer for a partner to arouse a woman if her sexual region is cold. If a man is low in "fire energy" (male sexual Yang energy), he will not have enough energy to melt the "ice" and will not be able to bring the woman to her "boiling point."

For men the recycling of sexual energy is very important. Such techniques as Testicle Breathing, Scrotal Compression and the Big Draw recycle a man's sexual energy and increase his Yang (hot) sexual potential. These techniques are presented in the book *Taoist Secrets of Love: Cultivating Male Sexual Energy*.

2. Emotional Level

Often when a man and woman first meet there is an unexplained attraction for one another. The reason might be that at the time they both have a high energy level, as well as emotional and spiritual levels. It is as if a strong magnetic force has drawn them together. Sometimes after marriage stress occurs because of family troubles, children, etc., and their energies are drained, gradually wearing out their magnetic forces until there no longer is a strong attraction between them. During this period the man and woman seem far apart and alone. We see many people starting out in the practices of the Microcosmic Orbit and Taoist Secrets of Love become aware of and improve the foods they eat and do regular exercises to increase their romantic forces and reestablish a close feeling with their partner. Orgasms come much easier then.

3. Spiritual Level

If a couple can find time to do meditation together, sit with each other, or do palm-to-palm touching of one another, they will quiet down and be able to feel the energy of the partner. Energy can still be exchanged with your partner even if he is low in energy and unable to move it. You can expand your Microcosmic Orbit into his, and he can do the same with you so that you can help one another move the energy.

If he is in a low mood, you can assist him by sending him your smiling energy. If you learn the Fusion of the Five Elements, you can actually absorb his negative emotions and fuse them to return good life-force back to him. He can do the same to you.

A good sexual relationship can involve many other factors, but it must have a good beginning, like fine wine.

I. The Goal of Taoist Meditation

1. The Discovery of CHI

Long ago it was discovered that the most effective way to observe the subtle workings of the Tao and the inner nature of men and women was through quieting the mind in sitting meditation. It was the practice of sitting meditation that revealed the existence of CHI as a subtle electromagnetic force flowing within the body. The pathways the CHI followed revealed the meridian system of the human body.

2. The Body is Composed of Three Parts

Through such meditation the early Taoists developed a greater refinement and increased awareness of the body as a composite of three parts: the physical body, soul body and spirit body. (Figure 1-2) These three bodies were studied to differentiate each one's nature and purpose.

Unlike other meditative traditions of Asia, which cultivate the soul and spirit at the expense of the physical body, the ancient Taoists considered all three bodies important. The Taoists found a way to climb consciously into the spiritual realms, and equally important, to climb back into the physical world to be creatively active here.

3. Developing the Physical Body

The novice in the Healing Tao System begins with a wide range of exercises which develop the physical body into an efficient and healthy organism, capable of living peacefully in the world, and yet free of the tensions and stresses of ordinary daily life. The aim of the first level is to develop self-awareness of the physical body and its energy relationship with the environment and other people. At this level one learns to heal oneself by learning to sense and direct the circulation of CHI within the meridian system of the body (the Micro-

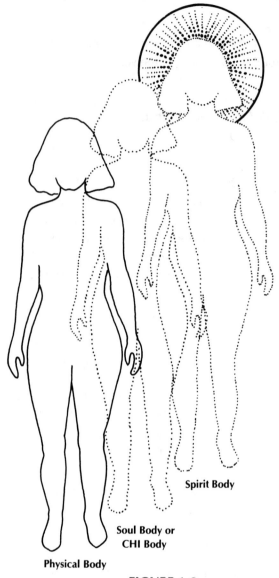

Spirit Body

**Soul Body or
CHI Body**

Physical Body

FIGURE 1-2

The Three Bodies

cosmic Orbit Meditation). The practice of loving self-awareness gener-
ates a positive energy condition in which greater respect and love for
others radiates constantly without conscious effort. The healthier the
body is, the more CHI it can produce and transfer into spiritual energy.
By practicing in this life to transfer CHI energy into spiritual energy, we
give birth to ourselves, raise our souls and spirits, and educate them.

The first level of Taoist practice is accomplished by utilizing the Microcosmic Orbit Meditation, Six Healing Sounds, Inner Smile, Fusion of the Five Elements, Tai Chi Chi Kung, Five Elements Nutrition, and Iron Shirt Chi Kung. As the awareness of the physical body is developed, increased levels of energy are made available by controlling and transforming sexual energy through Seminal Kung Fu and Ovarian Kung Fu practices.

4. Giving Birth to the Self, the Soul Body

Giving birth to the self, the goal of Taoist meditation, is awakening that part of oneself which perceives and acts free of the boundaries of environmental education and karmic conditioning. The birth of the self is not a symbolic image or poetic metaphor; it is an actual process of energy conversion leading to the formation of a subtle body with the capacity to develop reasoning, feelings and a will of its own.

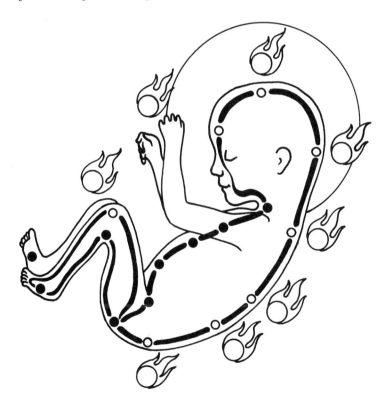

2. WOMEN'S SEXUAL ANATOMY

The publication of Masters' and Johnson's *Human Sexual Response* in 1966 opened the floodgates for books, articles, and seminars that interlocked with the sexual revolution of the sixties and seventies. The little-known profession of sexology burgeoned.

Gradually, sexologists began to pay attention to the particular sexual needs of women. They noticed that it was a rare man who went to his grave without ever having an orgasm, yet there were quite a number of women having little experience in sexual orgasm. Lonnie Barbach addressed herself to "pre-orgasmic" women in her book *For Yourself.* In *The Hite Report* Shere Hite disclosed how women brought themselves to orgasm, based on the anecdotal responses of hundreds of women to her vast questionnaire. Compiled by the Federation of Feminist Women's Health Centers, the book entitled *A New View of a Woman's Body* took a new look at women's genitals and redefined the clitoris.

It is a social fact that most women have never looked closely at another woman's genitals. Of the women who picked up a mirror to scrutinize their own (after making sure the door was locked or that no one else was home), many were left with the feeling that somehow they were not put together entirely correctly. The sexual isolation of women results in the complete absence of a socially acceptable word that encompasses everything we can see in a mirror. "Down there" is probably the closest we have come to saying that there exists a large area that we recognize as being our sexual organs. (Figure 2-1)

A. The Mount of Venus

Starting at the front and top is the Mount of Venus (also called the mons veneris, or mons, for short). (Figure 2-2) The color, amount, texture and distribution of hair will depend a great deal upon age and

46

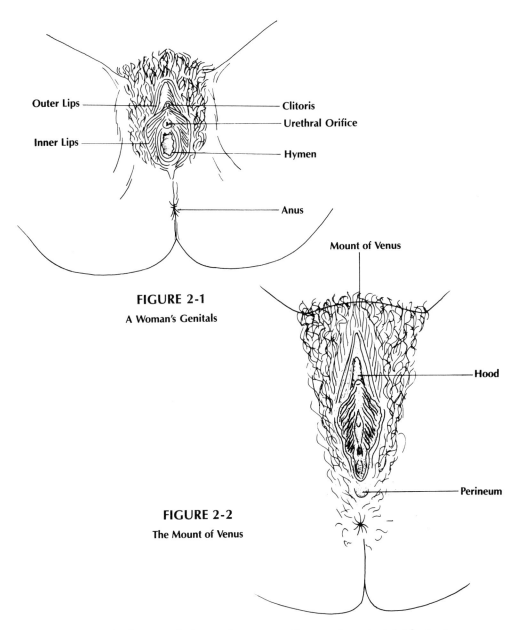

Outer Lips

Inner Lips

Clitoris

Urethral Orifice

Hymen

Anus

FIGURE 2-1

A Woman's Genitals

Mount of Venus

Hood

Perineum

FIGURE 2-2

The Mount of Venus

inherited characteristics and can vary from a few straight hairs to a bushy growth extending up the abdomen or down the thighs. The mons is a cushion of fat protecting the pubic bone underneath. The pubic bone is the place where the pelvic bones are joined together by cartilage, which during pregnancy softens so that the bones can separate, if necessary, during childbirth. The mons divides and separates into what is called the outer lips, or labia majora, which are of similar skin and hairiness as the mons.

47

B. The Inner Lips

Inside the outer lips are the inner lips, the labia minora. The skin of the inner lips is very different in color and texture because of their relation to the mucous surfaces in the same way that the lips of the mouth are different from the skin of the face. In an unaroused state the inner lips can vary in color from pink to dusky pink to dark maroon or purple. Sometimes the inner lips are pink and ridged, and sometimes they are long and wavy. Some women's inner lips are larger than the outer lips, and when these women are standing up, the inner lips can be seen protruding from between the outer lips. During sexual arousal the inner lips, richly supplied with blood vessels, become engorged and swell to two or three times their resting size. As orgasm approaches they can go through a dramatic color change, sometimes turning crimson or a dark wine color.

C. The Glans of the Clitoris

Following the small lips to the top, they join together to form the hood that protects the glans of the clitoris. Usually the glans in the unerect state is nestled under the hood. (Figure 2-3(a)) You can see it by pulling back on the hood. The glans of the clitoris is loaded with nerves, and for most women the glans is the most acutely sensitive spot in their sexual anatomy. Some women find that it is so sensitive that direct stimulation can be irritating. The shaft of the clitoris feels like a strong rubber band under the surface between the glans and the mons. As sexual excitement mounts, the shaft thickens and shortens, and the glans, shaft and supporting structures become erect. As with men, there can be a dramatic change in size and shape. (Figure 2-3(b)) Some women find that with intense prolonged arousal the swollen inner lips can obscure the glans almost entirely.

D. The Urethra and Vagina

Down from the glans is the opening to the urethra. Below this is the opening to the vagina. A woman's urethra is about one and a half inches long from the outside to where it opens into the bladder. This short distance from the outside to the inside helps explain women's propensity toward bladder infections (cystitis).

48

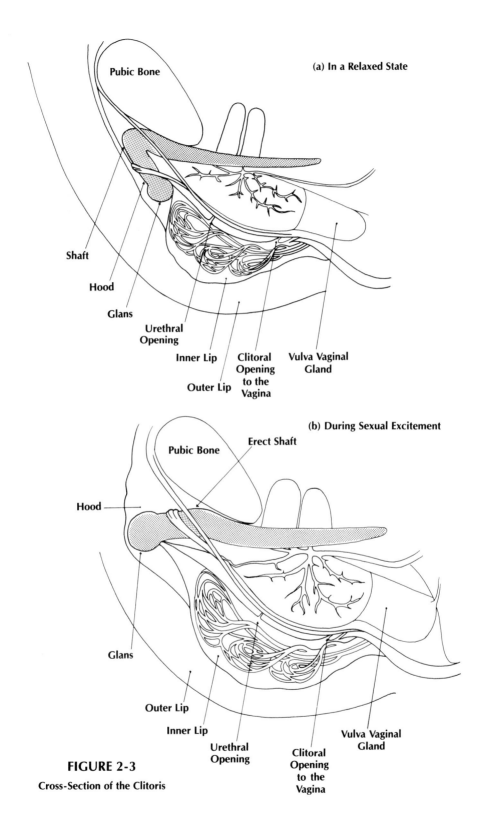

(a) In a Relaxed State

Pubic Bone

Shaft

Hood

Glans

Urethral
Opening

Inner Lip

Outer Lip

Clitoral
Opening
to the
Vagina

Vulva Vaginal
Gland

(b) During Sexual Excitement

Erect Shaft

Pubic Bone

Hood

Glans

Outer Lip

Inner Lip

Urethral
Opening

Clitoral
Opening
to the
Vagina

Vulva Vaginal
Gland

FIGURE 2-3

Cross-Section of the Clitoris

E. The G-Spot

Surrounding the urethra is a plexus of blood vessels. Since these blood vessels had no name in medical books, a group of women named the area the urethral sponge. (See *A New View of a Woman's Body*.) During sexual excitement the blood vessels engorge and a bulge can be felt through the vaginal wall. This bulge has been named the "G-Spot," after Grafenberg, one of the first sexologists. It can be explored by feeling around the front and upper part of the inside of the vagina. (It has also been said that the G-Spot is located one-half inch deeper than a woman's longest finger.)

The G-Spot can be difficult to reach during intercourse in a face-to-face position, except with those men whose penises, when erect, press up against their bellies. A change in position may be necessary if a woman wants her G-Spot stimulated more directly. Rear entry is one way. Fingers are often effective and direct. A woman stimulating herself might choose to squat or lie down with her legs up in the air in order to reach it better. Her partner might find it easier to reach if she is lying on her stomach. During coitus, if the woman is on top she can position herself pretty precisely for such stimulation. (Figure 2-4(a) and (b))

Some women, while holding their partners tightly, enjoy the sensation of an erect penis pushing on their lower abdomen, immediately above the pubic bone, stimulating the G-Spot from the other side.

When the G-Spot is massaged, often a woman's first impression is that she has to urinate. Sexologists assure women that if the pressure is continued there will be a transition to sexual arousal.

One of my students reported: "When I worked in a women-controlled clinic, we always talked rather glowingly of the virtues of the diaphragm. Every once in a while a woman would tell us that she didn't like the diaphragm because it interfered with her sexual enjoyment, that it covered up something. That was before the G-Spot became well known, and I think now that that was probably what these women were talking about."

Some women find that stimulation of the G-Spot can trigger an orgasm, while many women enjoy G-Spot stimulation as part of the whole panoply of sexual stimulation.

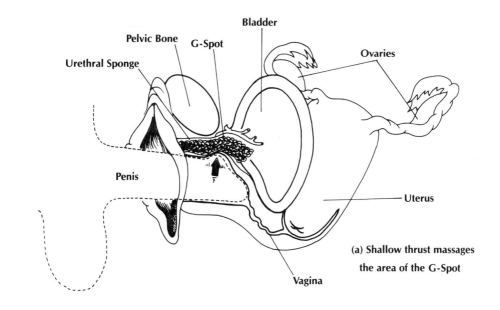

(a) Shallow thrust massages the area of the G-Spot

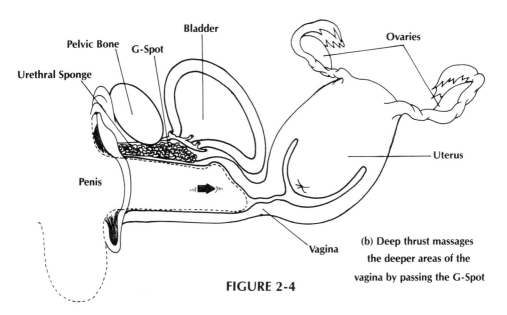

(b) Deep thrust massages the deeper areas of the vagina by passing the G-Spot

FIGURE 2-4

F. Female Ejaculation

An ancient Taoist Master discovered that a woman, when reaching a higher point of orgasm, had different responses which ejaculated different "waters." Three waters, or types of fluid, involved in female orgasms were found to exist. The lubrication experienced during arousal is considered the first water; the fluids emitted during a nor-

51

mal orgasm are the second water; and the third water of a female ejaculation, never experienced by many women, is released from the G-Spot. However, with or without G-Spot stimulation, there are women who ejaculate when they have an orgasm. This ejaculation, which can be quite copious, produces fluid that is much like seminal fluid. It is definitely not urine. However, many women who have experienced ejaculation report that they were dismayed and embarrassed, feeling certain that they had urinated. They then learned to withhold this reaction. Now that the fact of women's ejaculations is known, there will probably be much relief, relaxation, and increased pleasure by the women who have this capacity. As yet, no research has discovered where this fluid is made or stored.

G. The First Lubricative Fluid of the Vagina

Inside the vagina the walls rest against each other, but the potential for space exists. With a plastic speculum, flashlight and mirror, you can look inside the vagina yourself. You will probably first see the pink, ridged walls of the vagina. The many folds account for its tremendous elasticity. During sexual arousal, lubricative fluid oozes out of the walls in a kind of sweating action. At the back of the vagina is the cervix, the only portion of the uterus visible in the vagina. The cervix is round with a hole or slit in it. This is the opening of the cervical canal which goes into the uterus. Most sexologists agree that women have little sensation beyond the outer third section of the vagina. However, many women strongly disagree, saying that they experience terrific pleasure with deep penetration either by penis or finger at the back of the vagina, and many women feel pleasurable contractions of the uterus during orgasm.

There may be mucous dispersing from the cervix. The source and purpose of the mucous will be discussed in the next section.

H. The PC Muscle and Chi Muscle

Feeling around the periphery of the vagina at about the depth of one knuckle, you may be able to discern the edges of the Pubococcygeal Muscle (PC), also sometimes referred to as the Love Muscle.

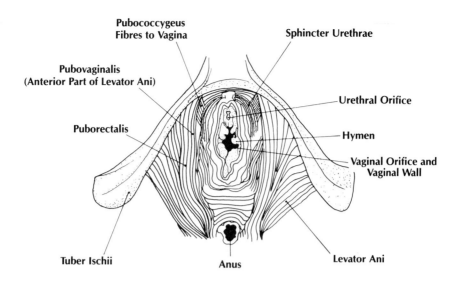

FIGURE 2-5

The Love Muscle includes the Pubococcygeus
(PC Muscle), Pubovaginalis and Pubo-Rectalis

(Figure 2-5) A contraction of the vagina is a contraction of the PC Muscle. You can tell for sure that that is what you are feeling if you can squeeze your fingers with it. The PC Muscle is one part of a group of muscles we refer to as the Chi Muscle. The Chi Muscle surrounds the anus, vagina, and urethra and provides support for the reproductive organs. (Figure 2-6) This is the muscle of Perineum Power and is asso-

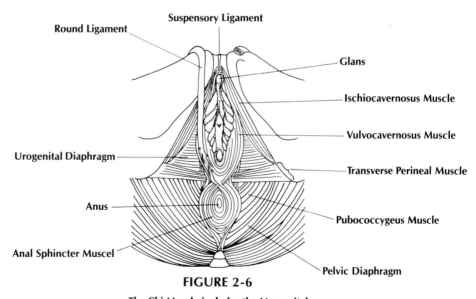

FIGURE 2-6

The Chi Muscle includes the Urogenital
Diaphragm, the Pelvic Diaphragm, the Anal
Sphincter Muscle and the Pubococcygeus (PC)
Muscle

ciated by the Taoists with many organs of the body, as will be described in Chapter 5.

A well-exercised PC Muscle is considered by some sexologists to be the key to healthy sexual functioning for both men and women. Poor muscle tone leads to sexual difficulties as well as other physiologic problems, such as difficulty in childbirth and urinary incontinence. In fact, the first professional to publicize the importance of good PC tone taught exercises to women in preparation for childbirth. His name, Kegel, is still associated with these exercises. The PC Muscle is crucial to Ovarian Kung Fu exercises.

You can test the tone of the PC Muscle by interrupting a stream of urine. This ability is due solely to the P-C Muscle. Many women have become dexterous at squeezing this muscle because they found it enhanced their sexual pleasure.

Sexologist Bryce Britton, in her book *The Love Muscle: Everywoman's Guide to Intensifying Sexual Pleasure*, includes detailed descriptions of how to use the PC Muscle as well as outlining an exercise program for sexual fitness.

FIGURE 2-7

The Perineal Sponge

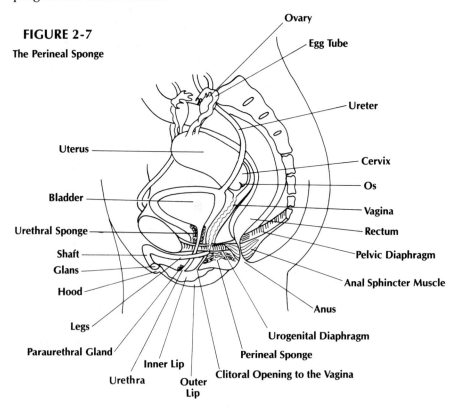

I. The Perineal Sponge

Inside the back part of the entrance to the vagina is another area of blood vessels called the perineal sponge. (Figure 2-7) During sexual arousal the perineal sponge thickens, narrowing the entrance to the vagina.

J. The Perineum

The perineum region includes the anus and sexual organs, but the point of the perineum is located between the back of the vaginal opening and the anus. (Figure 2-8) The anus is a sexual orifice for some

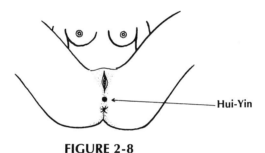

Hui-Yin

FIGURE 2-8
The Perineum (Hui-Yin)

women, and quite sexually taboo for others. To prevent vaginal and bladder infections all women should know that fingers or penis should be washed after anal contact.

3. THE SEXUAL RESPONSE CYCLE

Women's sexual responses were described by Masters and Johnson as being in four phases: excitement, plateau, orgasm, and resolution. These phases are demarcated by physiological changes in the sexual organs. In the excitement phase the vagina sweats, and the broad ligament which supports the uterus pulls up; this in turn enlarges the back of the vagina in the plateau phase. A myriad of changes occur during orgasm, including for some women changes in skin color on the back and chest, or tingling or contractions in the hands and feet. In the resolution phase there is a gradual return to the resting state. (Figure 3-1)

Most writings on women's sexual responses describe women as having a long arousal period. Yet in Shere Hite's research (*The Hite Report*) most women describe themselves as reaching orgasm within minutes after they start masturbating. Does this long arousal period indicate the flexibility of women's sexual responses? Or is it due to inept lovers or women's reticence to tell their partners what would please them?

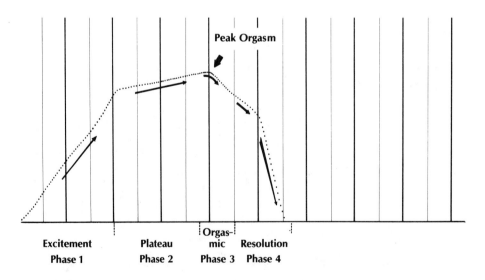

Peak Orgasm

| Excitement | Plateau | Orgas- mic | Resolution |
| Phase 1 | Phase 2 | Phase 3 | Phase 4 |

FIGURE 3-1

Ordinary Peak Orgasm

56

A. The Clitoris and Vaginal Orgasm

Most sexologists and other people limit the definition of the clitoris to the glans. The vagina and the inner lips are seen as separate and distinct entities, the inner lips having no purpose other than to protect the urethral and vaginal openings. Even though Masters and Johnson described the vivid changes of the inner lips during sexual excitement, they still did not identify them as being part of the woman's sexual organs.

For over half a century a battle raged over the location of women's orgasms. Freud and many of his followers maintained that clitoral orgasms were experienced by girls, but that adult women transferred their sexual response to the vagina. Masters and Johnson concluded from their studies that all orgasms are clitoral in origin.

Feminists, concerned about the effects on women's psyches and sex lives, did a lot of research, both in medical libraries and among themselves in self-help groups, and they talked to numerous women about their sexual experiences. From all these sources they concluded that women have one unified sex organ, but that all parts react during sexual arousal no matter what part is being stimulated.

When all the aspects of this sexual organ are viewed together, we see the erectile tissue of the small lips, glans and shaft, urethral sponge and perineal sponge. Add this all together and inch-for-inch women seem to have about as much erectile tissue as men. This similarity in structure suggests a similarity in function also, and further suggests a possible similarity in men's and women's sexual drives and responses. How much is related to how we are constructed, and how much is from our socialization?

B. The Depletion of Sexual Energy

Most men are aware of the depletion of energy they feel as a result of ejaculation, and most women are also aware of a depletion. The Taoists observed that while men lose their energy through ejaculation, women lose most of their energy through their menstrual periods. Although many women do not perceive a loss of energy, certainly those whose periods are preceded by a week or two of breast tenderness, water retention, or pelvic congestion, or whose periods are accompanied by strong cramps, heavy bleeding, backache, nausea, diarrhea, or outbreaks of herpes, etc., will notice the draining effect of these cyclical functions.

C. *Ovarian Kung Fu*

The Ovarian Kung Fu exercises are practiced in two parts:

The first part, Ovarian Breathing, retrieves the biological energy that goes into making eggs, uterine lining, cervical mucous, and the attendant hormones produced in the ovaries and the adrenal and pituitary glands.

The second part, the Orgasmic (Inward and) Upward Draw, involves the transformation of sexual energy, i.e., the circulation of the

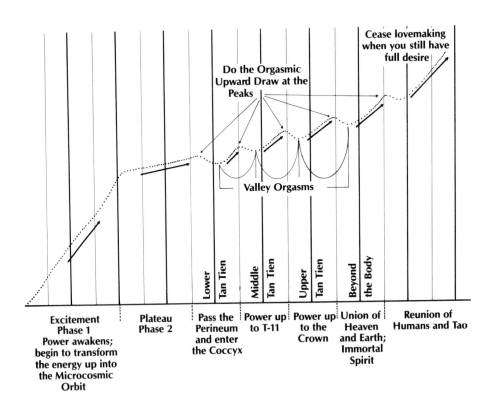

FIGURE 3-2

aroused energy back into the body rather than the discharge of it into the universe.

Both exercises involve bringing the energy from the reproductive and sexual organs up the spine to the brain. Once the brain is filled with energy, the energy will travel down the front of the body to the heart, and then continue down to be stored at the navel. The first exercise helps reduce the loss of energy from menstruation, enabling women to experience shorter, less troublesome periods. The second exercise conserves the biological energy lost through orgasm, prolongs and emphasizes the orgasm, and brings it up into the organs as well as to a higher energy center, there to attain a higher state of consciousness. It also brings intense pleasure. (Figure 3-2)

In the process of learning these exercises women come into closer contact with their cycles, learning to make finer discriminations in their muscle movements and energy flow, and to increase, deepen and extend their sexual pleasure. Ultimately they will zero in on the process of transformation, recognizing and achieving the link between sexuality and spirituality.

4. THE MICROCOSMIC ORBIT

"Reject all reasoning about sex; practice special exercises. To be able to make love and not emit is the secret of returning the semen. Increasing and aiding the semen is then the way of the life-force." — Plain Woman's advice to the Yellow Emperor, second century B.C.

In centuries past the Emperor of China invariably called in the court sages, usually Taoist, to obtain advice on his sex life. Before accepting the advice of any sage, so the story goes, the Emperor required any prospective Master to prove his sexual control. He did this by offering the would-be advisor a full glass of wine and demanding the sage insert his penis into it. If he was truly a Master, he could absorb the wine into his penis, and then release it back into the wine glass. This was taken as absolute proof that the sage could also absorb a woman's sexual fluids, her Yin essence, and therefore knew the secrets of immortality.

Today women can learn the secrets of the Taoist Immortals, be in control of their sexuality, and embark on a journey with a partner that will enrich them both. When they master these techniques for retaining their sexual power and then willingly share it, they will feel differently about themselves and each other.

A. Learn to Circulate your CHI in the Microcosmic Orbit

By far the most powerful energy exchange between two partners occurs at the level of subtle energy. The Taoists have been studying the circulation of subtle energy through certain energy points in the body for thousands of years and have verified, in detail, their importance. These energy points form the basis for acupuncture. Although Western medical research has acknowledged acupuncture as being clinically effective, scientists admit they cannot fully explain why the system works. The circulation of energy through these energy points, or meridians, is called the Microcosmic Orbit. (Figure 4-1)

FIGURE 4-1

The Microcosmic Orbit

All students of the Healing Tao System are taught to circulate their CHI in the Microcosmic Orbit, a necessary step to understanding the cultivation of Ching from the raw physical level of eggs to the refined subtle energy of a Shen, or spiritual being. Once they have opened their Microcosmic Orbit, they have already experienced a minor enlightenment. The mind has begun to realize it has control over its own subtle energy. Ultimately one learns that the movement of subtle energy is totally a power of the mind.

B. The Discovery of the Microcosmic Orbit

A few thousand years ago everything in the world was so simple: there were no televisions, radios, theaters, or nightclubs as entertainment, and no houses to care for, all of which drain energy and disturb the mind. The air was pure. Natural energy was abundant to humans.

When the sun set, people could not fall asleep right away, and they dared not roam around the jungle in the dark. One way to occupy their time was to sit down and quiet themselves. Once they were able to quiet their minds to a certain extent, their body functions started to quiet down as well. They started to notice the flow of something in the body. The flow began in the navel, traveled down to the perineum and up the spine to the head, down the front through the tongue, to the throat and then down to the navel. The circulation of energy through this route came to be known as the Microcosmic Orbit.

The more they were able to still their minds and bodies, the more intense the flow would be. As they continued to still their minds, they began to discover more paths opening and to feel the energy flow in a straight direction, up and down. From the perineum up to the head, the flow was then felt passing through the major organs in three channels, which later became known as the Thrusting Channels. As their practice continued, they felt the energy start to flow in a circular motion, similar to a belt, around a major energy center that they discovered in the navel, the Belt Channel.

As time went on they discovered that there existed in their bodies 32 energy channels, each one corresponding to a specific organ. They passed down this knowledge they had learned generation after generation until more and more people practiced it, and in this way identified the acupuncture meridians which became basic to the Taoist System.

Every person has the same body, the same channels, and has a soul and spirit. After many hundreds of years of practice, trial and error, improving and passing down, the Taoist Esoteric Yoga System came into being.

C. The Two Major Energy Channels of the Microcosmic Orbit —Functional and Governor

It is much easier to cultivate your energy if you first understand the major paths of energy circulation in your body. The nervous system in humans is very complex and is capable of directing energy wherever it is needed. However, the ancient Taoist Masters discovered there are two energy channels that carry an especially strong current.

One channel, the "Functional" or "Yin" Channel, begins at the base of the trunk midway between the vagina and the anus at the perineum point. It goes up the front of the body past the mons, abdominal organs, heart, and throat and ends at the tip of the tongue. The second channel, the "Governor" or "Yang" Channel, starts in the same place. It flows from the perineum upward into the tail bone, then up through the spine into the brain and back down to the roof of the mouth. (Figure 4-2)

The tongue is like a switch that connects these two currents— when it is touched to the roof of the mouth just behind the front teeth, the energy can flow in a circle up the spine and back down the front. The two channels form a single circuit that the energy loops around. This vital current circulates past the major organs and nervous systems of the body, giving cells the juice they need to grow, heal, and function.

D. Sexual Energy

1. The Primordial Energy

The sexual energy that moves in the Microcosmic Orbit is a primordial energy. Human life begins with the union of an egg and a sperm cell. This is the original act of Kung Fu in the balancing of Yin and Yang. Ovarian Kung Fu is the re-creation of that act within the female body. However, instead of forming a fetus from a fertilized egg growing inside the womb, the ovarian energy mounts to higher energy centers inside the body, and we give birth to ourselves on a spiritual level. The sexual energy is drawn upward through the Microcosmic Channel where it literally gives rebirth, a "new life"—and brings the confidence of controlling a powerful flow of creative energy and the satisfaction of a deep sense and higher balance of harmony with the world.

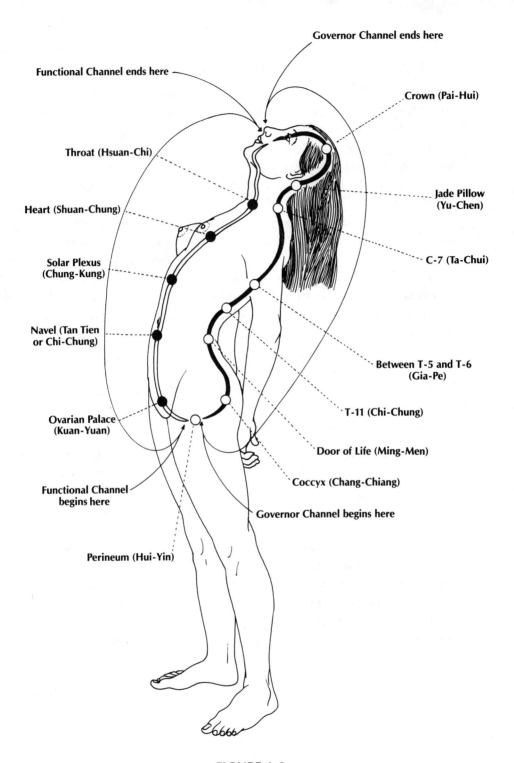

Governor Channel ends here

Functional Channel ends here

Crown (Pai-Hui)

Throat (Hsuan-Chi)

Jade Pillow (Yu-Chen)

Heart (Shuan-Chung)

C-7 (Ta-Chui)

Solar Plexus (Chung-Kung)

Navel (Tan Tien or Chi-Chung)

Between T-5 and T-6 (Gia-Pe)

T-11 (Chi-Chung)

Ovarian Palace (Kuan-Yuan)

Door of Life (Ming-Men)

Functional Channel begins here

Coccyx (Chang-Chiang)

Governor Channel begins here

Perineum (Hui-Yin)

FIGURE 4-2

The Functional and Governor Channels

2. A Powerful, Versatile Energy

The methods of CHI cultivation explained in detail in this book—from Ovarian Breathing to the Ovarian Upward Draw method to Beyond Orgasm—all involve drawing sexual energy stored in the ovaries up the spinal column and into the brain. When the brain is full, this energy will travel down the front into the throat, heart and navel. The brain and pituitary gland will aid in distributing this powerful energy to wherever it is needed. This is a unique attribute of sexual energy, or Ching, over other types of CHI that have their own special functions, e.g., liver CHI. Sexual energy is extraordinarily versatile and can be transformed into many different functions. This is one reason it is so nourishing to our spiritual being. Our inner spiritual being can easily digest it, almost as if it were baby food.

The loop of energy circulating about the body in the Microcosmic Orbit, carrying the sexual current from the ovaries and spreading vitality to other parts of the body, also has a profound effect on health in a specific way. It is this energy that triggers the glands to release the sex-stimulating hormones which regulate body chemistry and ultimately affect your ability to do anything. It has an especially strong influence on the quality of your lovemaking, because on the biological level sex is largely a question of hormonal balance.

The benefits of the Microcosmic Orbit extend beyond facilitating the flow of sexual energy; they include the prevention of aging and the healing of many illnesses, ranging from high blood pressure, insomnia and headaches to arthritis. Whether it be for fighting off an illness, answering a child's question, painting, or making love, the energy that flows in the Microcosmic Orbit is available when we need it.

E. Sealing the Energy within the Body

After opening up the Microcosmic energy channel, it is important to keep it clear of physical or mental blockages, thereby making it possible to pump a greater amount of sexual energy up the spine. If this channel is blocked by tension during the sexual excitement of lovemaking, ovarian energy will not be able to rise to the brain. The sexual power is then lost until the body goes through the long and physically taxing process of manufacturing more ovarian energy. The Microcosmic Orbit is an important step to sealing this energy within the body so that it will circulate and revitalize all parts of the mind and body. Otherwise, when intense sexual energy pressure builds in the head, much of it escapes out of the eyes, ears, nose and mouth and is lost.

F. Opening the Microcosmic Energy Channel

The easiest way to open the Microcosmic energy channel is to sit in meditation a few minutes each morning and relax. Allow your energy to automatically complete the loop by letting your mind flow along with it. Start in the eyes, and mentally circulate your attention with the energy as it goes down the front through your tongue, throat, chest and navel, and then up the tail bone and spine to the head.

At first it may feel like nothing is happening, but eventually the current will begin to feel warm in some places as it loops around. The key is simply to relax and try to bring your mind directly into the part of the loop being focused on. This is different from visualizing an image inside your head of what that part of the body looks like or is feeling. Experience actual CHI flow. Relax and let your mind flow with the CHI in the physical body along a natural circuit to any desired point, e.g., your navel, perineum, etc.

Even if you do not sit daily and circulate the Microcosmic current, just being aware that it exists in your body and functions automatically during these practices should help you more quickly master the methods of Taoist loving. You may even learn it through your lovemaking; all it takes is attention. The best lover is a fully relaxed woman who understands what is going on inside her.

A way to become more in touch with your energy is to lie next to your partner with your ear or nose near your partner's nose. Synchronize your breathing and begin to feel the mingling of your breaths and energies. You might also hug each other for a prolonged period and begin to feel the energy in the abdomen with each breath. The woman who masters this easy flow of energy inside her body's Microcosmic Orbit will find tapping into her sexual powers a simple and natural step.

The more conscious you become of the functioning of subtle CHI energy in your body, mind, and spirit, the greater your freedom to creatively love and be yourself.

Those interested in fully mastering this method of relaxation and opening the Microcosmic Orbit can refer to my first book, *Awaken Healing Energy Through the Tao*.

Study of the Microcosmic Orbit is highly recommended to all students of Sexual Kung Fu who seek to truly master the techniques taught here. Progress to the higher levels of transforming sexual energy without first learning the Microcosmic Orbit is very difficult. Many people may already have open channels and simply need to be made aware of them. Anyone can start to relax in a pleasing, natural setting.

Mastering the Microcosmic current also prepares the serious student for utilizing other energy-conserving techniques that complement Sexual Kung Fu, such as Iron Shirt Chi Kung I, II, and III, a method of packing and storing CHI energy into vital organs. Another powerful technique is Tai Chi Chi Kung, a condensed form of Tai Chi Chuan that circulates CHI energy among body, mind, and spirit, and strengthens muscles, tendons and bones.

5. CULTIVATING OVARIAN POWER

I. THE ACTIVATION AND CONTROL OF OVARIAN ENERGY

A. The Importance of Sexual Organs' Exercise

America is presently exercise oriented. However, with the exception of sexual intercourse, few exercises strengthen the crucial pelvic muscles. Pelvic exercises do exist which can increase CHI in these areas, thereby greatly strengthening the reproductive organs and the complex network of tendons surrounding them.

Strength in this region is of inestimable importance. Leading into the pelvis is a vast number of nerves, blood vessels and lymph glands. Here terminate tissues communicating with every square inch of the body. All of the major acupuncture meridians, which carry CHI to the vital organs, pass through this area. If it is blocked or weak, energy will dissipate, and the organs, as well as the brain, will suffer. This is what happens to many people in old age. As their rectal and pelvic muscles sag and become loose, their vital CHI energy slowly drains out, leaving them weak and feeble.

1. Celibates

No matter who you are, sexual energy is constantly building up and accumulating in the sexual region. Some negative evidence has been collected regarding the health of celibates based on studies of priests and nuns who use only willpower to suppress the sexual fire within. It has been found that the practice of celibacy by women has brought on the eventual deterioration of the sexual organs caused by long-term congestion in the ovaries or breasts, in turn affecting the internal organs.

Some celibates are able to transform their sexual energy naturally, and as a result no problems arise in the celibate state. A woman who is not so naturally enlightened will find an accumulation in her body and sexual organs of too much sexual energy. This energy tends to need a release, and if the woman has no way to handle the problem properly, the energy can affect her adversely, multiplying her negative emotions. Without properly cultivating sexual energy and opening the energy channels between the lower and upper body, the sexual energy is blocked, thereby congesting blood and hormones in the woman's genitals, ovaries, and cervix. Such problems can be avoided by practicing the Ovarian Breathing and Orgasmic Upward Draw exercises.

B. Ovarian Breathing Cultivates Ovarian Power

1. A Woman's Menstrual Cycle

It is said that anatomy is destiny: women are born to be mothers. A baby girl's ovaries are immature, small and smooth, but they contain the power necessary to create the 300-500 eggs she will produce in her reproductive years and a reserve of potentially 450,000 eggs.

Every woman has a profound connection with her menstrual cycle. Women students of the Healing Tao System have revealed how sensitive they are to what seems to be subtle changes in their cycles; they notice right away if their periods are one day early or late, if they last a day longer or are a day shorter, and if the consistency or color varies from what they have come to expect.

Apparently many women remember an event that occurred the day they received their first periods. Those memories may be pleasant or unpleasant, but they remain indelible. One woman remembers it was the first time a man tried to pick her up; another woman remembers that her mother slapped her face (a gesture of welcome into the world of being a woman); another woman hit a home run in a softball game that day.

Many women's cycles become a source of much confusion and uncertainty. They are unsure about fertile times, are ashamed of secretions and odors, are discontent with available birth control methods, develop anger at common childbirth practices, or harbor a simultaneous dependency on and distrust of the medical profession.

Some women go through life with few problems during their cycles, having easy periods, uncomplicated births, or smooth transitions into menopause. Others have distressing problems with their periods, such as recurrent vaginal infections, abnormal Pap smears, difficult births, hysterectomies, or they take synthetic hormones because of disabling hot flashes.

Major changes can occur in the menstrual cycles as well as in many other aspects in the lives of some women simply by practicing Ovarian Breathing.

The point is that, even if a woman has two or three children and does not plan to have more, her body continues cyclically to produce ovary energy. Instead of wasting that energy, it can be conserved through transformation into another form for later use. The ovarian exercises provide a way to use that ovarian power.

2. Yang Energy and the Menstrual Cycle

There are three distinct parts to the menstrual cycle. First, there is the period itself. Following menstruation, an ovary spurts several immature eggs into action, and usually one egg matures completely. Surrounded by a jelly-like covering, it breaks out of the ovary. That period of time, from the end of the bleeding until ovulation, is the time of maximum ovary power. During this part of the cycle the Taoists believe that the ovaries' energy is at its most Yang, or most hot.

After ovulation the ruptured area of the ovary heals and forms the corpus luteum, or yellow body. This yellow body produces progesterone. The function of progesterone is to keep the uterine lining from sloughing off. If the egg unites with a sperm and a pregnancy starts, progesterone will be secreted during the entire pregnancy. If there is no fertilization, the ovary will produce a spurt of estrogen, and the menstruation cycle will begin.

The Taoists note, and women's experiences to date confirm, that the part of the cycle between menstruation and ovulation is the time that a woman will receive the maximum benefit from the practice of Ovarian Breathing, with continued practice then being optional until the next cycle. The process of Ovarian Breathing will draw energy out of the egg. Imagine having access to an energy that is powerful enough to bestow life!

C. The Diaphragms

The body possesses not one but several diaphragms. Everyone is familiar with the thoracic diaphragm in the chest, separating the heart and lungs from the abdominal organs and assisting us in breathing. When you inhale, this diaphragm lowers, thus increasing the space in the chest and allowing the lungs to fill; the deeper the breath, the lower the diaphragm moves.

Less is known about the pelvic and urogenital diaphragms, which separate the pelvis from the perineum. To practice Ovarian Breathing properly you must use not only the chest diaphragm, but also the pelvic and urogenital diaphragms. (Figure 5-1) These serve as flood-

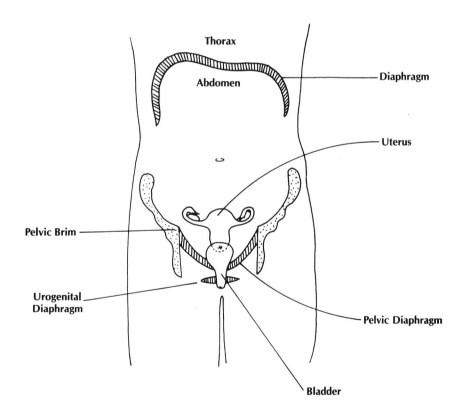

FIGURE 5-1

True deep breathing issues from the pelvic and urogenital diaphragms

gates, opening to spurt energy to the organs, or as pistons, pumping the energy up to higher centers. True breathing comes from these lower diaphragms. It is an exceedingly important element in the Taoist practice of transmitting the energy generated from the sexual organs into a higher energy form.

1. The Pelvic Diaphragm

The pelvic diaphragm is a muscular wall that extends across the lower part of the torso. It is suspended between the symphyses pubis (pubic bones) in front and the coccyx (at the bottom of the spine) in back. (Figure 5-2) There are several organs that penetrate this muscular partition as it lies between the pelvic cavity and the perineum. These organs are the urethra, the vagina and the rectum. One function of the pelvic diaphragm is to support these organs; therefore, control over this diaphragm provides you with greater control over these organs. The pelvic diaphragm is also the floor of the abdominal cavity, which contains the stomach, small and large intestines, liver, bladder, and kidneys. It lifts up and helps shape these vital organs.

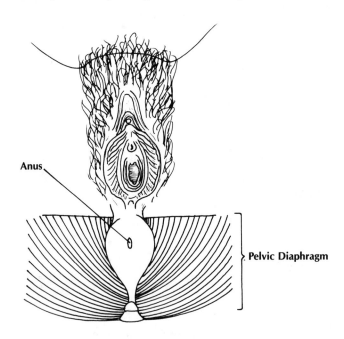

FIGURE 5-2

Pelvic Diaphragm

2. The Urogenital Diaphragm

At the perineum, the point midway between the anus and vagina below the pelvic diaphragm, is another muscular diaphragm, the urogenital diaphragm. This is penetrated by the urethra, and on its underside is attached the shaft of the clitoris. (Figure 5-3)

These two diaphragms seal and hold the life-force, or CHI, energy to prevent its escape through the lower openings in the body. When the openings passing through these diaphragms are tightly sealed, CHI pressure will be increased in the abdomen. When CHI pressure (pounds per square inch, or psi) strengthens, it will invigorate the vital organs, helping to improve the flow of CHI and blood.

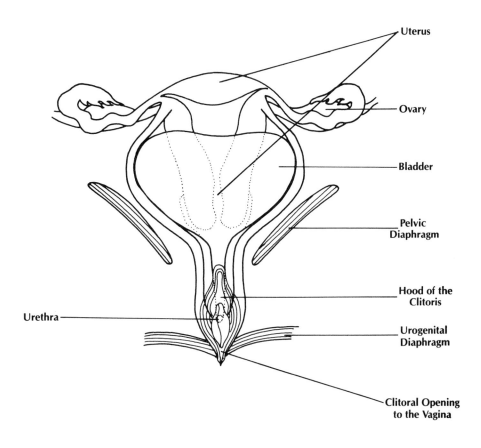

FIGURE 5-3

Urogenital Diaphragm

The importance of these anatomical structures will become apparent as you study the Healing Tao System in its entirety. As previously mentioned, Iron Shirt Chi Kung exercises also help to develop power and strength in these areas and are a perfect complement for anyone seeking a daily regimen that will assist in the practice of Ovarian Kung Fu. (See the section at the end of this book entitled "The Healing Tao System" for a further description.)

D. The Sacral and Cranial Pumps Move CHI up the Spine

Contained and protected within your spinal column and skull is the very "heart" of your nervous system. (Figure 5-4(a)) Cushioning it is the cerebrospinal fluid, "cerebro" for the head and "spinal" for the vertebrae. This fluid, as described by the Taoists long ago, is circulated by two pumps. One is located in the sacrum and is known as the Sacral Pump. The other is in the region of your upper neck and head and is known as the Cranial Pump. (Figure 5-4(b)) Many people who have activated these pumps have reported the sensation of a "big bubble" of energy traveling up their spine during Ovarian Breathing.

1. The Sacral Pump

Taoists regard the sacrum, containing the Sacral Pump, as a point at which the sexual energy coming up from the ovaries and perineum can be held and then transformed as it is given an upward push. It can be compared with a way station that refines the ovaries' energy, or Ching CHI, as it circulates in the body. If the opening of the sacrum to the spinal column (the sacral hiatus) is blocked, the life-force cannot enter and flow up to the higher center.

2. The Cranial Pump

The cranium of the skull has long been regarded by Taoists as a major pump for the circulation of energy from the lower centers to the higher centers. Medical research has recently confirmed that minute movements of the joints of the eight cranial bones occur during breathing. Cranial movement is responsible for the production and function of the cerebrospinal fluid surrounding the brain and spinal

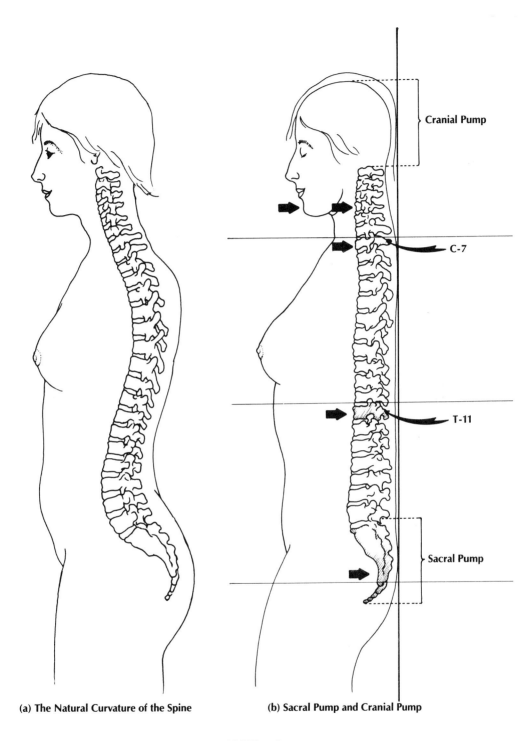

(a) The Natural Curvature of the Spine

(b) Sacral Pump and Cranial Pump

Cranial Pump

C-7

T-11

Sacral Pump

FIGURE 5-4

cord, and this is necessary for normal nerve and energy patterns in the entire body. Strengthening the cranial joints can increase energy and alleviate symptoms such as headaches, sinus problems, visual disturbances and neck problems.

In Taoism, cultivation of the movement of the pelvis, perineum, urogenital diaphragm, anus, and the Sacral and Cranial Pumps is very important and necessary in helping to move the sexual energy up the spine.

In Ovarian Breathing, we use the mind and a slight tensing of the neck and jaw to help activate the Sacral and Cranial Pumps. In the Orgasmic Upward Draw we use a stronger power lock of the neck, teeth and muscles, a deep breath, and eye movement to assist in the activation of these pumps.

E. The Chi Muscle Assists in Controlling the Flow of CHI

As we have already learned, one of the main objectives of the Taoist practice is to increase the flow of CHI, our life-force, to our organs and glands. The Inner Smile and Microcosmic Orbit Meditation are very important methods of reaching this objective, especially in the Healing Love practice, because they can help you open the channel through which the sexual energy has to flow up, assisting you in controlling the flow of sexual power. However, without directing sexual healing energy to the organs, lovemaking becomes a normal social act, ending up in the loss and depletion of gland and organ energies. Crucial to the ability to control this flow of sexual energy is the development of a strong Chi Muscle.

1. Perineum Power

Included in the perineum region are the anus and sexual organs. The perineum region is known as the seat of Yin (cold) energy, and is closely connected to the organs and glands. (Figure 5-5) The Chinese term for perineum, Hui-Yin, means the collection point of all Yin energy, or the lowest abdominal energy collection point. It is also known as the Gate of Death and Life. This point lies between the two main gates. The front gate, or sexual organs' gate, is the big life-force open-

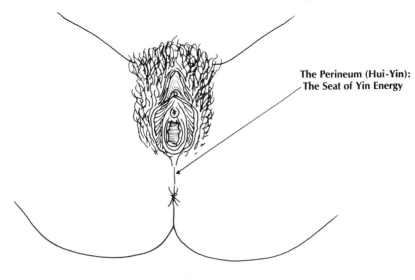

The Perineum (Hui-Yin):
The Seat of Yin Energy

FIGURE 5-5

ing; here the life-force can easily leak out and deplete the organs'
function. Although the walls of the vagina are tight during youth and
after a refreshing sleep, they become looser as we age or when fatigued. The walls of the vagina, housing the PC Muscle, must be strong
in order to permit the life-force energy to flow and increase their
strength. The second gate, the back gate, is the anus.

Taoists regard the perineum region as the lowest diaphragm, one
that functions like a pump. Control of the Chi Muscle, consisting of the
PC Muscle, the muscles of the pelvic and urogenital diaphragms, the
sphincter muscle of the anus, and many involuntary muscles located
in this perineum region, influences the pumping action. As Ovarian
Breathing floods this region with energy, the perineum, vagina and
anus begin to tighten almost immediately. In the Tao practices, especially in Iron Shirt Chi Kung, the perineum's power to tighten, close
and draw the life-force back up the spine is an important factor.

2. The Anus is Connected to Organ Energy

The various sections of the anus region are closely linked with the
organs' and glands' CHI. When not sealed or closed tight, we can easily
lose the nutrition needed for our life-force and sexual energy through
"a river of no return"; they will flow out and will not recycle.

77

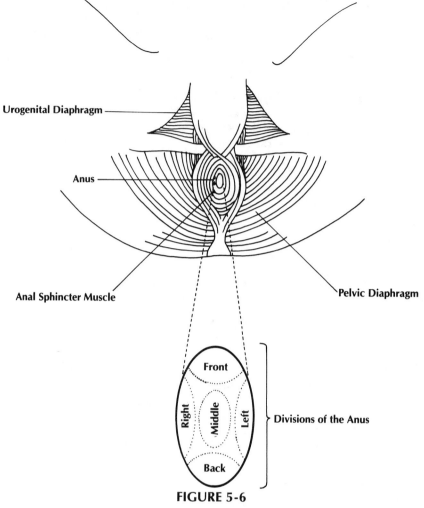

Urogenital Diaphragm

Anus

Anal Sphincter Muscle

Pelvic Diaphragm

Front

Right | Middle | Left

Back

Divisions of the Anus

FIGURE 5-6

The Anus is Divided into Five Regions

3. The Anus Region is Divided into Five Sections

The anus is divided into five sections: (a) middle, (b) front, (c) back, (d) left, and (e) right. (Figure 5-6) By contracting and pulling up the various sections of the anus, you are also pulling up the perineum region, which partially consists of the anus.

A. THE MIDDLE PART

The middle of the anus CHI is connected with the organs and glands as follows: the vagina-uterus; aorta and vena cava; stomach; heart; thyroid, parathyroid, pituitary and pineal glands; and top of the head. (Figure 5-7).

78

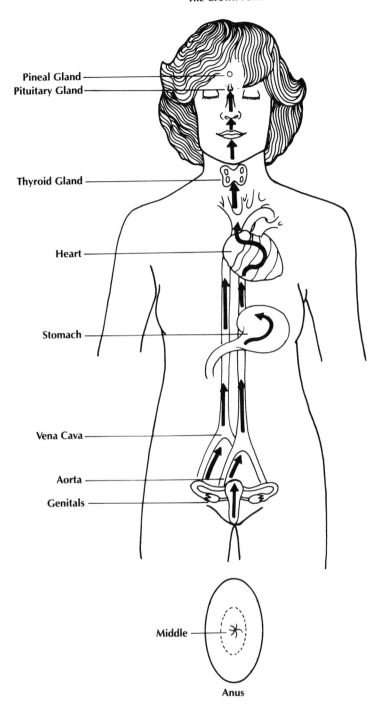

The Crown Point

Pineal Gland

Pituitary Gland

Thyroid Gland

Heart

Stomach

Vena Cava

Aorta

Genitals

Middle

Anus

FIGURE 5-7

The Middle Part Anus Pull Up

B. THE FRONT PART

The front of the anus CHI is connected with the following organs and glands: the bladder; cervix; small intestine; stomach; thymus and thyroid glands; and front part of the brain. (Figure 5-8)

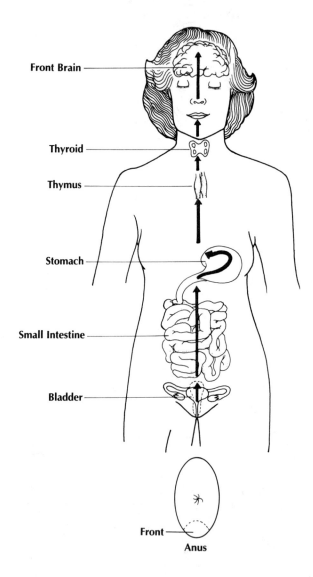

FIGURE 5-8

The Front Part Anus Pull Up

C. THE BACK PART

The back part of the anus CHI is connected with the organ and gland energies of: the sacrum; lower lumbars; twelve thoracic vertebrae; seven cervical vertebrae; and small brain (cerebellum). (Figure 5-9)

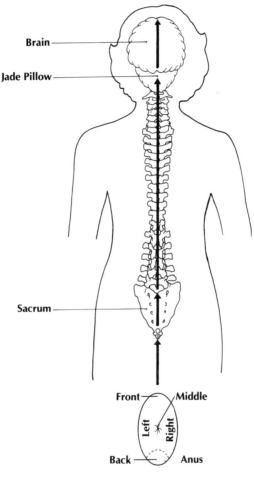

FIGURE 5-9

The Back Part Anus Pull Up

D. THE LEFT PART

The left part of the anus CHI is connected with the organ and gland energies of: the left ovary; large intestine; left kidney; left adrenal gland; spleen; left lung; and left hemisphere of the brain. (Figure 5-10)

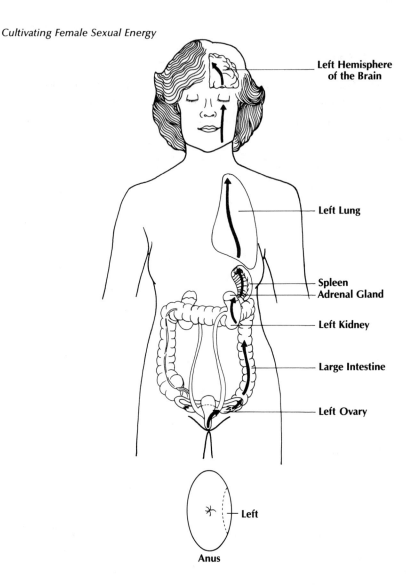

Left Hemisphere
of the Brain

Left Lung

Spleen
Adrenal Gland

Left Kidney

Large Intestine

Left Ovary

Left

Anus

FIGURE 5-10

The Left Part Anus Pull Up

E. THE RIGHT PART

The right part of the anus CHI is connected with the organ and gland energies as follows: the right ovary; large intestine; right kidney; right adrenal gland; liver; gall bladder; right lung; and right hemisphere of the brain. (Figure 5-11)

82

Once you are well trained in controlling the Chi Muscle, you can easily guide the sexual healing energy to the particular organs or glands that you need to heal, or guide the energy to help your partner during lovemaking. In the latter part of the Orgasmic Upward Draw, you will learn how to guide your orgasms to the organs and glands.

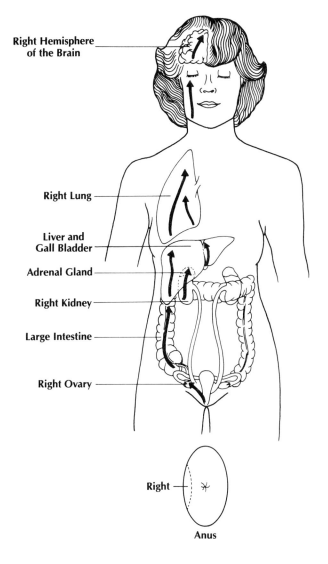

Right Hemisphere of the Brain

Right Lung

Liver and Gall Bladder

Adrenal Gland

Right Kidney

Large Intestine

Right Ovary

Right

Anus

FIGURE 5-11

The Right Part Anus Pull Up

F. Yang Ovaries' Energy—Healing and Creative Power

The ancient Taoists had extraordinarily astute powers of observation, and their findings on the subject of sex are surprisingly consistent over long stretches of time, which in China means not hundreds but thousands of years. This is significant because many groups did not know of any others' abilities, whereabouts, or even existence, since these esoteric practices were kept very secret.

They noted that the ovaries, as the factory that produces sexual energy in the form of eggs and female hormones, are of prime importance, because all of the vital organs, such as the brain, must contribute some of their own reserves to create and maintain them. Further, their records point out that in the first part of a woman's cycle, there is a tremendous storage taking place of hot life-force energy which they called Yang Ching Chi (Ovarian Chi). (Figure 5- 12) As previously noted,

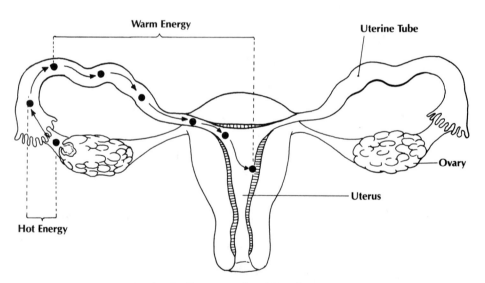

During the first stages of ovulation the energy is
hot. As the egg travels toward the uterus the
energy turns warm

FIGURE 5-12

The Energy of Ovulation

Yang energy activates and charges an egg during a woman's ovulation with full potential life-force, and this is a sign of a strong and youthful energy with the power to create and heal.

Ovarian Chi, or Ching CHI, is denser than the life-force, or CHI, that normally circulates in the Microcosmic Orbit. Since it is thicker and slower to move, this energy needs all the help it can get to move upward to a higher energy center. Therefore it is important to be sure the channel of the Microcosmic Orbit is open and the CHI is flowing before proceeding to Orgasmic Breathing or the Orgasmic Upward Draw. Then the more inward the orgasm, and the more you can bring it upward, the more you will heal and revitalize as the Ching CHI (sexual energy) travels through the channel in its loop up the spine to the head and down the front through the navel, genitals and perineum, linking the various organs and glands with each other and with the brain. This energy can also be used to heal and revitalize your partner.

As the woman's cycle continues and the egg moves out of the body, the experience of heat gives way to what has been described as a mildly warm quality. All sexual energy, whether male or female, is Yin in its latent or resting state. At this time the aroused sexual energy, now more Yin in nature, is more healing than creative. It is important to use this sexual energy and not let its vitality pour outward. If it does, you have to start the process all over again.

II. SINGLE CULTIVATION: OVARIAN BREATHING, OVARIAN AND VAGINAL COMPRESSION

Ovarian Breathing: The Ovarian Breathing exercise that follows will help you to open and utilize the channels of the Microcosmic Orbit, a process described briefly in Chapter 4 and in depth in the book *Awaken Healing Energy Through the Tao*. In Ovarian Breathing you use your mind to draw the warm, Yang, vital egg energy up the spine to your head and to the third eye (located mid-eyebrow), down through the tongue, the heart, the solar plexus, finally to be stored in the navel. You will be drawing on the energy generated by the ovaries, eggs and hormones themselves. At first the process is slow, but later a simple thought will send delightful waves of energy up your back to your head.

Ovarian Compression: The second exercise, Ovarian Compression, trains you to have more control of the Chi Muscle to build up warm Ching energy in the ovaries and to move this energy safely upward.

Orgasmic Upward Draw: A third exercise, the Orgasmic Upward Draw, is the subject of Chapter 6. You will learn how to contend with the Ching energy when it is aroused, and how to extend the orgasm inward and upward. This is the most powerful way to energize and revitalize the organs, glands and brain. Like a wild mare, this energy is the most difficult to control. It is recommended that in the beginning you practice this exercise alone, using self-arousal, before attempting to tame your sexual energy at its most explosive time, i.e., with a lover during lovemaking.

A. Ovarian Breathing

1. An Overview of the Exercise

The Ovarian Breathing exercise involves a gentle contraction of the Chi Muscle, as delicate as the closing petals of a flower, and so minimal that any less would do nothing at all. The various postures will be described below, although it would be best to try this exercise standing up or sitting on the edge of a chair.

You will be bringing your awareness to both ovaries. Then you will gather more energy in the area to be described as the "Ovarian Palace," from which you will move the energy through the uterus to the perineum. From there you will guide it up your back to the brain, and then using your tongue as a switch, you will guide it down to your navel, where it can be stored.

We have noted that the energy of the ovaries is regarded as hot energy and, as such, can be stored in the heart center or navel center. Some people store too much energy in the heart and find it causes heartburn and difficulty in breathing. This means there is excess energy that is not circulating sufficiently. Therefore, in the early stages of your practice, we advise you to store the sexual energy in the navel, and as your practice continues, store it in the heart to increase love, joy and compassion.

2. Postures

There are three postures in which to practice Ovarian Breathing: sitting, standing and lying.

A. SITTING

For simplicity and comfort, sit on a chair. (Figure 5-13) Sitting lends ease to a practice that favors relaxation and good concentration.

Sit on the edge of a chair with both the legs and buttocks supporting your weight. Do not put all the weight on the sitting bones because in time this can create sciatic nerve pain. The vagina and perineum should not be constricted but should be covered with comfortable underwear or loose clothing to protect them from any draft. As a helpful technique used since olden times, a woman can place a hard, round object, perhaps a ball, in such a way that it presses directly on her vagina and clitoris during practice, or she can sit on the heel of one foot, pressing it tightly against the clitoris to help the CHI activate easily. If you practice the Microcosmic Orbit circulation and Iron Shirt

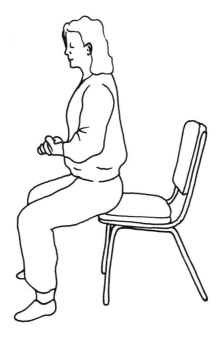

FIGURE 5-13
Sitting Posture

Chi Kung, you should be well practiced at directing energy upward and can omit this step.

Raise the tongue to the roof of the mouth; this is essential in circulating the CHI and completing the loop between the front and back channels of the Microcosmic Orbit. (Figure 5-14) The feet are firmly planted on the floor with the hands resting palms-down on the knees. The back should be quite straight at the waist, but slightly round at the shoulders and neck. This very minor forward curvature of the upper back tends to relax the chest, and helps the power flow through the

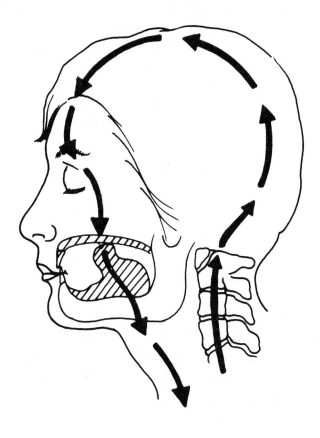

FIGURE 5-14

The tongue touches the palate so the energy

can flow down

neck, chest, and abdomen. Keep the chin slightly tucked in. Military posture, with shoulders thrown back and head held high, tends to lodge power in the upper body and prevent its circulating back down to lower centers.

A variant of the sitting position is to sit cross-legged, either in the lotus position or American Indian style. We appreciate the esoteric virtues of the lotus position, but Chinese practice attributes serious disadvantages to this sitting position. Some monks suffered severe sciatic nerve pain or were crippled by lengthy meditation in the lotus position. Also, turning the soles of the feet away from the ground prevents you from directly drawing in through the feet the earth's Yin power. When you are very good at controlling and directing the energy, you can sit in any position and still direct the energy as you wish. However, the human body is designed to absorb earth energy through the kidney (K-1 point) and other meridians in the feet and filter it before passing it up to the coccyx and brain. Some people can develop problems if they absorb too much "raw" earth CHI directly into their perineum and sacrum, as occurs in the lotus position. Eventually they become allergic to this undigested energy and experience numerous unpleasant reactions. Nevertheless, the lotus position may be used by those accustomed and devoted to it, as long as they are comfortable and can apply their whole attention to the exercise. Few cross-legged positions afford the relaxation of the perineum provided by sitting on the edge of a chair.

B. STANDING

Another good position is standing. The above instructions on raising the tongue tip to the palate and maintaining correct posture apply equally to this position.

Standing is particularly favorable for Ovarian Breathing because the sacrum and pelvis can relax. Standing up straight in a relaxed manner encourages good posture. The hands are at the sides and the feet are shoulders' width apart. Discipline yourself to relax if you feel too tense, or the CHI power may stick in the heart region and make you irritable.

C. LYING

In the beginning, before you learn to control the energy, do not lie flat on your back when performing these exercises. In this position the chest sits higher than the abdomen and receives too much energy. Nor should you lie on the left side. Both of these positions unduly stress the heart. The proper lying position is on the right side. A pillow placed beneath the head should raise it about three or four inches, so that the head sits squarely on the shoulders. The four fingers of the right hand are placed immediately in front of the right ear, while the thumb sits behind the ear and folds it slightly forward to keep it open. The ear must stay open to permit air to flow through the Eustachian tube and keep the left and right ears' pressures balanced. This is important because you can create a lot of CHI pressure during this practice. The left hand rests on the outer left thigh. The right leg is straight; the left leg, which rests on the right, is slightly bent. (Figure 5-15)

Lions often sleep in a similar position. Animals have a wise instinct since this position frees the spinal column from the pressure of gravity, allowing it to assume its natural curvature. Lying on the right side can relieve the spine from stress.

FIGURE 5-15

The best way to practice Ovarian Breathing
lying down is on the right side of the body with
a pillow beneath the head, the right leg
extended, the left leg resting on the right thigh,
and the right hand supporting the head

As mentioned previously, when you have mastered the energy well, you can lie on your back to practice, but make sure that the energy is not stuck in the chest and the heart. Do not lie on the left side.

3. A Step-By-Step Guide

In this section we will explain each step in great detail. In Section 4 we guide you through the practice. Finally, in Section 5 we give a summary of the practice, to be used as a guideline only when you are more advanced.

Unless otherwise specifically indicated, all breathing is to be done through the nose. Nasal breathing affords better control of the air inhaled. It filters and warms the air and supplies life-force of a well-balanced quality.

Sit erect on the edge of your chair with your feet flat on the floor approximately shoulders' width apart. Remember to wear loose pants or comfortable underwear to protect the vaginal opening from drafts and to avoid leakage of CHI. Do not practice naked in a cold room, or you will lose a lot of CHI.

Make sure you feel very relaxed. If you are tense, do some stretching exercises or take a walk first in order to disperse tension.

A. BRINGING ENERGY INTO THE OVARIAN PALACE AND DOWN TO THE FIRST STATION: THE PERINEUM

(1) BRINGING ENERGY INTO THE OVARIAN PALACE

Begin the exercise by locating the Ovarian Palace. Place both thumbs on the navel and use your index fingers to form a triangle. The place where the index fingers touch is the Ovarian Palace. Spread out your little fingers evenly; underneath the points where they rest are the ovaries. (Figure 5-16) As your little fingers rest on them, become aware of them. Rub the ovaries until you feel them warming. Concentrate in order to produce more energy from the ovaries and eggs. Simultaneously use your mind to control the P-C Muscle to close and open slightly the vagina as delicately as the petals of a flower. The energy may begin to manifest itself with such sensations as warmth, tightness, swelling, tingling, etc. Each person can react differently

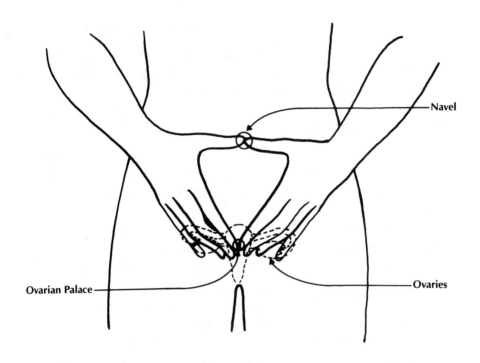

FIGURE 5-16

Locating the Ovaries and the Ovarian Palace

from the energy. When you start to feel something, inhale and bring the energy to the Ovarian Palace (where the index fingers touch). The gentle opening and closing of the vagina and the concentration of your mind gradually will enable you to collect and absorb the ovaries' energy into the Ovarian Palace.

(2) THE FIRST STATION: THE PERINEUM

Inhale a short sip of air only (and inhale in this manner every time you are asked to inhale throughout this exercise). As you inhale, pull the ovaries' energy down from the Ovarian Palace to the perineum by contracting both the outer and inner lips of the vagina, pulling downward toward the perineum, and then contract and pull up the front of the anus (perineum). Remember that contraction of the vagina is a contraction of the PC (Puboccygeal) Muscle, one part of a group of muscles we refer to as the Chi Muscle. This action initiates the contraction of the entire Chi Muscle group, which continues when the anus is contracted and pulled up. Since the anus belongs to the area known as the perineum, we can say that "to contract and pull up the anus" is "to contract and pull up the perineum." To avoid confusion from this point on in describing the contractions used in Ovarian Breathing, we will describe the contraction of the Chi Muscle as "to contract and pull up the perineum." You might feel the route the energy follows, i.e., traveling from the top of the uterus down into the uterus, through the cervical canal and vagina, and down to the perineum. The energy might make a detour to the shaft and glans of the clitoris before arriving at the perineum. In any case, you should feel the energy move from the Ovarian Palace to the perineum, whether or not you experience the exact route it follows. Hold your breath, inhale in short sips, close the vagina tightly and retain the ovaries' energy at the front part of the perineum for a while. (Figure 5-17)

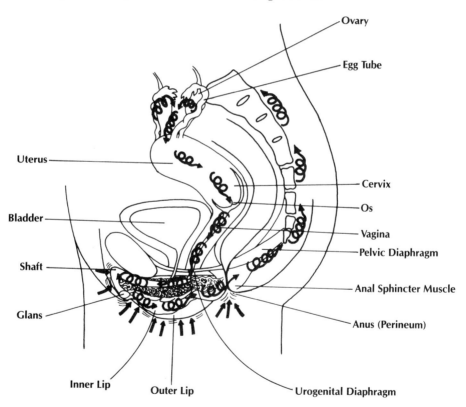

FIGURE 5-17
Ovarian Breathing

93

Exhale. Now concentrate on that warm feeling and mentally guide it from your ovaries to the front part of your perineum, letting the energy flow to the perineum via the uterus, down through the cervical canal and along the back wall of the vagina. Feel the flow as it travels the few inches to the perineum, an action induced by setting your mind at the perineum to hold the energy there. It is important to learn to maintain your attention at the perineum, because if you release it, the warm sexual energy will leak out. Be aware of the energy now flowing from the Ovarian Palace to the perineum. With each inhalation and exhalation counting as one, repeat the process nine times per session. Each time return to the ovaries, and while there inhale and exhale several times to build up more energy before you begin the process again.

(3) THE RETENTION OF SEXUAL ENERGY AT THE PERINEUM POINT

Think of drinking a full glass of water through a straw. You cannot draw all the water in one sip; you have to break the flow in order to breathe, and if you do not hold or retain the water that you already have in the straw, the water will flow out. In order to drink again you will have to begin drawing through the straw all over again. However, if you place your finger over the top of the straw while you breathe short sips of air, you can hold the water inside it. Similarly, the retention of the Ching CHI at the perineum is very important, for if you release your attention, the warm energy will drop down to the sexual organs and leak out of the vagina. By practicing, you will learn to use the power of the mind to hold the energy there. Practice for several days or until you are successful.

(4) RETURNING TO THE OVARIAN PALACE

As you strive to reach each energy transformation point in Ovarian Breathing, you must begin each time by returning to the Ovarian Palace to collect the ovaries' energy. Practice Ovarian Breathing by opening and closing the vagina slightly in order to collect the energy in the Ovarian Palace. Once you feel that enough ovaries' energy has been collected, repeat the process of bringing energy to the perineum: each time inhale a little sip of air, and close the vagina with minimal movement of the Chi Muscle. At the same time that you close the vagina, pull slightly downward toward the perineum, and then contract and pull up the front part of the perineum. Hold your breath, inhale in short sips, close the vagina tightly, and use your mind to create an awareness of the perineum point, thereby drawing the ovaries' energy to this point. Retain the energy at the front part of the perineum. Upon exhalation rest for a while, mentally guiding and feeling the Ching CHI as it travels from the Ovarian Palace down to the vagina, clitoris and perineum, while maintaining your awareness of the perineum point and continuing to hold energy there.

In the Taoist practice sexual energy is the primary energy. If you only exercise the muscles and have no knowledge about life-force and sexual energy, then the benefits are less. Practice to this point for one to two weeks, or until you can definitely feel the energy at the perineum, the ovaries and the Ovarian Palace. There will be a sensation of energy traveling down to the vagina, and then there will be a strong feeling as the energy travels gradually to the clitoris.

Remember, unless specifically indicated otherwise, all breathing is to be done through the nose since nasal breathing affords better control of the air inhaled. Also, all inhalations are short sips of air.

The whole body must relax. Allow all tension to flow out of you as if you were in meditation. Use the mind alone to raise and lower the sexual energy. With practice you will learn to identify the hot Ching CHI stored in the ovaries' area. Always start your breathing and collecting in the ovaries first, until you get in touch with the energy.

B. MOVING THE ENERGY UP THE SPINE THROUGH THE SECOND STATION: THE SACRUM, THE FIRST ENERGY TRANSFORMATION POINT

Along with the ability to hold sexual energy, the sacrum also helps transform it into the first stage of life-force energy.

(1) GUIDING ENERGY TO THE SACRUM

Guide the ovaries' warm energy down from the Ovarian Palace to the perineum and up to the sacrum by first inhaling a short sip of air, slightly contracting and closing the vagina's outer and inner lips, pulling downward toward the perineum, and then contracting and pulling up the front part of the perineum. Pause for a while, holding your

95

breath, inhale in short sips, close the vagina tightly and retain the ovaries' energy at the front part of the perineum. Be aware of the Ching CHI as it flows to this point. Exhale and return to the ovaries, maintaining a part of your awareness at the perineum to retain the energy that you have brought there. Practice Ovarian Breathing by opening and closing the vagina slightly, and collect the energy in the Ovarian Palace. Once you feel that enough ovaries' energy has been collected, inhale and close the vagina, pulling downward toward the perineum, and then contract and pull the front part of the perineum upward to bring energy to this area. Rest briefly and be aware of the energy that travels from the ovaries down to the vagina, clitoris and perineum. Inhale slightly. Now pull up the middle part of the perineum, and at the same time pull up the back part of the perineum toward the coccyx at the very bottom of your spine.

(2) ACTIVATING THE SACRAL PUMP

Slightly arch your lower back outward thereby tilting the sacrum downward to bring the energy to this point. As you pull the ovarian energy up the front, middle and back parts of the perineum to the coccyx and then to the sacrum, hold the sacrum down to help activate the Sacral Pump (Figure 5-18), which action will be further accentu-

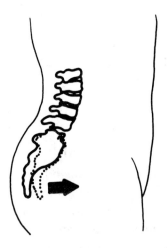

FIGURE 5-18

Activating the Sacral Pump involves tilting the
sacrum down without moving the hip bone

ated if you gently tighten the back of your neck and skull bones. In the beginning use a wall as a guide by pushing the sacrum against the wall, thereby exerting force on it. Hold the energy at the sacrum for a while, then exhale, but continue to focus your attention on this point.

(3) OPENING THE SACRAL HIATUS

The hiatus opening of the sacrum is an indentation in the bone of the sacrum located a little up from the tip of your spine, and is the place through which, once opened, you will draw your warm, ovarian energy into the spine. (Figure 5-19) It is usually a little difficult to work

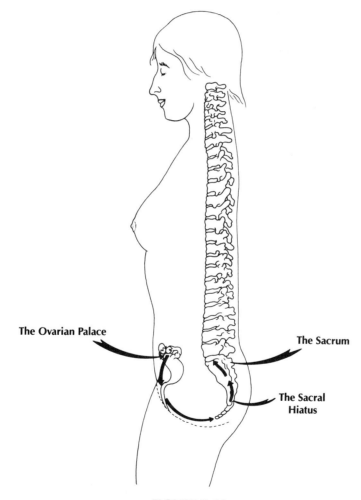

The Ovarian Palace

The Sacrum

The Sacral Hiatus

FIGURE 5-19

Guiding Energy Through the Sacral Hiatus and Up the Sacrum

because ovarian energy is denser than CHI and has to be pumped through. Some people experience pain, a tingling sensation, or "pins and needles" when this energy enters the hiatus. If this happens to you, do not be upset. You can help pass the energy through the hiatus if you are having trouble by gently massaging the area with a silk cloth from time to time.

(4) RESTING TO FEEL THE ENERGY MOVE UNASSISTED

Now let your sacrum and neck relax back to their normal positions. As they relax you will feel the energy move by itself, assisted by the activation of both the Sacral and Cranial Pumps. At the same time practice Ovarian Breathing. Bring the energy up to the sacrum again and hold it there until you can feel the hiatus at the sacrum open and the energy gradually move up. You will actually feel the warm energy move up a little at a time. Practice nine times, then rest. The resting period is very important. Many times while you are resting the energy will rise up through the point you had been focusing on. If you can, still your mind and use it to guide the energy along the pathway you have been working on for a while, and then rest your mind and let the energy move by itself; the energy will automatically flow through this pathway.

(5) AN EXERCISE TO HELP OPEN THE SACRUM

If you have trouble feeling the energy at the sacrum, the following exercise can be helpful in opening the sacrum. Try rocking your sacrum back and forth and then hold the hips stationary, moving the sacrum only. The sacrum and the hips are three separate pieces of bone which eventually become fused because we do not exercise them. (Figure 5-20) Use both hands to hold the hips and try to rock the sacrum. In the beginning it is difficult to do, but after a while you will gradually separate the hips from the sacrum. You can also ask a friend to hold your sacrum with one hand while his other hand is on your hip in order to let you know if it is the hip or the sacrum that you are moving. After this exercise hold still and observe the effect of the pumping.

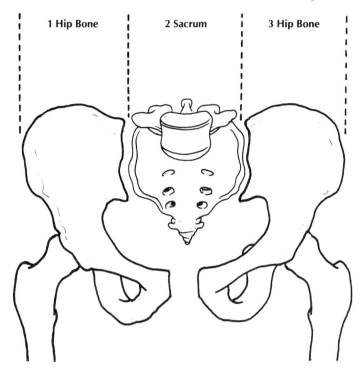

1 Hip Bone	2 Sacrum	3 Hip Bone

FIGURE 5-20

The sacrum and the hip bones are three
separate pieces of bone which, through lack of
exercise, become fused

(6) THE SACRUM ASSISTS IN TRANSFORMING RAW SEXUAL ENERGY INTO LIFE-FORCE ENERGY

The Taoist masters discovered that the sacrum has the ability to transform sexual energy into a life-force energy that is more readily accepted by the organs and glands. Therefore, the practitioner must be aware of the state of the energy entering the middle part of the body. Some people practice by pulling up only the middle part of the perineum, causing the raw ovaries' energy to shoot up the middle part of the body and become stuck in the organs and glands. Unaccustomed to handling this kind of raw sexual energy, the organs and glands will suffer from such disorders as indigestion, overheating (especially the liver), pain in the kidneys and back, and worst of all, heart congestion. These and other symptoms have come to be known as the "Kundalini Syndrome," and they occur because the person is not open enough to channel this raw sexual energy before it enters the vital organs. This phenomenon is mentioned in the books entitled *Kwantida—Psychotic or Transcendental*, by Lee Sanella, M.D., and *Stalking the Wild Pendulum*, by Itzhak Bentov. These books contain examples of many people who suffer from the inability to control the rising energy. The energy they hold in their hearts or in their heads is either too raw or too hot for those organs, with parts of the organs having an allergic reaction to that energy. However, the symptoms disappeared once they learned about and felt the connection of the tongue to the roof of the mouth during the Microcosmic Orbit meditation. This connection allows the energy flowing up the spine through the major stations to transform into life-force energy and flow down to the navel. Many never know how to escape their problem of too much raw sexual energy rising up because they never learn how to bring the energy to the proper channels to circulate it back down.

Once you have practiced Ovarian Breathing and have felt the sexual energy circulate and become transformed, your organs will begin to adapt to and withstand the ovaries' raw sexual energy. This energy can then be directly transformed and refined whenever the body requires it without problems arising.

C. THE THIRD STATION: T-11, A SEXUAL-ENERGY TRANSFORMATION POINT

If you have managed to bring the energy up through the sacrum, spend the next week drawing the ovaries' energy to T-11 (the eleventh thoracic vertebra) in your mid-back opposite your solar plexus. T-11 also has the ability to transform the sexual energy into life-force energy.

(1) COLLECTING ENERGY IN THE OVARIAN PALACE

In the same manner as above, start with Ovarian Breathing, collecting the ovaries' energy in the Ovarian Palace by opening and closing the vagina with a minimal movement of the Chi Muscle. Inhale with a short sip, close the vagina slightly, pulling the energy downward toward the perineum. Then contract and pull up the front part of the perineum and pause for a while, holding your breath and retaining the energy at this point. Be aware of the Ching CHI that has been brought there. Inhale in short sips, close the vagina tightly and concentrate on retaining the ovaries' energy at the front part of the perineum. Exhale and return to the ovaries, but maintain a part of your awareness at the perineum to retain the energy that you have brought there. Continue to practice Ovarian Breathing by opening and closing the vagina slightly and collecting the energy in the Ovarian Palace.

(2) DRAWING ENERGY TO T-11

Once you feel that enough ovaries' energy has been collected, inhale using a short sip and close the vagina by pulling downward, thereby pulling the energy down to the perineum, and then contract and pull the front part of the perineum upward to bring energy to this area. Rest for a while and be aware of the energy that travels from the ovaries down to the vagina, clitoris and perineum. Inhale a short sip and pull up the middle and back part of the perineum toward the coccyx to bring the energy to the sacrum. Slightly tilt the sacrum outward as if you were pushing the sacrum to the wall. Pause for a while and feel the Sacral Pump activate. Inhale a short sip again without exhaling, and tilt your spine outward against the imaginary wall to straighten T-11. This will create an upward pumping action which will pull the ovaries' energy up to T-ll. (Figure 5-21) Retain the energy at this point until the area feels full and until you feel the energy continue to open T-11 and move up by itself. When you feel uncomfortable exhale and regulate your breath.

(3) FLEXING THE T-11 POINT ASSISTS IN ACTIVATING THE SACRAL AND CRANIAL PUMPS AND THE ADRENAL MINIPUMP

As previously noted, ovarian energy is denser than CHI. You will have to accommodate it by flexing the part of your back housing T-11 in and out, thereby straightening the spine at this point and loosening it for freer passage of the warm energy. Then allow your sacrum, T-ll and neck to relax back to their normal positions. This action will help to activate both the Sacral and Cranial Pumps, as well as another minipump located at the adrenal glands, a little at a time. If you have trouble feeling this, return again to the Ovarian Palace and repeat the

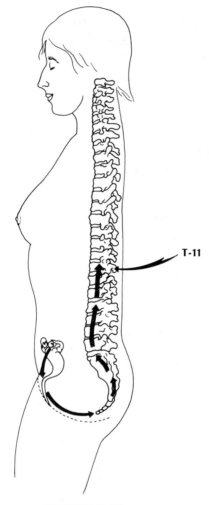

T-11

FIGURE 5-21
Guiding Energy Up to T-11

process. Practice nine times, then exhale and relax every part of the body. Concentrate on T-11 and feel the energy flow up to this point.

In Taoist practice we regard T-11 as the adrenal glands' energy center. The adrenal glands sit atop your kidneys and can act as a mini-pump. When you arch the T-11 point you create a vacuum (or minipump) in this area to push the energy up higher. The sacrum, T-11, C-7 and Jade Pillow in Taoism all are regarded as places that have the ability to transform sexual energy into life-force energy. In the T-11 area the Door of Life (the Ming Men, or mid-point of the spine) is also located. The Ming Men does not have this property, but in the Microcosmic Orbit it is regarded as a very important safety point, as well as the strengthening point of the kidneys.

D. THE FOURTH STATION: C-7, A SEXUAL-ENERGY TRANSFORMATION POINT

Your next stopping point is at cervical-7, or C-7, located at the point of your spine at the base of your neck. You can feel it as the vertebra that sticks out when you bend your head down. This point controls the energy provided to the hands and neck, and is the connecting point providing power to the scapulae and spinal cord. This point also has the ability to transform sexual energy into life-force energy.

(1) COLLECTING ENERGY IN THE OVARIAN PALACE

Practice in the same manner described above. Collect the ovaries' energy at the Ovarian Palace. Inhale with a short sip, close the vagina slightly, pulling the energy downward toward the perineum. Then contract and pull up the front part of the perineum and pause for a while, holding your breath and retaining the energy at this point. Be aware of the Ching CHI that has been brought there. Inhale in short sips, close the vagina tightly and concentrate on retaining the ovaries' energy at the front part of the perineum. Exhale and return to the ovaries, but maintain a part of your awareness at the perineum to retain the energy that you have brought there. Continue to practice Ovarian Breathing by opening and closing the vagina slightly and collecting the energy in the Ovarian Palace.

(2) DRAWING ENERGY TO C-7

Once you feel that enough ovaries' energy has been collected, inhale a short sip of air and close the vagina, pulling the ovaries' energy downward toward the perineum, and then pull the front part of the perineum upward to bring energy to this area. Rest for a while and be aware of the energy that travels from the ovaries down to the vagina, clitoris and perineum. Inhale a short sip and contract the middle and back part of the perineum, and then pull the energy up to the sacrum, T-ll and C-7. When you reach C-7, push slightly from the sternum to

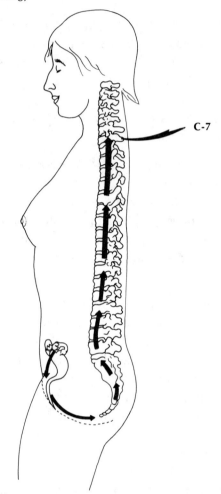

C-7

FIGURE 5-22

Guiding Energy Up to C-7

the back, and feel the push of C-7 and both shoulders as they activate
to draw the energy up. (Figure 5-22) This action will activate the thymus gland to increase the upward pulling power. Hold the energy at
this point as comfortably as you can. Now during practice you will
find that gradually you are able to hold your breath longer and increase your capacity to intake air. Exhale, and then let your sacrum,
T-ll and neck relax, returning to their normal positions. Concentrate
on C-7. This action will help to activate all three pumps (Sacral, Adre-

nal and Cranial) a little at a time. If you have trouble feeling this action, return to the Ovarian Palace and repeat the process. Practice nine times. Remember that you must return to the source of energy in order to bring it to the higher center.

E. THE FIFTH STATION: THE JADE PILLOW, A MINI-STORAGE AND TRANSFORMATION POINT FOR SEXUAL ENERGY

Your next stopping place is your Jade Pillow. This is located at the back of your head between cervical-1, or C-1, and the base of the skull. This point also can serve as a small storage and transformation point for sexual energy.

(1) COLLECTING ENERGY IN THE OVARIAN PALACE

Practice in the same manner as previously described. Collect the ovaries' energy at the Ovarian Palace. Close the vagina with a minimal movement of the Chi Muscle, pulling down the ovaries' energy to the perineum. Feel the sensation as the vagina closes, and then pull up the front part of the perineum to bring the ovaries' energy to this point. Hold your breath and retain the energy at the front part of the perineum. Be aware of the Ching CHI that has been brought there. Exhale and return to the ovaries, but maintain an awareness of the perineum to retain the energy that you have brought there. Practice Ovarian Breathing by opening and closing the vagina slightly in order to collect the energy in the Ovarian Palace.

(2) DRAWING ENERGY TO THE JADE PILLOW

Once you feel that enough ovaries' energy has been collected, inhale a short sip and close the vagina, pulling the ovaries' energy downward to the perineum, and then contract and pull the front part of the perineum upward to bring energy to this area. Rest for a while and be aware of the energy that travels from the ovaries down to the vagina, clitoris and perineum. Inhale another short sip and bring the energy up to the sacrum, T-11, and C-7, and then slightly push the chin down and pull it back, moving it toward the back of the neck at the base of the skull. (Figure 5-23) Feel this push create a force that activates the Cranial Pump, which will help to pump the dense ovaries' energy. Hold the energy at this point for a while, feeling it being stored and transformed. Exhale, then permit your sacrum, T-11 and neck to relax

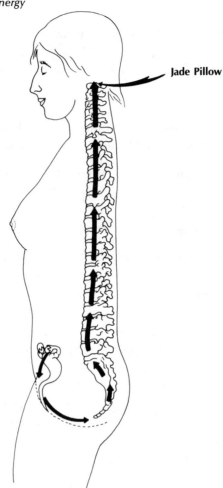

Jade Pillow

FIGURE 5-23

Guiding Energy Up to the Jade Pillow

in their normal positions. This action will help to activate the Adrenal, Sacral and Cranial Pumps again. Retain the energy at the base of the skull. Repeat this entire process nine times.

F. THE SIXTH STATION: THE CROWN POINT, A LARGER STORAGE POINT FOR SEXUAL ENERGY

Your next stopping point is called the Pai-Hui, located at the midpoint, or crown, of your head and is the center housing the pineal gland. This point is a larger storage point.

(1) COLLECTING ENERGY IN THE OVARIAN PALACE

Practice in the same manner, only this time you will fill the "straw" to the top. Collect the ovaries' energy at the Ovarian Palace. Close the vagina with a minimal movement of the Chi Muscle, pulling the ovaries' energy down to the perineum, and feeling the sensation as the vagina closes; contract and pull down the front part of the perineum to bring the energy there. Hold your breath and retain the energy at the perineum. Be aware of the Ching CHI that has been brought to this place. Exhale and return to the ovaries, but maintain an awareness at the perineum to retain the energy that you have brought there. Practice Ovarian Breathing by opening and closing the vagina slightly in order to collect the energy in the Ovarian Palace.

(2) DRAWING ENERGY TO THE CROWN POINT

Once you feel that enough ovaries' energy has been collected, inhale a short sip and close the vagina by pulling downward to bring the ovaries' energy to the perineum, and then contract and pull up the front part of the perineum to bring energy to this area. Rest for a while and be aware of the energy that travels from the ovaries down to the vagina, clitoris and perineum. Inhale and tilt the sacrum and T-ll to the back in order to straighten the spinal curve out a little bit and thereby help activate the lower Sacral Pump. At the same time push the sternum in toward the back, tuck your chin in a little, and squeeze the back of your skull; this will activate the upper Cranial Pump. Continue pulling up to the point at the top, the center of the head. (Figure 5-24) As you continue to inhale, bring the energy down to the perineum, up to the sacrum, T-ll, C-7, Jade Pillow, and then turn your eyes and other senses upward to help guide the energy up to the point of the Pai-Hui, or crown point, and the pineal gland.

(3) RESTING AND USING YOUR MIND TO GUIDE THE ENERGY TO THE BRAIN

Once the energy finally has completed its course up into your head, use your eyes and other senses to help retain it in the brain, holding it at the top of your brain as comfortably as possible. Exhale, then let your sacrum, T-ll and neck relax, returning to their normal positions. This will help to activate the three pumps: Sacral, Adrenal and Cranial. Use your mind to guide the energy station-to-station up

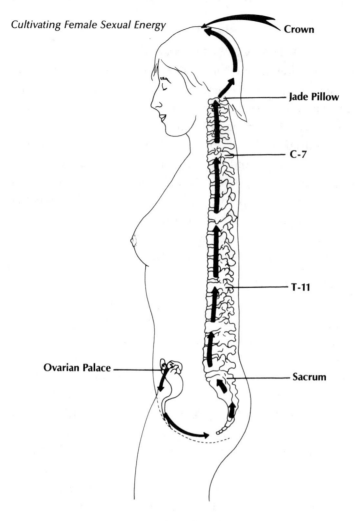

FIGURE 5-24

Guiding Energy Up to the Crown Point

the spine to the top of the head. Fix your attention and eyes at the crown point. Remember it is the resting period that is the strongest in guiding the energy to the brain. Repeat this process nine times.

G. CIRCULATING THE ENERGY IN THE BRAIN

(1) FILLING THE BRAIN CAVITY WITH CREATIVE SEXUAL ENERGY

When you have finished practicing nine times, and can feel the ovaries' sexual energy fill the brain, start to circulate the energy in the brain for nine, eighteen, or thirty-six counterclockwise revolutions. There is a very distinct feeling of spinning outward. (Figure 5-25(a)) When this circulation is completed, turn the energy back into the center of the brain for nine, eighteen, or thirty-six clockwise revolutions. (Figure 5-25(b)) This should feel pleasant and energetic and will help

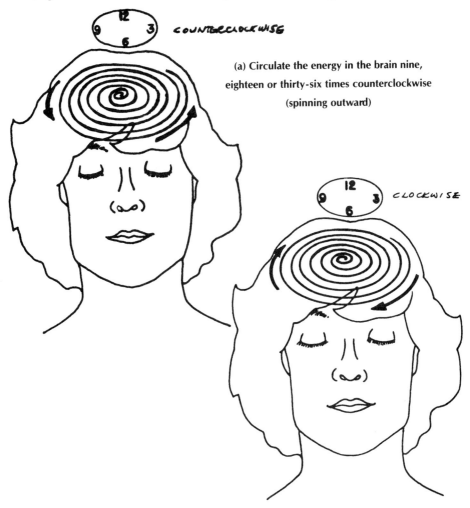

(a) Circulate the energy in the brain nine, eighteen or thirty-six times counterclockwise (spinning outward)

(b) When the counterclockwise turns are completed, circulate the energy nine, eighteen or thirty-six times clockwise (spinning inward)

FIGURE 5-25

to balance the left and right sides of the brain, vitalizing it to increase memory and think more clearly, and it will introduce you to the beginning stages of the ability to control sexual energy and emotional frustrations. As people age and use up much of their CHI, they gradually drain themselves of brain energy and spinal fluids, drying them up and leaving a cavity. Ovarian Breathing transports creative sexual energy to refill this cavity and thereby revitalize the brain. Taoists regard sexual energy as similar to brain energy.

(2) TOUCHING THE TONGUE TO THE PALATE TO PERMIT THE ENERGY TO FLOW DOWN TO THE NAVEL FOR STORAGE

Be sure the tongue is touching the palate (behind the front teeth will suffice), so that the warm ovaries' energy can flow down to the third eye, to the inside of your nose, and through the tongue from which it is now able to travel down the throat to the heart center. (Figure 5-26) Retain the energy in the heart center for a while, filling it with energy until it feels open; enjoy the feeling of love, joy and peace; then bring it down to the solar plexus and to the navel. Collect the sexual energy at the navel where it can be safely stored.

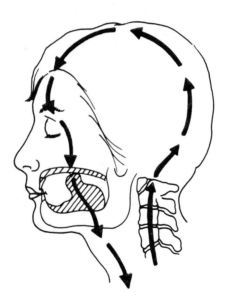

FIGURE 5-26

The tongue touches the palate so the energy

can flow down

H. COLLECTING THE OVARIES' SEXUAL ENERGY AT THE NAVEL

It is is very important to end by storing the energy in the navel. Most ill effects of the practice are caused by an excess of energy in the head or the heart. The navel can safely handle the increased energy generated by the ovaries.

(1) SPIRALING THE ENERGY AROUND YOUR NAVEL CENTER

To collect the ovaries' energy, concentrate on your navel area, which is about one and a half inches inside your body. Use your mind, eyes and other senses to mentally move the energy in and out, spiraling it around your navel 36 times. Do not spiral above the thoracic diaphragm or below the pubic bone. Start by spiraling counterclockwise outward. (Figure 5-27(a) Then reverse the direction of the spiral and bring it back to the navel, circling it clockwise 24 times. (Figure 5-27(b)) Use your finger as a guide the first few times. The energy is now safely stored in your navel, available to you whenever and wherever your body needs it.

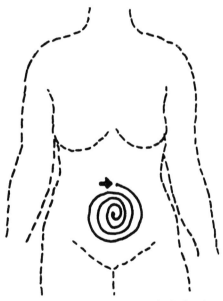

(a) Collect the energy in the navel, circling it 36
times counterclockwise, and

FIGURE 5-27

Collecting Smiling Energy in the Navel

111

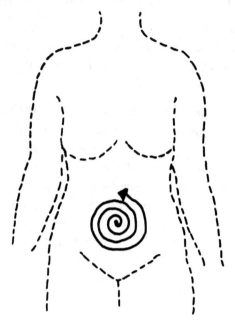

(b) 24 times clockwise

FIGURE 5-27

I. COLLECTING ENERGY IN THE HEART

The energy can also be stored in the heart. If you are a Yang body type (meaning your energy runs hotter than most people, perhaps manifesting in a hot temper), you should not start by storing the sexual energy in the heart center. Instead, begin by storing it in the navel. Once the navel is filled, this is an indication that the channels are open enough to begin to store energy in the heart without problems.

The heart center is a powerhouse for a woman. It is the seat of love, joy, happiness, and is the center of rejuvenation since it is the site of the thymus gland. With this center open a woman will experience these positive emotions along with an energetic approach toward herself, and she will be provided with abundant healing energy to heal herself and others. If the heart center is opened before she is ready, the Microcosmic Orbit will not be complete and the energy will not circulate properly. The sexual energy can adhere to the heart, and the heat generated and congested there can cause great problems such as uneasiness, shortness of breath, or pain in the chest. If these problems happen to you, practice the Healing Sound of the heart as detailed in the book *Taoist Ways to Transform Stress into Vitality,* lightly tap the chest and the heart, and use your hands to brush your chest downward until you belch to release the trapped energy.

(1) SPIRALING THE ENERGY AROUND YOUR HEART CENTER

To collect the ovaries' energy in the heart, concentrate on your heart center, located up one inch from the lower tip of the sternum, and about one and a half inches inside your body. It is approximately three inches in dimension. Use your mind, eyes and other senses to mentally move the energy in and out, spiraling around your heart center 36 times. (Figure 5-28(a)) Do not spiral above the diaphragm or

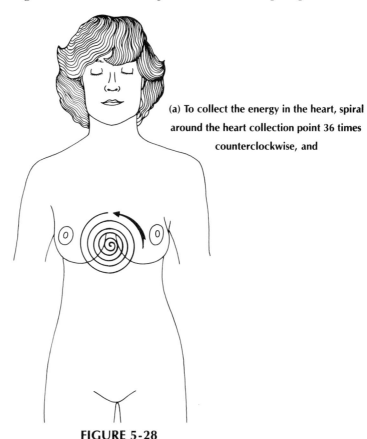

(a) To collect the energy in the heart, spiral around the heart collection point 36 times counterclockwise, and

FIGURE 5-28
Collecting Smiling Energy in the Heart

below the pubic bone. Start by spiraling counterclockwise outward. Then reverse the direction of the spiral, returning the energy to the heart center, circling it 24 times. (Figure 5-28(b)) Use your finger as a guide for the first few times. The energy is now safely stored in your heart center, available whenever and wherever your body needs it.

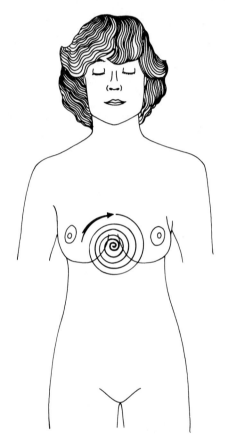

(b) 24 times clockwise

FIGURE 5-28

J. BRINGING ENERGY TO THE BRAIN WITH ONE ACTION

In the beginning travel from station to station, until you feel that the back channel, or Governor Channel, is more open. Once you have mastered the process you can practice the Ovarian Breathing exercise and the energy will travel up to the brain in one sweet drawing-up of the "straw," using a single, clean inhalation and one contraction of the vagina. Exhale, then inhale and bring the energy up again. Practice this a few times, but since the ovarian energy is warm, be sure to put your tongue up to your palate and bring the energy down to the navel. Eventually all you will need is your concentration on both your ovaries and the crown of your head to mentally move the sexual energy from the ovaries all the way up to the brain in one step.

K. EFFECTS OF OVARIAN ENERGY

This subtle exercise puts you in touch with your ovarian energy. Women report that they feel the energy moving up their spine; some say it feels wide, thick like honey, and slow. Most women who perceive the temperature at all say it feels warm. Some women experience it as cool at first, but after practicing for a while, notice it changes to warm. Some experience sensations in their genitals or on their thighs, usually describing them as warm to hot. Many women describe the energy as warmer, wider, heavier, or thicker than the organ CHI energy circulated in the Microcosmic Orbit. This is because the ovarian energy *is* heavier and denser.

It is not unusual that the energy feels cold when there is a lot of healing going on, such as in women who have menstrual problems. The sensations can vary over time. What is important to know is that if the energy feels warm, it must be circulated and not left up in the head.

One session of Ovarian Breathing should take about ten minutes. When completed four to seven times a week, women have reported noticeable changes in their menstrual cycles, such as less bleeding, less cramping, and a reduction in breast pain. With continued practice menstruation ceases. The energy conserved in such a manner becomes part of the vital energy of the body, increasing the available energy for transformation into a higher form. Also, there is historical evidence that the women who practice Ovarian Kung Fu, when they decide to have children, will produce very healthy, well-balanced children.

Some perform Ovarian Breathing and then proceed directly to the Microcosmic Orbit Meditation. The practice can be done any time and virtually anywhere, once you have achieved the direct pathway from the ovaries to the brain. When you find yourself with unstructured time, e.g., waiting in line, commuting, at your desk, looking at television, in bed, etc., carry out several series of contractions, as many as you choose to fill the time available. The main consideration is that the back be properly straight, the chest relaxed, and the vagina protected from the breeze. You must also remember to touch your tongue to your palate after you practice three or four times.

Take your time to really feel the warmth when you practice. Do not rush it, and always maintain the action of the pumps as you breathe in and out. Use a more mental than physical pull when you do the exercise. Let the warm feeling be your guide. Always remember to bring the energy down to the navel after a few breaths, since the navel is roomy and a safe place to store this warm vital energy.

It is highly desirable to use Ovarian Breathing to tone the pelvic diaphragm. The whole lower abdomen is deeply massaged each time the pelvic diaphragm flexes. Life-force flows into the region through periodic waves of breath which stimulate the glands and vital organs.

Ovarian Breathing has tremendous implications for women's control over their reproductive systems. There is not enough evidence to conclude that women can control their fertility through this method. History records, however, that when a woman practices the Orgasmic Upward Draw, she can control her cervix and urethra very well, squeezing the urethra (before the cervix) tightly so a man's sperm cannot enter the cervix to join with her egg.

There is too little evidence to come to any conclusions about the effectiveness or reversibility of this method when used for birth control. However, some women are experimenting with this method, trusting that it will be reversible just by stopping the practice for a couple of months. These women feel justified in using themselves as their own laboratories, since the method is gentle and appears to be under control. So many women, out of desperation to control their reproductive systems, have already accepted the wholesale experimentation of dangerous birth control methods, by supposedly trustworthy institutions, such as IUDs, DES, morning-after pills, sequential birth control pills, and forced sterilization.

4. Steps to Practice

The following is a step-by-step guide through the practice.

a. Sit erect on the edge of your chair with your feet flat on the floor about shoulders' width apart. Make sure you feel very relaxed. If you are tense, do some stretching exercises, practice the Inner Smile to the tense part, or take a walk to disperse tension.

b. Find the Ovarian Palace by placing both thumbs at the navel and forming a triangle with your index fingers. Spread your little fingers; the place where they come to rest is the site of your ovaries. Become aware of them. Rub the ovaries until they become warm. Concentrate to produce more energy from the ovaries and eggs. Use your mind and very little pressure on the P-C Muscle to close and open the vagina. When you feel enough energy has been generated, inhale a short sip of air, bringing the energy to the Ovarian Palace.

c. Inhale another sip of air and create a downward pulling action of the ovaries' energy to the perineum by contracting the outer and inner lips of the vagina. Then contract and pull up the front part of the perineum so that the energy will travel there. Maintain an awareness of the front part of the perineum for a while.

d. Exhale and breathe normally. Rest and guide the warm feeling from your ovaries to your perineum, letting the energy flow to the perineum via the uterus, down through the cervical canal and along the back wall of the vagina. At the same time feel it flow the few inches to the perineum, an action induced by putting your mind at the perineum and maintaining your attention there. Inhale and exhale several times from the ovaries to build up more energy. The retention of the ovaries' sexual energy (Ching CHI) at the perineum is very important, for if you release your attention, the warm energy will leak out.

e. Start at the Ovarian Palace and use Ovarian Breathing, inhaling and exhaling until you feel that the energy is ready. Inhaling in short sips, draw the warm energy from your ovaries to the perineum, and then by pulling up the middle and back of the perineum, draw the energy up to your coccyx, located at the very bottom end of your spine. The sacral hiatus, an area made mostly of bone and located a little up from the tip of your spine at the sacrum, is the opening through which the energy must pass.

Once you have pulled the warm energy of the ovaries down to the perineum, contracted the front of the perineum, and then pulled up the middle and back part of the perineum, follow by tilting the sacrum, slightly arching your lower back outward and pushing the bottom of your sacrum as if you were standing with your back against a wall and flattening against it. Then tilt the sacrum downward and hold it in this position in order to activate the Sacral Pump, which will be further accentuated if you gently tuck in your chin and straighten the back of your neck and skull. Hold the energy at the sacrum for a while, then exhale but continue to maintain your attention at the sacrum. Repeat the process nine times.

f. Once you have managed to bring the energy up through your coccyx and sacral hiatus, spend the next week drawing the warm energy to the eleventh thoracic vertebra (T-11) in your mid-back opposite the solar plexus. Practice in the same manner: inhaling short sips of air while pulling and guiding the energy from the perineum up your spine to the sacrum, and then to T-11. Pull up and retain the energy at T-11, tilt to the back, and feel the point fill with energy and continue to open as the energy moves up by itself.

T-11 is the energy center for the adrenal glands, which sit on top of your kidneys. In Taoist practice we regard the adrenal glands as a minipump. As you arch, you will create a vacuum here to push the energy up higher.

g. Your next stopping place is at the base of the neck, called cervical-7, or C-7. Practice in the same manner as described above: inhaling short sips of air and pumping energy from the ovaries down to the perineum and up to the sacrum and T-11. Slightly push from the sternum to bring the energy to C-7, and then pull and guide it there. Repeat this process nine times.

h. Your next stopping place is your Jade Pillow. This is located at the back of your head, between cervical-1, or C-1, and the base of the skull. Practice in the same manner as described above, inhaling short sips as you continue to pump the ovaries' energy down to the perineum and up to the sacrum, T-11, C-7, C-1 and Jade Pillow. There is a small storage place in this area where you can store the ovaries' energy for further use, although it is the upper part of the brain that is the largest storage place for energy. Repeat the process nine times.

i. Your next stopping point and a larger storage place for the energy is the Pai-Hui, located at the crown of your head. Practice in the same manner, only this time fill the "straw" to the top. Tilt the sacrum to the back in order to straighten the curve of the spine outward a little bit; this will help to activate the lower pump. At the same time push the sternum to C-7, tuck in your chin a little, and squeeze the back of your skull. This will activate the upper Cranial Pump. Continue to pull up to the point at the center of the top of the head. Repeat nine times.

j. Touch the tongue to the palate to permit the energy to flow down to the third eye, to the inside of your nose, through the tongue and down to the heart center. Pause for a while at the heart center and feel the energy fill and open this center as it transforms into loving energy. Then bring the energy down to the navel center for storage. Here spiral the energy 36 times counterclockwise and outward, then reverse and circle inward 24 times.

Once you finish the last set of nine, and you feel the ovaries' sexual energy fill the brain, begin to turn the energy to circulate it in the brain counterclockwise for nine, eighteen, or thirty-six revolutions, and then change directions, circulating the energy clockwise for nine, eighteen, or thirty-six revolutions. Use your mind, eyes and senses to assist you. Rest and mentally guide the energy from the Ovarian Palace to the top of the crown.

5. SUMMARY of Ovarian Breathing

a. Bring your attention to your ovaries and breathe into them.

b. Direct your attention to the Ovarian Palace, lying between the ovaries.

c. Contract the vagina slightly, pulling the ovaries' energy down to the perineum, then contract and pull up the front part of the perineum to bring the energy there while simultaneously inhaling a short sip of air. Rest, holding your breath, and feel the flow of the energy from the Ovarian Palace to the vagina, the clitoris and the perineum. Exhale, with your mind retaining the energy there. Repeat this procedure nine times.

d. Continue to retain the ovaries' energy at the perineum, and at the same time return your partial attention to the ovaries and the Ovarian Palace. Collect the energy there, then simultaneously inhaling short sips, very slightly contract the vagina, the front part of the perineum, then the middle and back part of the perineum, and inhale the ovaries' energy to the coccyx and up to the sacrum. Exhale. Repeat nine times.

e. Holding the ovaries' energy at the sacrum, return your attention to the ovaries, and bring the energy to the Ovarian Palace. Inhale short sips of air as you lightly close the vagina and simultaneously contract the front part of the perineum. Bring the CHI to the perineum, pause for a while, and inhale. Pull up the middle and then back parts of the anus. Pull the energy up to the coccyx and sacrum. Pause and inhale and push the sacrum back as if it were pushed against a wall to open the hiatus so that CHI can enter the spinal cord. Move the energy to T-11. Exhale. Repeat nine times.

f. Holding the ovarian energy at T-11, return your attention to the ovaries and the Ovarian Palace. Inhale short sips of air, lightly closing the vagina while simultaneously contracting the front, middle and back of the perineum. Move the energy from the ovaries to the perineum, sacrum, T-11 and C-7. Hold and retain it there. Exhale. Repeat nine times.

g. Holding the ovarian energy at C-7, return your attention to the ovaries and to the Ovarian Palace. Inhale short sips of air, slightly close the vagina while simultaneously lightly contracting the front, middle and back of the perineum, and move the energy from the ovaries to the perineum, sacrum, T-11, C-7 and Jade Pillow. Exhale. Repeat nine times.

h. Holding the ovarian energy at the Jade Pillow, return your attention to the ovaries and repeat the process, proceeding from the ovaries to the brain, to the top of the head, to the crown. Repeat nine times. When the energy has filled the brain, permit it to spiral in the brain nine, eighteen, or thirty-six counterclockwise revolutions and then nine, eighteen, or thirty-six clockwise revolutions. Place the tongue up on the palate and allow the energy to flow down to the third eye, tongue, throat and heart. Pause for a while at the heart and feel the sexual (creative) energy transfer into loving energy, and then move down to the solar plexus and the navel. Collect the energy at the navel.

REMEMBER! THE ENERGY FROM THE OVARIES IN OVARIAN BREATHING IS WARM ENERGY. BE SURE TO BRING IT DOWN AFTER FOUR INHALATIONS.

B. Ovarian and Vaginal Compression

1. Compressing Air into the Ovaries Increases Sexual Power

Many benefits of Ovarian Breathing are magnified when performed in conjunction with the Ovarian and Vaginal Compression exercise. This exercise reduces mental problems, strengthens the ovaries and the cervix, and increases the power of the vaginal muscles. It helps you consciously to direct energy into and out of the pelvic region. It builds your sexual power dynamically by using the vital CHI from the upper part pushed by the compressed air and packed by its charge into your ovaries to increase the ovaries' energy. By packing the CHI into the ovaries and the vagina, you warm up the sexual region so that you can be more sexually active, easily aroused, and easily have an orgasm. When the sexual region has less CHI, it gets cold and is difficult to arouse. This can be compared to attempting to boil ice water, as opposed to room temperature water; it takes much more heat to bring the ice water to the boiling point.

Of the three suggested positions, sitting or standing are preferable. Inhale a fairly large amount of air into the throat and swallow the air. Swallowing drives the air down to the solar plexus. From the solar plexus the air is rolled down into the pelvic region. From there it will be driven down both sides of the vagina to be compressed there. (Figure 5-29)) This is accomplished by contracting the abdominal muscles downward in a slow wave. The vagina seems to expand, a flush of heat is experienced, and after a short time the power driven into it flows up the spine to the head, which also becomes very warm.

2. Ovarian and Vaginal Compression Exercise Step-By-Step

a. Sit on the edge of your chair with your feet flat on the floor about as far apart as your shoulders' width. Feel the feet support a part of the weight; do not place it all on the sitting bones. Wear loose clothing so that it will be easy to compact the CHI.

b. Inhale through the nostrils into the throat. From there swallow the air down to the solar plexus, midway between your heart and your navel. Do not stop at the heart center. Imagine the air as a ball.

c. First the ball sits behind the solar plexus. From this point roll it down to the navel, then into the pelvis, and spread it out to both sides

121

FIGURE 5-29

Ovarian and Vaginal Compression

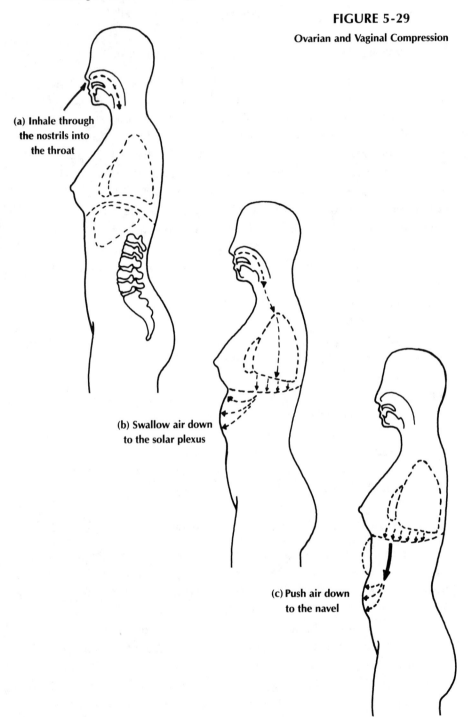

(a) Inhale through
the nostrils into
the throat

(b) Swallow air down
to the solar plexus

(c) Push air down
to the navel

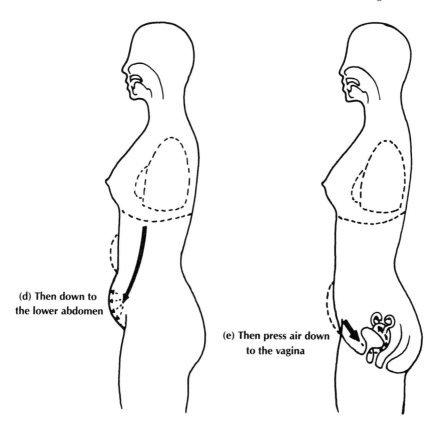

(d) Then down to the lower abdomen

(e) Then press air down to the vagina

of the ovaries. This is accomplished by contracting the abdominal muscles downward in a slow wave. Feel the CHI pressure drop around the ovaries, pack and compress the ovaries to energize them, and gradually pack the cervix. Squeeze the inner and outer lips of the vagina tightly, and keep on pushing into the vagina as if you were blowing up a balloon, until the vagina feels like it is expanding.

d. Forcibly compress the air into the ovaries for as long as you can. Once the air is driven into the ovaries, you will experience a flush of heat. After a short time the power driven into the ovaries flows up the spine to the head, which also becomes very warm. The minimum period for each compression should be 30 to 40 seconds. Slowly work up to at least one minute. Every single Ovarian Compression shoots tremendous energy into the vagina. With compression lasting an entire minute the exercise takes full effect. The anal sphincter and perineum

123

muscles must be squeezed tightly during this exercise to prevent leakage of energy.

e. When you have finished the compression, exhale and relax completely. Saliva accumulates in the mouth during compression; swallow it before exhaling.

f. After complete exhalation, take a number of quick, short breaths to recover your wind. Dart the air in and out of the nostrils to quickly regain capacity for another compression. Remember to breathe through the nose, and do not inhale unduly large quantities of air. This process is called "Bellows Breathing" because you must pump your lower abdomen in and out quickly in order to do it.

This exercise quickly charges the whole body. If you feel ill or out of sorts, several Ovarian Compressions will restore you to good form. Perform the exercises in the following sequence:

(1) First practice one Ovarian Compression. (2) Then, rotate the waist with the arms at shoulder level. (3) Rest for a moment and repeat the exercise.

Remember to keep the tongue up on the palate when compressing the air. In the beginning perform two to three compressions, gradually increasing to five.

When you have grown stronger, you may do five compressions in succession, and then rest by rotating your body from the waist. Begin a second series of five compressions. Keep the breathing between compressions short and shallow so you do not lodge power high in the body.

Practice Ovarian Breathing and Ovarian and Vaginal Compression twice a day for approximately fifteen minutes in the morning and fifteen minutes in the evening. Regular practice of these breathing techniques yields many benefits in addition to those already mentioned, such as a decrease in insomnia and nervousness, and an improvement in overall energy.

The exercise should start to take effect within three days after its commencement. The ovaries feel warm and may itch, or feel somewhat tingly, an indication that the ovaries are receiving unusually high amounts of vital force. These signs occur only if the exercise is done properly. A month or two of exercise will produce substantial increases in strength and well-being.

3. SUMMARY of Ovarian and Vaginal Compression

    a. Choose your preferred position.

    b. Breathe in very slowly through the nose, concentrating on the throat. Compress the air in the throat until you can inhale no further.

    c. Swallow strongly to the solar plexus and hold the air there as if it were a ball.

    d. Press the ball of air down to the navel region.

    e. From the navel press the ball of air down to the pelvic region.

    f. Press the ball strongly and continuously into the ovaries until you can hold your breath no longer. At the end of your breath capacity, swallow the saliva strongly.

    g. Rest by taking quick, shallow breaths through the nose.

    h. Relax by rotating the waist several times.

    i. Start with 5 repetitions and increase slowly to 36 at a sitting.

    j. Keep the tongue up on the palate.

C. Venting Exercises for High Blood Pressure

After practicing Ovarian Compression for two to six weeks, some women with high blood pressure notice a large flow of CHI energy to the head. They feel tension in the head because the blood has followed the upward flow of the vital power. This is not unlike a mild symptom of the "Kundalini Syndrome," in which freed energy races about the body out of control.

If you suffer from high blood pressure and have not practiced meditation to open the Microcosmic Orbit, which distributes the energy evenly throughout the circuits of the body, you can meditate on two points to vent excess pressure. These are the Ming-Men, or Door of Life, on the spine directly opposite the navel (between lumbar 2 and 3), and the Yuang Chuan (K-1 point), the kidney point, on the soles of your feet.

To locate the Ming-Men, place a string around the waist like a belt. Make it perfectly horizontal and place it across the navel. The Ming-Men lies where the string meets the spine. When you bend over backward from the waist, the point feels like a hole in the spine. (Figure 5-30)

125

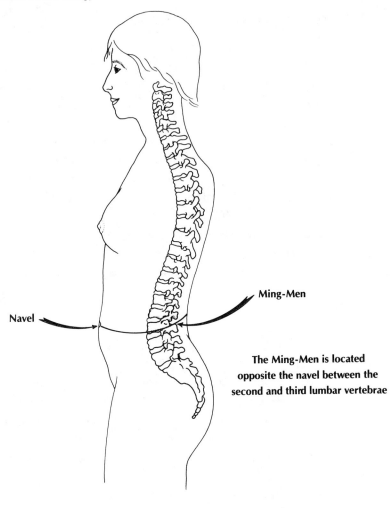

Navel

Ming-Men

The Ming-Men is located
opposite the navel between the
second and third lumbar vertebrae

FIGURE 5-30
The Ming-Men Point

The other point, the Yuang Chuan, lies on the foot. When clenching
the toes, it is the deepest central point on the sole of the foot. (Figure
5-31)

The Ming-Men Point: To help bring the excess energy in the head
down the front of the body, use the Microcosmic Orbit. This can be
accomplished by placing the left palm directly on the Ming-Men point
and placing the right palm on top of the head. Mentally guide the

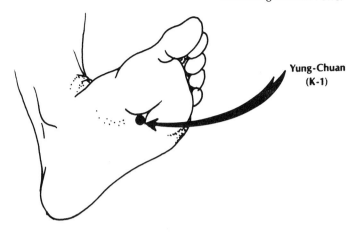

FIGURE 5-31
The Yuang Chuan (K-1) Point

excess energy down to the Ming-Men. This draws the CHI and blood there. The hand can help to induce the CHI flow. The right hand, like a pitcher, sends out energy; the left hand, like a catcher, receives the energy. In this way the energy can be brought down more easily.

The Yuang Chuan Point: The Yuang Chuan point is the Yin-energy entry point. The Taoists regard the soles of the feet as the roots of the body, and the root is important as the foundation for the work of the spirit body. Once you have found the points on both feet, tape onto them spiny little balls such as prickly chestnuts or plain tree seed pods. Place both soles on the ground and press firmly on the spiny balls while concentrating on the kidney-1 point (also known as the "bubbling spring"). You can help guide the energy down to the soles by placing your left palm on the sacrum, and the right palm on the top of the head; guide the energy from the crown to the Ming-Men, down to the sacrum, down to the backs of the knees, and finally to the soles through the backs of the legs.

After a short time of practice you will feel the power flow to the Ming-Men. Direct it down through the spine and backs of the legs to the Yuang Chuan. Press down on the balls of the feet so that you feel the soles very distinctly. In severe cases it may take a month or two to get the power into the Ming-Men and bring it down to the Yuang Chuan.

If blood flows too strongly to the head during or after compression, vent the power by practicing the Ming-Men and Yuang Chuan exercises right after compression. Imbalanced force will flow down the body through these two points. After practicing the exercises, many students open the Microcosmic Orbit so that their energy flows in a continuous circuit, and there will be no need to bring the energy down through the back to the soles. You can also bring it down the front of the body through the heart and navel, down to the perineum, and down to the backs of the knees to the soles. This alone has often ended high blood pressure.

Many benefits of Ovarian Breathing are magnified when performed in conjunction with the Ovarian Compression exercise. If the ovaries are too cold, there will be a reduction in desire for sex. Ovarian Compression, by warming the ovaries, will warm your heart as well. It helps you calm down when sexually over-excited by teaching you to consciously direct energy into and out of the pelvic region. It builds your sexual power dynamically by using the vital CHI taken from the air and packing its charge into your Ching CHI.

Refer to Chapter 6 for more safety tips in performing the exercises in this chapter.

6. THE ORGASMIC UPWARD DRAW

A. Sexual Energy and Women

In ancient times the Taoists saw men and women as worthy partners and adversaries. Their sexual union reflected the union of Yin and Yang on the cosmic level. Their different approaches to life and problem-solving brought harmony to the earth.

Taoists regard man as fire and woman as water. Fire, when started, burns very fast and does not last long. As we mentioned earlier, it takes time for water to reach its boiling point, just as it takes time to bring a woman to her boiling point. Once she reaches that point, she will maintain it for a long time.

Taoists have described women as sexually superior to men, yet we see today that many women are sexually unhappy. Because the response times of men and women are different, the sexual embrace occurs, many times, without the full arousal of the woman. The vaginal spasms which occur at this arousal level are mistaken as the total orgasm. However, since the woman has reached only half of her potential for orgasm, she reports feeling let down, frustrated, alienated, angry, restless, and isolated.

To experience the multilevels of a complete orgasm, a woman must be aware that there are many steps she must climb, with each step energizing certain parts of the body. The complete orgasm is desirable because it energizes and brings pleasure to the entire body. Conversely, the repeated interruption of orgasm at lower levels creates energy imbalances, since only some of the organs and glands are stimulated and not the entire body. If a man can prolong his erection, he can help bring the woman to higher levels with simple movements, and the couple will be able to reach the highest harmony they can attain in lovemaking.

The Orgasmic Upward Draw (more simply referred to in this chapter as the Orgasmic Draw) exercise taught here is a way to increase the sexual potential of a woman by warming up her sexual region ahead of time to avoid this depressing chain of events.

In all of the basic sexual studies conducted, many parallels have been made between a man's orgasm and a woman's orgasm, especially in what is called rhythmic pulsations, which have been measured at eight-tenths of a second. Research has also found that when a woman's sexual organs are considered as one functioning unit, the amount of erectile tissue is about the same as for a man. Therefore, there is no reason to believe that women's orgasms are any less strong or powerful than men's.

The Taoist sages noted that through internal alchemy, women, using the same method used by men of turning their aroused sexual energy inward and upward, can transform this energy into a power which fills certain reservoirs in their bodies, eventually enabling them to reach the ultimate spiritual accomplishment. The Orgasmic Draw is a preparation for the spiritual practice of Kan and Li, which rely on the power of the stored sexual energy (Ching) to be transferred into a new life-force energy (CHI), and CHI into spiritual energy (Shen).

Women have the capacity for virtually inexhaustible sexual pleasure, far greater than the capacity of men. Even though women do not lose very much energy during intercourse as a result of orgasm, that small unit of sexual energy multiplies, and the longer an orgasm lasts, the more sexual energy can be produced. If thought of in units, the energy can be multiplied by the woman from 10 units to 100, 1000, or to hundreds of thousands of units. However, if this small unit of energy is disposed of, it no longer is within reach, and there will be no opportunity to transform it to the higher energy level.

On a day-to-day level, this storehouse of sexual energy expresses itself as an abundance of loving and healing energy—enough for each woman to not only love and heal herself physically and psychically, but to extend that loving and healing to various relationships in her life and commitments in her community and global sphere. It is no accident that women become involved in professions such as nursing and teaching, occupations which require the generation of tremendous amounts of loving, caring, and healing energy.

Aside from being a thrilling experience, the Orgasmic Draw is a technique reaping benefits such as organ and gland rejuvenation. Every time aroused sexual energy is routed to the brain, memory improves, cells are nourished, and a wonderful feeling engulfs the body from the top of the scalp to the tips of the toes.

B. Ovarian Breathing and the Orgasmic Draw

Up to this point you have learned Ovarian Breathing as a means to pump quiet sexual energy created in the ovaries to the brain. The Orgasmic Draw will teach you how to draw the far denser "aroused" sexual energy upward. The means by which you will accomplish this initially is muscle power. You will use it not only to stop the outward movement of the orgasm, but to actually change the direction of the energy inward and upward. Eventually the control will become more internal, the muscles of the pelvic diaphragm will begin to develop, and you will be controlling the Orgasmic Draw with your mind.

The temperature of sexual energy is the second major difference between Ovarian Breathing and the Orgasmic Draw. The aroused sexual energy cultivated in the Orgasmic Draw is cooler than the biologic, reproductive (or sexual) energy that is produced by the ovaries and harnessed during the process of Ovarian Breathing. It is also cooler than aroused sexual energy in men, which is considered hot Yang energy. It is the cool quality of this energy that enables it to be stored in the brain for future use.

As in Ovarian Breathing, the Chi Muscle plays a great role in directing the energy. To review briefly: contracting the front of the anus (part of the perineum region) brings the energy from the ovaries (the Ovarian Palace) to the perineum point. Pulling up the middle and contracting the back of the anus (the perineum region) directs the energy from the perineum to the coccyx. This maneuver is useful while you are still at the basic level of practice. As your practice continues, the control becomes both automatic and internal.

1. Single and Dual Cultivation

Even though most people settle upon a particular formula of how they like to have sex and stick to this formula, this does not mean that they would not like another means of gratification if it were offered in a safe and caring way. A woman can enrich her life both physically and spiritually by learning the Orgasmic Draw as taught here using two pathways: Single and Dual Cultivation, which are by no means mutually exclusive. Single Cultivation is usually practiced by the woman who does not have a sexual partner, or whose sexual partner is not practicing the Big Draw (the man's version of the Orgasmic Draw). Many women who practice Dual Cultivation, i.e., with a partner who practices the Big Draw, find that the route of Single Cultivation (Ovarian Breathing, the Orgasmic Draw and meditation, as well as Iron Shirt Chi Kung and Tai Chi) cannot be overlooked.

A woman who practices alone begins to feel the spaciousness inside of her, the blending of her body with the universe, and an increased sensitivity to those around her. Sometimes these experiences are mere glimpses, but with continued practice they can become part of her living reality.

A woman practicing with a partner can learn how to share energy with her partner and can begin to approach the experience of the "Valley Orgasm" or "Beyond Orgasm" state, an experience of heightened awareness for both partners. As the two different souls or two spirits (Yin and Yang) unite, an alchemical fusion of energy occurs that gives birth to a new consciousness for both partners. As they reach the point of "Beyond Orgasm," each having opened their Microcosmic Orbit, Thrusting Channel and Belt Channel, both will feel the sexual energy shoot out of their hearts to the tops of their heads.

A. SOLO PRACTICE

The importance of Single Cultivation, especially at the beginning, is strongly recommended. With solo practice you will be better able to tune into your own responses and thereby have more control over your sexual energy. Between the time you start to experience sexual excitement and the time an orgasm is imminent is a gap you can play within. If you start the Orgasmic Draw when you are only slightly aroused, you will not feel very much sensation. If you wait until you are at the point of pouring the energy out, you may or may not be able to capture and prevent it from leaving your body. Your solo practice is invaluable in enabling you to sense these distinctions and turn them into reflexes.

After you have practiced and feel you have learned the Orgasmic

Draw well, you can try it with a partner, but it should be a partner who is interested in these practices or who is aware that you want to recycle your sexual energy. It is important to be perfectly frank with your partner so that both of you know what is going on.

B. PRACTICING WITH A PARTNER

If you have a partner who is also practicing the Big Draw and Testicle Breathing, you are one of the luckier ones. You will have the opportunity to experience the exchange of energy with your partner and the possibility of entering into the "Beyond Orgasm" state mentioned above. If, however, you have mastered the techniques of the Healing Love exercise, and your male partner does not practice these Taoist Secrets of Love techniques, you will be far superior to him. Then, if you use the Orgasmic Draw on him, you will drain his life-force from him, possibly causing him great harm and creating negative forces within yourself.

The word Tao means "way" and, as described above, those who seek union with the Tao are trying to find the "way" of the universe from which all of nature proceeds. There are many paths to travel along this "way," and many have sought a path in which sex is perceived as spiritually undesirable. Such people recoil from Taoist Dual Cultivation and label those who practice it as following the "Left-Hand Path" (as opposed to the "Right-Hand Path" of celibacy). Dual Cultivation, properly practiced, is a safe path, reaping benefits for the body, mind and spirit.

C. Overview of the Orgasmic Draw

In the Ovarian Breathing exercise you moved warm reproductive sexual energy (ovarian energy or Ching CHI), that lies in the ovaries in its Yang state, up to the head and then down into the body. With the Ovarian Compression exercise you forced the CHI energy that is produced in the vital organs and glands—heart, lungs, spleen, thymus gland, etc.—down to mix with the warm Ching CHI resting in the sexual organs to heat up this region. Then you moved the resulting warm energy upward and circulated it.

In the Orgasmic Draw you will arouse yourself in the direction of an orgasm, collect all the organs' and glands' energy to mix with the sexual energy, move that orgasmic feeling inward and extend it longer and at a higher center, to be then moved into the organs, glands and finally the nervous system, so that the orgasm reaches every cell of the body. As a result you will experience a new kind of orgasm which you have never experienced before. The cool, Yin, sexual energy stored in the ovaries is at your command. You can gather it quickly and build rapidly to a climax, turning it inward and thereby extending the orgasm for as long as you desire, or you can deposit it in the "slow cooker" for a longer and more voluptuous experience. Ultimately, the erection of the clitoris and the internal sensations of fullness and expansion will result in a rhythmic outpouring release. Once you master this Taoist technique, you will find the easiest flowing channel in the body flows directly up to the brain and higher center of the body. Practice is essential since initially you must learn to control the anus Chi Muscle and the involuntary muscle of the pelvic diaphragm to change the rhythmic outpouring of energy into an inward and upward draw of energy, and to help push the sexual energy up through the spine into the upper body.

1. The Four Levels of the Orgasmic Upward Draw Practice

A. BEGINNING STAGE

You will use the muscles of the fists, jaws, neck, feet, perineum, buttocks, and abdomen to help activate the Sacral and Cranial Pumps, divert the ovarian energy and orgasmic feeling, and push the energy upward into the organs and glands in the aroused state.

B. INTERMEDIATE STAGE

You will use less muscular tension of the fists, jaws and feet, increase your reliance on the Chi Muscle of the perineum, pelvic diaphragm and sphincter, and employ the Sacral and Cranial Pumps to help move the sexual energy upward.

C. ADVANCED STAGE

Less muscle tension of the Chi Muscle of the perineum will be required and more use of the Sacral and Cranial Pumps to provide greater power for the mind to move Ching CHI to the crown center. By concentrating power at the upper part of the crown, you will draw the energy from the lower center to the higher center.

D. MOST ADVANCED STAGE

You will only use pure mind control; there is no need for use of muscles. The mind's power will command the ovaries' sexual power to move up and down into the organs, glands and nervous system, and to envelop, pack and revitalize it at your will.

2. Explanation of Procedure

In this exercise you will need to arouse yourself 95 to 99 percent of the way to orgasm. As you master the Orgasmic Draw, you may fine tune your orgasm and gradually cultivate it to go beyond 100 to 200 percent arousal, even up to 1,000 percent. To initially achieve arousal you will massage the breasts. Once you feel that orgasm is imminent, you will stop and practice the Orgasmic Draw method three to nine times per session, or until the orgasm turns inward, flowing into the Microcosmic Orbit and entering into the organs and glands as the lower-center arousal subsides. This will count as one exercise. You will repeat this procedure: stimulating yourself, and then practicing the Orgasmic Draw until the arousal subsides and the orgasmic feeling moves upward.

Practice makes perfect. Once you totally gain control of your sexual organs and the energy involved in solo practice, you will naturally have full control during sexual intercourse. You can continue to have sex and practice at the level you have reached. Some will naturally become skillful much more quickly than others if they have trained their minds through yoga, meditation, or other mental disciplines. If you are not involved in a program of daily physical discipline, do some warm-up exercises and stretching before practicing the Orgasmic Draw. Iron Shirt breathing and packing directly assists in the execution of the Orgasmic Draw. These exercises will tone up the energy in your organs, making it easier to feel your internal CHI energies, and thus speed up the command of your sexual energy.

People spending years and years earning a doctorate in medicine or a Ph.D. in any high technological science know that such knowledge is important to making a living in this worldly life. However, people must also consider learning the high technology about themselves, one involving an energy body and a spiritual body, and earning a doctorate in preparation for the next life. All of the energy practices of this life can be transferred to your next life if you start to practice while you still have an abundance of that energy. Consciously you will transfer your own identification to a spiritual body. Therefore, it is worthwhile to spend time on practice to earn this highest of human technological degrees.

D. The Orgasmic Draw, or How to Transform Aroused Sexual Energy into Total Body Orgasm

1. Practice in an Unaroused State

A. PRE-EXERCISE

While learning the exercise, first practice in an unaroused state.

(1) LOWER ABDOMINAL BREATHING

From your practice of the Microcosmic Orbit you may now find yourself breathing normally in the lower abdomen, with little or no movement of the chest and shoulders. Lower abdominal breathing is the way we breathe when we are babies, and the way we breathe when we are asleep or in deep relaxation. Many of us have to relearn how to breathe into the lower abdomen when awake and alert. Lower abdominal breathing causes the diaphragm to move lower during inhalation, thus elongating the lungs and providing more lung area to be filled with air. Check yourself at random during the day and discover from which area you are breathing. You can practice lower abdominal breathing anytime. In addition to increasing lung capacity, abdominal breathing will also greatly strengthen the lower abdominal muscles, which will help you to control lower abdominal energy. (Figure 6-1)

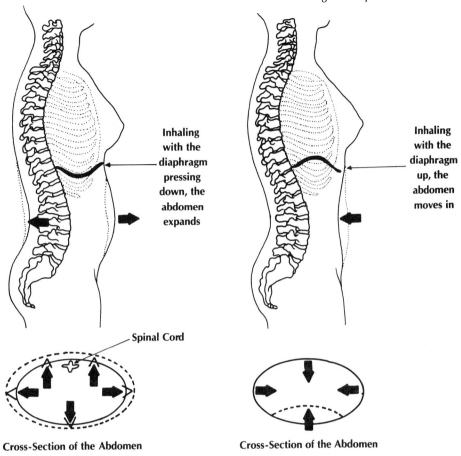

Spinal Cord

Cross-Section of the Abdomen   Cross-Section of the Abdomen

FIGURE 6-1

Lower Abdominal Breathing Breathe as a round shape,
expanding all sides and not the stomach only

(2) THE DIAPHRAGM

Sit or stand in a comfortable position. Exhale, flatten your abdomen, and exhale once more, relaxing the diaphragm down to press against the organs, especially the adrenal glands (located on top of each kidney). Relaxing the diaphragm in the exhale position requires practice. Your mind can help to guide the diaphragm and you can use the Inner Smile to smile to it. The diaphragm can become stuck on the rib cage if it is too tight, and this will make it difficult to move it up and

137

down. You can assist its movement by rubbing along the bottom of the rib cage until the tightness and pain are gone. This will enable the diaphragm to stretch and you will find your breath becoming deeper, making it easier to practice abdominal breathing.

(3) THE ENERGY BALL

Now inhale without expanding the abdomen. You should feel a pressure on the lower abdomen which serves to pack the organs into a smaller place. This will help to concentrate the energy in the lower center, and pack and condense the energy into an energy ball, which we call a "crystal" ball. Exhale and relax. This condensed energy will be of tremendous use in later, higher practice of the Taoist system as you form the energy body and spiritual body that give birth to the soul and spirit.

B. THE RELATIONSHIP OF THE PALATE TO THE ORGANS

The palate and the tongue are closely related to the organs and glands. Knowing how to activate the palate, the floor of the Cranial Pump, will enable you to trigger that pump's action, thereby assisting the flow of CHI.

(1) THE FRONT PALATE

The front part of the palate near the teeth and the inside gum is related to, and is the reflex point of, the heart and small intestine.

(2) THE MIDDLE PALATE

The middle part of the palate before the soft palate is related to, and is the reflex point of, the liver and gall bladder.

(3) THE BACK PALATE

The soft palate located toward the back of the mouth is related to, and is the reflex point of, the kidneys and bladder.

(4) THE FRONT OF THE MOUTH

The point at the front of the mouth between the upper and lower teeth is related to, and is the reflex point of, the lungs and large intestine.

(5) THE JAW LINE

The jaw line between the lower teeth and gums is related to, and is the reflex point of, the spleen, stomach and pancreas.

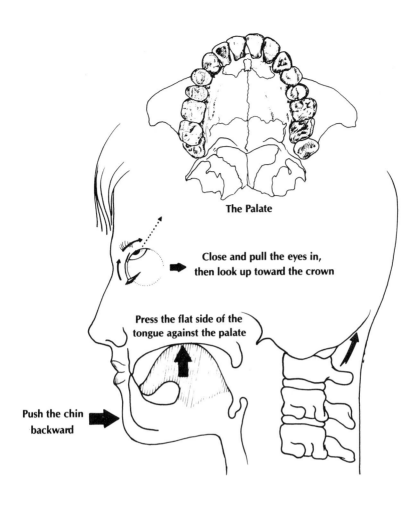

The Palate

Close and pull the eyes in,
then look up toward the crown

Press the flat side of the
tongue against the palate

Push the chin
backward

FIGURE 6-2

Activating the Cranial Pump

C. ACTIVATING THE PUMPS

In these exercises, we combine lower abdominal breathing together with muscle power locks.

(1) ACTIVATION OF THE CRANIAL PUMP (FIGURE 6-2)

The muscle power lock that is responsible for activating the Cranial Pump is accomplished by squeezing the muscles of the tongue against the palate and teeth, while simultaneously squeezing the muscle at the back and base of the skull, thereby activating the Cranial Pump as well as all of the pumps in the body.

139

(A) TEETH

Clenching the teeth will help to squeeze the temporal bones, and when released will activate the Cranial Pump. The cranial bone, located at the palate, is called the palatine bone. Clenching the teeth will also stimulate the lungs and large intestine.

(B) TONGUE

Press the flat side of the tongue to the middle of the palatine bone and the tip of the tongue against the lower front corner made by the gum and teeth. Pressing the tongue firmly to the palate, the floor of the Cranial Pump, will help activate the Cranial Pump and stimulate the palate, the reflex point of the liver and gall bladder. It also stimulates the jaw line, the reflex point of the spleen, stomach and pancreas, and the tip of the tongue. (Figure 6-3)

(C) CHIN

Activate the back side of the Cranial Pump by pushing the chin backward (not up or down). You will feel a tightening at the back and base of the skull, or occipital bone. In the beginning, you will have to squeeze the muscle at the back of the skull to activate the base of the Cranial Pump.

(D) EYES

The eyes contain many muscles around the orbital bones (the cavities of the skull containing the eyes) which will also help to increase the pumping action. Rolling and pulling up the eyes and squeezing the muscles into the orbital bones will also help to activate the Cranial Pump. Look up and slightly pull the eyes up toward the crown at the top of the head. You will feel a pressure there. This will activate the top of the Cranial Pump.

You are now clenching the teeth and pressing the tongue to the palate, pushing the chin to the back, looking up with your eyes and focusing them on the top, or crown, of the head. Once the Cranial and Sacral Pumps are properly activated, the pulling-up action (or suction) will increase, thereby helping to pull the sexual energy up. In the higher part of spiritual practice, the pumping action of the Cranial Pump is very useful in thrusting the spiritual body out of the physical body through the crown.

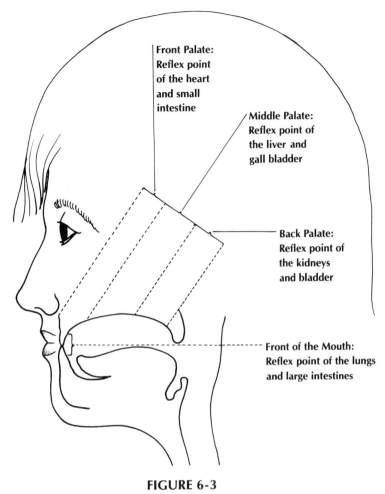

Front Palate: Reflex point of the heart and small intestine

Middle Palate: Reflex point of the liver and gall bladder

Back Palate: Reflex point of the kidneys and bladder

Front of the Mouth: Reflex point of the lungs and large intestines

FIGURE 6-3

Relationship Between the Palate and the Organs

(2) ACTIVATION OF THE MUSCULATORY PUMP

Activating the Musculatory Pump will create a pumping action to draw the sexual energy upward. Taoist Masters discovered that as you create other muscle power locks by squeezing the muscles to the bones of various parts of the body and then releasing them, you will increase the pumping action of the fluids in the body. As you continue in your practice to train your mind to perform this squeeze, the pumping action of the body will greatly improve.

We often feel our hands and feet as the first parts of our bodies to grow cold. Since the arms and legs are the body's extremities, the circulation of fluids to them tends to slow down as time goes by, resulting in the accumulation of many toxins in these areas.

(A) ARMS

To activate the arms' pumping action, start by clenching your fists and rolling four fingers of each hand (excluding the thumb) under, pressing them firmly to the palms. When you feel the pressure, roll the fingers as if you were rolling paper. Press your thumbs firmly to the fingers. (Figure 6-4) Inhale and squeeze the lower arms' muscles to the ulnae and radii (two forearm bones). Hold for a while and release. You will gradually feel a strong pumping action beginning. Gradually increase the squeeze to include the upper arms, squeezing the muscles around the humeri (upper arm bones). Practice until you master this, and then continue to the next step. These movements will assist in drawing the sexual energy up.

(B) LEGS

To activate the legs' pumping action, start by pressing the soles of the feet to the floor firmly and spreading out the toes. First spread the small toes outward, then the fourth, third, second and finally, the big toes. (Figure 6-5(a)) This spreading action will greatly activate the muscles and tendons of the legs to create the pumping action. Since the feet have very dense tendons, pressing the toes firmly to the floor will feel like a clawing action. Now curl the toes up, keeping them spread apart with the soles still touching the floor. (Figure 6-5(b)) Feel as though you are inhaling through your feet, and squeeze the muscles of the legs to the tibiae and fibulae bones (lower leg bones). Hold for a while, then release them. Gradually move up to the femurs (thigh bones), squeeze the muscles tightly to the bones, and release them to increase the pumping action. These movements will assist in drawing the sexual energy upward when you perform the Orgasmic Upward Draw.

(C) BUTTOCKS

The buttocks consist of many large muscles and are a major factor in assisting the upward flow. Activate these muscles by inhaling as if through the buttocks and pulling up both buttocks, squeezing them toward the anus. You will physically feel as though lifted from the chair you are sitting on. Continue the squeeze, which now moves into the pelvic bones. Hold for a while, and release. Practice a few times, until you master it.

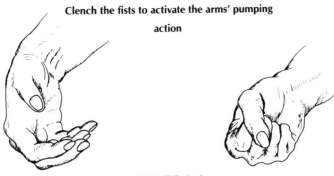

Clench the fists to activate the arms' pumping action

FIGURE 6-4

Arms' Pumping Action

Although the squeezing described seems like many separate actions, mastering them in this way, step-by-step, enables you ultimately to put them together in such a fashion that they become one effort.

FIGURE 6-5

Legs' Pumping Action

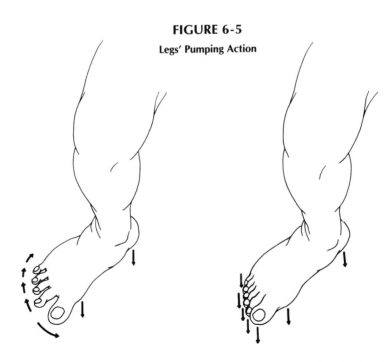

(a) Press down and spread out the toes to activate the muscles and tendons of the legs

(b) Curl the toes up, keeping them fully in contact with the ground

(3) COMBINING THE STEPS

(a) Sit on the edge of a chair or stand with the feet comfortably apart and the knees slightly bent. Feel yourself relax and smile to yourself. Then, make your body tense, and relax again. Such activity will induce greater relaxation.

(b) Begin abdominal breathing nine, eighteen or thirty-six times. Exhale, flattening the abdomen, and inhale without expanding the abdomen.

(c) Clench the teeth. Press the tip of the tongue against the lower front corner of the jaws and teeth and the flat part to the palate, and push the chin to the back. Squeeze the fists and arms' muscles, spread the toes, press the toes and the feet to the ground, and squeeze the muscles to both leg bones. Hold for a couple of moments. Again, although these steps seem disjointed when practiced individually, as they all are mastered and then combined, they will become one unified action easily performed.

(d) Exhale and relax.

(e) Now inhale, hold, and clench the feet, fists, teeth, perineum, and buttocks. Exhale and relax.

(f) Inhale again, hold, and clench the teeth, fists, feet, perineum, and buttocks; tilt the sacrum back, slightly arching the back to help the energy flow more easily into the spine. Exhale and relax.

(g) This time, add an upward movement of the eyes; looking up will help focus the energy toward the brain. Practice again: inhale, hold, clench everything, and look up. Exhale and relax.

(h) Now it is time to add the last item, which will force the energy up into the brain. Perform all the clenching, and then a series of nine strong contractions of the perineum. These contractions are essential to keep the orgasm in the body and propel it upward.

2. Practice in an Aroused State

A. AN OVERVIEW

Now that you have practiced all the clenching exercises, you are ready to try the Orgasmic Draw in an aroused state. To reach an aroused state you will massage the breasts, and stimulate the clitoris, in whatever position you are accustomed to. As you approach what you consider to be a high state of arousal, provide enough time before you know you will climax. Then clench everything, and while holding your breath, simultaneously execute nine hard contractions. Later when we fully describe the Orgasmic Upward Draw, we will go into detail on how to move the sexual energy up.

You will notice that after your first Orgasmic Draw there will be a transfer of aroused energy upward, first moving up the spine to the top of the head and to the pineal gland (through the Governor Channel), then down (through the Functional Channel) as the energy continues in the Microcosmic Orbit. When you feel the energy fill the Orbit, you will start to move the orgasm's aroused energy into the ovaries, then into the left and right kidneys, to the liver, spleen and lungs, and finally up to the left and right sides of the brain, completing what we call the "organs' and glands' orgasm." Additional stimulation will again raise the level of sexual arousal, and you will be able to practice another Orgasmic Draw. If you wish, you can then continue to complete a set of three to six draws. Practice three to six repetitions once or twice a day, and you will quickly refine your ability to do the Orgasmic Draw. Practice until you can fully control the manner of transferring the orgasm upward, using your mind to circulate the orgasm through the Microcosmic Orbit to all of the glands and organs, thereby increasing the amount of energy going to the brain. You will find that as control of the Orgasmic Draw gradually moves inside, the process will require less and less physical clenching. Ultimately, after perhaps six months to a year of practice, the control will be totally internalized.

B. THE IMPORTANCE OF VIRTUE ENERGY

Raising the organs' and glands' CHI to increase the ovaries' sexual energy is one of the most important ways to rejuvenate the organs and glands and start the return of youthful feelings. The most rejuvenating energy, virtue energy, is generated from the organs:

(1) Gentleness from the kidneys and bladder; (2) Kindness from the liver and gall bladder; (3) Honor, respect, joy, and happiness from the heart and small intestine; (4) Fairness from the spleen, stomach and pancreas; (5) Righteousness from the lungs and large intestine.

The sexual organs are linked to all of the major organs and glands. With proper stimulation, as the Taoists classically state, the energy of the glands and organs will contribute to full sexually aroused energy, and all the good virtue energy emerging from them will combine into the best energy we know: the energy of compassion. If you can re-direct the energy of compassion back to the organs, you will charge them to their fullest extent, and negative energy will have no room to remain. If you have too much negative energy in the organs and do not try to remove it, when you begin to multiply your sexual energy, the negative energy will increase, and so will your negative emotions.

The Microcosmic Orbit Meditation, Inner Smile, Six Healing Sounds, and Healing Love practices all help to transform negative emotional energy into good virtue energy. A more extensive practice of transforming negative energy into good virtue and blending all virtues with the energy of compassion will be explained in a later practice of the Healing Tao, called Fusion of the Five Elements. When fully aroused sexually, the glands, organs and nervous system will be exer-cised to their fullest extent as well.

C. MASSAGING THE BREASTS WILL RAISE THE ORGANS' AND GLANDS' CHI

When you massage the breasts or the clitoris, be aware of the CHI energy that is activated as you stimulate the many nerves they contain. The nerves are connected to all the major organs and glands of the body, beginning at the top of the crown with the pineal gland. From this point you will begin to feel the stimulation of all the glands and organs as the sensation descends and flows throughout your body. Use your mind to guide the glands' and organs' CHI to flow to the breasts, blending their energies to produce the best possible glands' and organs' CHI. This special blending of organs' and glands' CHI can have a very powerful creative and healing effect.

(1) GLAND CHI AROUSAL

When certain glands are stimulated to secrete their hormones (Fig-ure 6-6), the organs with which they are associated become activated, and eventually every cell of the body is affected. Stimulation of the breasts especially affects the pineal, pituitary and thymus glands.

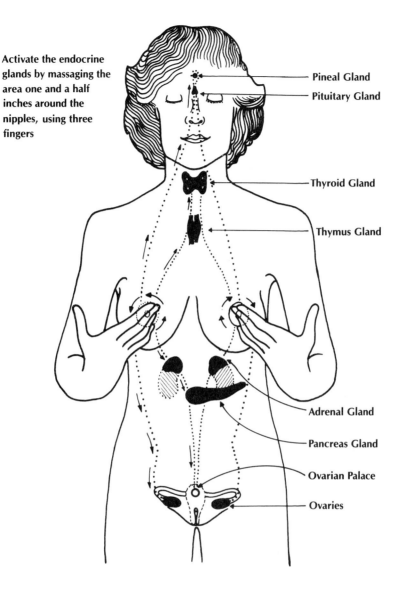

Activate the endocrine glands by massaging the area one and a half inches around the nipples, using three fingers

Pineal Gland

Pituitary Gland

Thyroid Gland

Thymus Gland

Adrenal Gland

Pancreas Gland

Ovarian Palace

Ovaries

FIGURE 6-6

Activating the Endocrine Glands

(A) PINEAL GLAND CHI

The kidney meridian passes through the breasts (Figure 6-7), and as you use your fingers to gently massage the nipples, their stimulation activates the kidneys and bladder as well, which, in turn, help to activate the sexual glands. The clitoris, having a direct relationship to

147

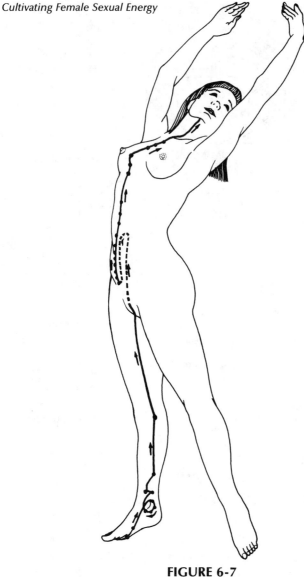

FIGURE 6-7

The Course of the Kidney Meridian

the pineal gland at the crown energy point at the top of the head, the uppermost point of the hormonal pathway, responds and brings the sensation to this point. The pineal gland is the body's time clock and compass and in later practice has the ability to reflect light. When it is fully developed, it can see the true light of creation and will guide the spirit back to the place of its origin. (Figure 6-8)

148

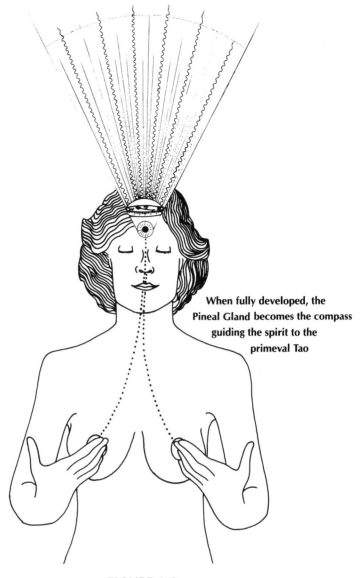

When fully developed, the
Pineal Gland becomes the compass
guiding the spirit to the
primeval Tao

FIGURE 6-8

(B) PITUITARY GLAND CHI

From the pineal gland the sensation descends into the next gland along the hormonal pathway, the pituitary gland, situated at the hind part of the third eye energy center. This gland has a wide range of effects upon growth, metabolism and other functions of the body. Taoists believe the pituitary gland governs intelligence, thought and memory. The pituitary is the master gland from which all other glands are activated.

149

(C) THYROID AND PARATHYROID GLANDS CHI

As the energy continues to descend the hormonal pathway, the thyroid and parathyroid glands become activated. The thyroid gland is situated on either side of the trachea, or windpipe, close to the larynx and arising from the same tissue, and almost from the same spot, as the anterior of the pituitary gland. Opposite the C-7 point, the thyroid gland corresponds to the C-7 energy center. It is the gland that is vitally important to growth. Heavier in the female than in the male, this gland becomes enlarged during sexual excitement, menstruation, and pregnancy. The Taoists consider this an energy gland, regulating the metabolism of the cells in the body, and one of the most important centers because it controls the growth and development of the body and mind. It is also considered the great link between the brain and the reproductive organs.

(D) THYMUS GLAND CHI

Next in the descending order of the hormonal pathway is the thymus gland, or gland of rejuvenation, located at the heart energy center, and descending from, covering and overlapping the upper portion of the heart. This is a lymphoid organ (related to the lymphatic glands) which reaches its greatest size at the beginning of puberty and gradually diminishes in size and activity as time goes on. The Taoists consider this to be a gland that, when properly activated and harmonized with the energy from the pituitary gland energy center and the generative force of the sexual organs, can reverse the aging process.

(E) PANCREAS GLAND CHI

The energy then descends to the pancreas, located between the lower part of the stomach between the liver and spleen. The pancreas is a gland that maintains control over digestion, body temperature and blood sugar levels.

(F) ADRENAL GLANDS CHI

Next, in descending order, are the adrenal glands situated atop the kidneys at the adrenal glands' energy center, or T-11. The adrenal glands', or energy glands', function is to support the kidneys, but they are also the major producers of adrenalin in the body. Adrenalin is a hormone which stimulates the heart, thymus gland, liver, spleen and pancreas. In addition, the adrenal glands support the functions of the kidneys, spine and nervous system, brain, bones and bone marrow. Stimulation of the adrenal glands adds strength and alertness to both physical and mental activity.

(G) SEX GLANDS CHI

Stimulation of the kidneys occurs when the kidney meridian running through the breasts is massaged. In turn, all the other glands become stimulated until finally the sexual organs, last in descending order of the hormone pathway, become energized. Hormone secretions from the sex glands are responsible for sexual response, sexual energy and reproduction. The sex glands include the vagina, uterus and breasts, but it is the Ovarian Palace which houses the woman's sexual energy center. All other energy now is awakened.

Balancing and raising the energy level of the glands in the body is an important part of the Taoist way of developing, healing and strengthening the physical body. This is crucial to the higher levels of practice in which all the glands provide nourishment to the formation of a spiritual body.

(2) ORGAN CHI AROUSAL

With the glands activated, a response can be felt in the organs. This response will have physical and mental manifestations described as follows:

(A) LUNG AND LARGE INTESTINE CHI (FIGURE 6-9)

The first CHI that can be felt is the CHI of the lungs and their associated organ, the large intestine. The properties of the lungs are dryness and coolness; their virtue energies are courage and righteousness. The feeling of righteousness can be as different as each person. It might feel straight or tall, or like a bright white color, pure, fresh and uplifting. Feel this energy generate from the lungs.

The negative emotions of the lungs are sadness and grief. The feelings can be experienced as flat, or like a collapsed ball; they can be gray, musty, cold and low, with no force; downtrodden. Since you do not like to feel this way, cultivate good virtue and connect yourself with the good feelings of the lungs mentioned above: pure, fresh, uplifting. Bring these good feelings to the breasts.

The lungs' CHI readiness is manifested physically by faster breathing and copious saliva, which you feel must be swallowed quickly. These signs indicate that the CHI of the lungs is ready to come forth.

151

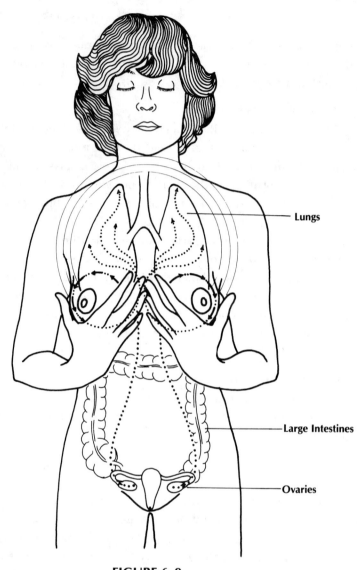

Lungs

Large Intestines

Ovaries

FIGURE 6-9
Lungs and Large Intestines CHI

(B) HEART AND SMALL INTESTINE CHI (FIGURE 6-10)

Second is heart CHI; the heart's associated organ is the small intestine. The heart contains hot energy. Its virtues are honor, respect, joy and happiness. These virtues are manifested in feeling straight and open; they are bright red, warm, full, comfortable, secure and satisfying. The negative manifestations of heart and small intestine CHI are impatience, hastiness and cruelty. This can feel spiney or sharp, muddy, burnt, noisy, irregular and irritating, all feelings that you do not like to have in your system.

The physical manifestations of heart energy are revealed by observing the tongue becoming mobile, saliva seeming to overflow, and a growling sound emanating from the throat. These are signs that the CHI of the heart is prepared.

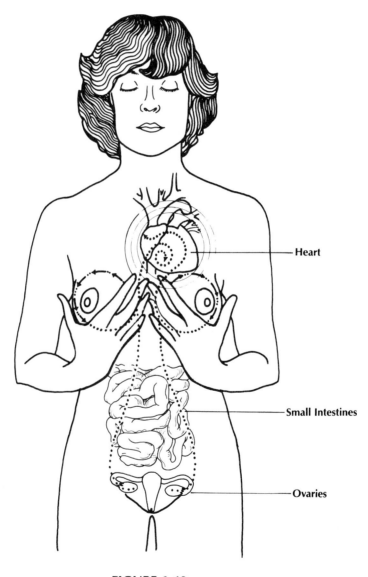

FIGURE 6-10

Heart and Small Intestines CHI

153

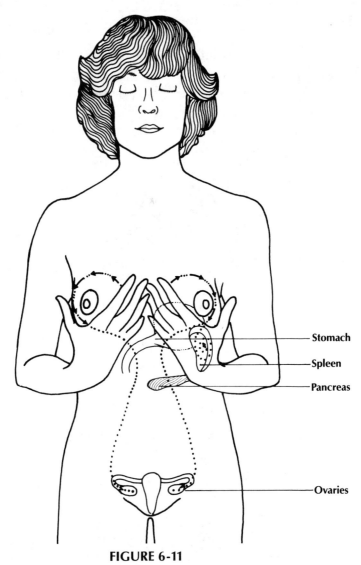

FIGURE 6-11

Spleen, Stomach and Pancreas CHI

(C) SPLEEN, STOMACH AND PANCREAS CHI (FIGURE 6-11)

The third CHI is felt from the spleen and its associated organs, the stomach and pancreas. Mild, harmonic energy is the property of the spleen. Fairness is its good virtue, and the feeling can be a wide-open chest, clean, soft and balanced, even smooth. The negative emotion of worry feels irregular, cloudy, humid, uncertain and out of proportion.

The physical manifestation of these organs' energy can be observed when your hands have the desire to grasp and squeeze the breasts. This indicates that the spleen energy is in readiness.

154

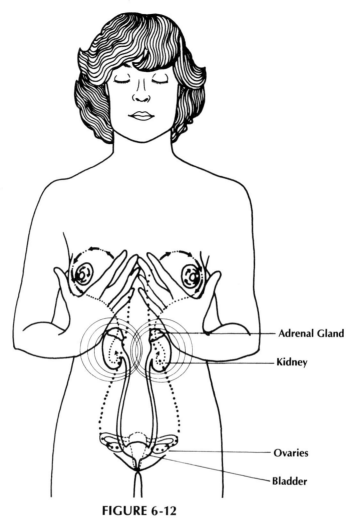

FIGURE 6-12

Kidneys Adrenal Glands and Bladder CHI

(D) KIDNEYS AND BLADDER CHI (FIGURE 6-12)

Next is the CHI of the kidneys and their associated organ, the bladder. Their property is cold energy, and their virtues are gentleness, alertness and stillness. This can feel round, full, expansive, bright blue, fresh, cool and comfortable, pleasant to the ear, mild, and honey-like in taste. The negative feelings are fear, stress, fright, awkwardness, tiny, compressed, dark, gray, cloudy, a cold chill, tight or closed in, and scattered.

The physical manifestation of these organs' CHI can be observed when you feel as if you are drowning with fluid in the vagina. This means that the CHI of the kidneys is ready.

155

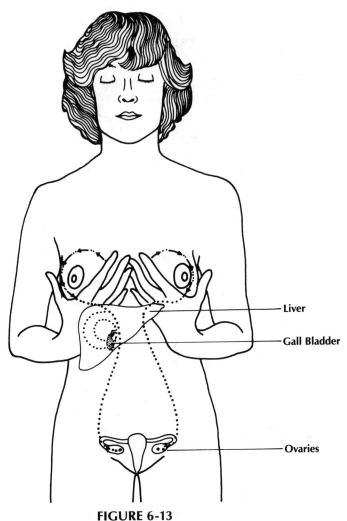

FIGURE 6-13
Liver and Gall Bladder CHI

(E) LIVER AND GALL BLADDER CHI (FIGURE 6-13)

Liver CHI will be felt next. The liver's associated organ is the gall bladder. Its properties are warm and energetic. The virtues are kindness and self-expansion. They can feel round, smooth, soft, green, sweet, fragrant, warm and pleasant, nurturing, and as if they were gently expanding. The negative emotions are anger, aggression, arrogance and can feel spear-like or sharp, cloudy, hot and explosive, loud, painful, tough, rough, and bitter.

The physical manifestation of these organs' CHI can be observed when the eyes become watery. This is the indication that the CHI of the liver is ready.

156

(F) BONE CHI

The next CHI that will be felt is bone CHI. When you feel like sucking the tongue, the CHI from the bones is prepared.

(G) TENDONS AND SINEWS CHI

Tendons and sinews CHI is ready and will manifest itself when you feel like raising your legs.

(H) BLOOD CHI

Blood CHI is ready when you are moved to touch your vagina and clitoris.

(I) CHI OF THE FLESH

Finally you will feel the CHI of the flesh. You will feel that this CHI is ready when the urge is to massage the nipples, vagina and clitoris.

3. Procedure of Massaging the Breasts

Begin the procedure by massaging the breasts to activate the ovaries' sexual energy, which in turn will activate the energy of the glands and organs. This exercise can be performed while sitting on a chair or on the edge of a bed.

A. BEGIN IN A SITTING POSITION

Be seated. As in Ovarian Breathing, you will want a steady and fairly firm pressure on the vagina's opening, especially on the clitoris. Sit on a fairly hard, round object such as a ball or a rolled-up washcloth. You may immediately experience a pleasant sensation due to the stimulation of the genital area. If you are well-practiced in Iron Shirt and the Microcosmic Orbit, you will not require an object.

B. BRING CHI UP THE SPINAL CORD

At this stage of your practice, you should be able to pull the middle and the back part of the anus up, thereby bringing the CHI up through the spinal cord, and then all the way up to the pineal gland. Hold it there for a while. Then pull up the left and right sides of the anus, and bring the CHI to the left and right nipples.

C. WARM YOUR HANDS

Inhale and rub your hands together vigorously. This will create heat in your hands by bringing the energy of your body into your palms and fingers. Place your hands on your breasts in order to feel the heat from your hands entering the skin.

D. MASSAGE THE GLANDS

(1) Place the tongue on the roof of the mouth.

(2) Maintaining constant contact with the skin, very lightly massage your breasts using the second, middle and fourth fingertips of both hands. Moving your right hand clockwise and your left hand counterclockwise, gently press the breasts against the rib cage, proceeding very slowly down to the area of the xyphoid process under the base of the sternum. Bring your awareness there.

(3) To activate the glands, press your three fingers to the kidney point located approximately one and a half inches in from the nipple. This point is determined by taking the second joint on the middle finger of each hand and placing it directly on the nipple with the hands against the sides of the body. The fingers will automatically fall so that the tips are at this kidney point. Use the same three fingers and massage, circling around toward the center (right hand clockwise, left hand counterclockwise). That circle will touch the kidney, liver, pericardium and spleen meridians.

(4) Continue to massage your breasts with your fingertips barely touching the skin and gently rotating. Massage them very slowly in an outward, circular motion (right hand clockwise, left hand counterclockwise). Bring your awareness there.

(5) When you feel the clitoris is activated, the sexual energy will surge to the head and activate the pineal gland. You might feel a pressure present in the head as the energy begins to radiate, like a beacon from a lighthouse, to the pituitary gland.

(6) Continue massaging and move your attention down to the pituitary gland, feeling the intense pressure in the forehead as it radiates a blue light.

(7) Permit the activated energy to descend to the thyroid and parathyroid glands. Feel the expansion of these two glands as they become activated by the CHI of the sexual, pineal and pituitary glands, and

then feel them radiate the energy outward. Blend their CHI together with the CHI of the two higher glands. Let this special blend of glands' CHI flow down to the thymus.

(8) Continue to gently massage the breasts and settle your mind on the thymus gland, activating that gland. Feel it expand and blossom like a flower. Blend all the glands' CHI gathered together thus far and permit their energy to radiate to the breast. Use your mind to blend their CHI in the breasts.

(9) Let the specially blended CHI flow down to the pancreas and feel the pancreas activate. Let the pancreas energy flow to the breasts.

(10) Allow the mind to concentrate on the adrenal glands, letting the special blend of energy you have created activate the adrenal glands. As you feel them activate, expand and release this special energy; bring this energy up to the breasts, where all the glands' energy is blending together. This glands' energy will help to activate the organs' CHI.

E. MASSAGE THE ORGANS

(1) Be aware of your nose and lungs, and continue to rub your breasts slowly, feeling the CHI from the thymus activate the breasts' and lungs' CHI. Feel the energy of righteousness as straight, bright white, pure and expanding. Fill the lungs and direct their CHI to the breasts.

(2) Be aware of your tongue and heart. Feel the CHI from the heart in the form of joy, happiness, respect and honor, and direct this energy to the breasts. Think of the breasts as melting pots that will melt the glands' and organs' energy, fusing them into a very special kind of hormonal energy and the kind of compassion which is capable of rejuvenating the glands, organs and whole system.

(3) Direct your attention to your mouth; move your mouth around and be aware of the sexually aroused energy as it activates the spleen energy. Raise the virtuous energy of fairness, and feel it manifested in a wide open feeling in the chest. Feel the CHI of the spleen and direct it to the breasts. Feel the virtues fuse.

(4) Now direct the sexual CHI, which started from the clitoris and the breasts, to the kidneys. Activate the kidneys' CHI and expand the virtuous energy of gentleness, alertness and stillness, bringing it to the

breasts. As you rub your breasts and activate each organ's CHI, this CHI will automatically be drawn to the breasts. Feel the CHI start to fuse with all the other CHI virtues, combining into a very special CHI.

(5) Direct the sexual CHI to the liver to activate the liver's CHI. Raise the kindness virtue and the feeling of self-expansion, also drawing these feelings to the breasts. At this time you should feel the vagina moistening from a sweating action of the vaginal walls, plus the secretion of glandular fluid. Soon the clitoris will become engorged with blood and will become erect, and the nipples will become firmer. The outer lips of the vagina will become swollen to nearly twice their size. The inner lips will also swell.

(6) Then, place the palms of the hands on the knees, place your attention upon your breasts, and experience the energy there. By now you have accumulated a lot of energy in the breasts, where it all has melted together into compassion CHI. The nipples have become hard and erect with the swelling of the breasts. Let the energy flow like a funnel into the nipples as you feel the tingling warmth of sexual arousal. Wait a few moments as the breast energy accumulates in the nipples, and then using your concentration let the energy drop like a plumb line down into the ovaries. Your "inner eye" can help to direct the CHI there. Pause and feel the accumulated breast energy and ovary energy.

(7) Become aware of your breathing and concentrate your attention on the ovaries, sending each exhalation directly to the ovaries. Concentrate on the ovaries, and use your mind and some muscles to move the lips of the vagina until you feel them swell. The PC Muscle will be tense, and then will relax and begin to pulsate. Feel an increase in the pulsation of the vagina, and feel it open and close like the petals of a flower. When this energy becomes strong, let the vagina close in and draw the energy from both ovaries to merge in the Ovarian Palace (located three inches below the navel at the cervix). You can slightly squeeze, tensing the cervix, and concentrate the sexual energy at this point. You are entering the orgasmic phase. With these practices you can direct the orgasm inward, and you can extend the orgasm more than you have ever dreamed you could.

You have now completed stage one of the Orgasmic Draw. The CHI, which is ready, is now comprised of the organs', glands', virtues' and sexual energies. Practice this stage, activating the clitoris and the thymus and pineal glands, for a week before you proceed with the Orgasmic Draw. You will actually feel the CHI in these areas. Then continue with this exercise, now moving to the lungs, the heart and spleen, etc., for another week. Once you are able to practice the entire sequence well, activating and collecting the glands' and organs' CHI will take only five to ten minutes per session.

When you feel that the sexual CHI is ready at the Ovarian Palace, you can begin the Orgasmic Draw.

4. Procedure of the Orgasmic Draw: Moving the Aroused Organs' and Glands' CHI Upward Step-By-Step

A. BEGIN WITH THE BREAST MASSAGE

Use the same sitting position as you did previously for the breast massage. If sitting on a chair, have your feet flat on the floor. If you need some more stimulation you can use the hard, round object previously described to press against the opening of your vagina, touching your clitoris. Stimulate yourself by rubbing your breasts, activating the organs' and glands' CHI. Fuse this with the sexual energy to become the energy of healing and compassion. Direct the sexual energy from the nipples down to the ovaries, and expand the energy into the ovaries and genitals, finally concentrating it in the Ovarian Palace.

B. PERFORM MUSCLE CONTRACTIONS AT THE POINT OF ORGASM

Inhale deeply through your nose when you are near or in the midst of orgasm. Simultaneously clench both fists and claw your feet down, making them feel like vacuum pumps sucking at the floor. At the same time clench your jaw, tighten the Cranial Pump at the back of your neck, and press your tongue firmly to the roof of your mouth.

C. BRING THE SEXUAL ENERGY DOWN TO THE PERINEUM (HUI-YIN)

Inhale once more and draw up the entire genital-anus region, concentrating on the Hui-Yin (perineum), urogenital diaphragm, and especially the front part of the perineum. Pull the energy from the Ovarian Palace downward to the perineum by squeezing the vagina's outer and inner lips as tightly as possible, feeling the force squeeze the clitoris. Holding your breath for a while, inhale again, contract and pull down the front part of the anus, holding your breath for a while. Feel the sexual energy being pulled down and collected at the perineum. With all muscles flexed, inhale, clench, and pull up your Ovarian Palace and sexual region repeatedly, holding the energy at the front part of the perineum. Practice nine of these hard contractions, inhaling without exhaling. Each time pull down from the Ovarian Palace to the front part of the perineum. Retention of the energy at the perineum is very important. If it is released, the sexual energy will drop down to the sexual organs or leak out the vagina, and you will have to start the exercise again. To retain the energy at a certain point means you must settle your mind and concentrate on that point. When you become out of breath, exhale and release all the muscles in the body. You may feel energy rush up, down and around the sexual region, especially during this resting period. Use your mind to guide the energy from the Ovarian Palace to the front part of the perineum.

After practicing this exercise for a week or two, you may begin to feel the muscle contractions automatically pull your vagina in and squeeze the clitoris. The anus will feel as though closed very tightly. Remember that unless otherwise indicated, all breathing is through the nose. The whole body must relax on the exhale. Allow all tension to flow out of you as if you were in meditation. Practice this exercise for at least one week.

D. RAISE THE SEXUAL ENERGY TO THE SACRUM BY ARCHING THE SACRUM AND ACTIVATING THE SACRAL PUMP

Start with arousing the breasts to stimulate the glands' and organs' energies to fuse with the sexual energy. Clench the fists, feet, neck and jaws on inhalation. Draw up the entire genital area, urogenital diaphragm, anus, and especially the vagina. Squeeze the energy tightly to the clitoris and pull it up to the perineum. Rest for a while, inhale again and contract the front part of the anus, drawing the sexual energy down from the ovaries to the perineum. Holding your breath for awhile, inhale again, and contract the middle part of the anus. At the same time contract the back part of the anus and pull up toward the coccyx, a little up from the bottom tip of your spine, drawing the sexual energy up through the perineum, and continue to draw it up to your coccyx. Feel it enter the hiatus in the sacrum.

Activate your Sacral Pump by arching the sacrum back and outward thereby straightening the sacrum. This makes it easier for the CHI to rise. Hold the energy at the sacral area and continue to inhale and pull the sexual energy in from the Ovarian Palace and sexual organs, until you feel the energy in your clitoris and your vagina begin to subside. Sometimes this requires three to nine inhalations with increasingly harder contractions. Squeezing the buttocks more tightly may help you force the sexual healing energy (Ching CHI) into the sacrum. When you are out of breath, exhale. Then relax and let your sacrum and neck return to their normal positions. This resting period will induce the activation of the Sacral and Cranial Pumps. You will gradually have the sensation of something entering into the spinal cord as the sacrum begins to open for more CHI to flow.

If you are well practiced in Ovarian Breathing, or have already opened your Microcosmic Orbit, this step of the Orgasmic Draw will be much easier. Otherwise, the sacral area is usually a little difficult to pump the energy through since, as previously noted, sexual energy is denser than other types of CHI, and aroused sexual energy is denser still. This is where the Sacral Pump enters in. As mentioned in the Ovarian Breathing exercise, some people will experience pain, tingling, or a "pins and needles" sensation when the sexual energy enters the sacral hiatus. This should not be alarming. Remember you can assist the sexual energy in its upward push past the coccyx by gently massaging the area with a silk cloth from time to time.

E. DRAW THE SEXUAL ENERGY TO T-11 BY BOWING THE SPINE OUTWARD

Once you are able to move the energy through your sacrum, spend the next week drawing the energy to T-11 (on the spine, opposite your solar plexus). Repeat the same procedure: arousing, clenching, and inhaling. Pump the energy up to the perineum, sacrum, and then to T-11. Again, because sexual energy is denser than life-force (CHI), you have to accommodate it by bowing your spine outward, as if you were backing up against a wall and pushing toward it to straighten your spine. This will increase the pumping action and allow for a freer passage of Ching CHI. Retain the energy at T-11 until this point feels full of energy. Practice nine hard contractions. Each time bring the energy from its source at the Ovarian Palace to T-11; each time inhale without exhaling. Then exhale and relax every part of your body, mentally guiding the CHI to flow from the Ovarian Palace to T-11.

F. PUSH FROM THE STERNUM AND BRING THE SEXUAL ENERGY TO C-7

Your next station is C-7 (at the base of your neck). Practice in the same manner as described above: continue to draw the energy down to the perineum and up to the sacrum (arching the sacrum), up to T-11 (bowing the spine outward), to C-7, and push the top of the sternum back toward C-7 at the base of the neck. This will help increase the pumping action of the spine, activate the thymus gland, join the thoracic and cervical vertebrae, and help push the sexual energy up.

G. STRAIGHTEN THE SPINE AND BRING THE SEXUAL ENERGY TO THE BASE OF THE SKULL (JADE PILLOW)

The next stopping place is your Jade Pillow (located at the back of your head between C-1 and the base of the skull). Practice in the same manner as previously described: continue to draw the energy down from the Ovarian Palace to the perineum, up to the sacrum (arching the sacrum), up to T-11 (bowing the T-11 outward), up to C-7 (pushing from the sternum to C-7), thereby straightening the entire spine. Inhale and pull up to the Jade Pillow, then push the chin in toward the back and base of the skull. This will activate the Cranial Pump. At this point clench the teeth, squeeze the muscles at the back of the skull, and press your tongue hard to the palate. All of these movements will increase the cranial pumping action. The Cranial Pump, as it fills with energy and begins to move the energy through, may pound furiously.

H. ACTIVATE THE CRANIAL PUMP AND BRING THE SEXUAL ENERGY TO THE CROWN (PAI-HUI)

The next station for energy is the Pai-Hui (located at the crown of your head). Draw two imaginary lines from the tip of your nose and the tip of an ear straight up to the top of the head. The point where they meet is the center of your head, or crown. Press around this area and find the most sensitive spot. This is the Pai-Hui. You will be able to confirm this as the proper spot when you feel the energy reach this point.

Repeat the same process of arousing the sexual energy by massaging the breasts. When you are ready, bring the energy down from the Ovarian Palace, draw it up to the sacrum, T-11, and C-7, straighten the spine, and draw the energy up to the Jade Pillow. Tuck your chin in slightly and squeeze the skull to further activate the upper Cranial Pump. Maintain a straight upper spine. Turn your eyes and all your senses up to the top of the crown. Press your tongue firmly to the palate to help activate the Cranial Pump located there. Persist in pulling the energy to the top of your head until you feel the aroused energy at the lower center subside, all the energy having been transferred to the higher center. Practice nine hard contractions and continue to inhale, each time pulling the energy from the Ovarian Palace up to the crown. Use your mind, eyes and all of your senses to spiral the sexual creative energy nine, eighteen, or thirty-six times, first in a clockwise, and then in a counterclockwise direction. Some people feel the energy first start to flow counterclockwise. If this is the case, simply let it flow. When the spiraling has finished, rest for a while and be aware of the sensational feeling as the energy enters the brain. Let the extra energy flow down the front channel, or Functional Channel, to the third eye, nose, throat, heart center, solar plexus, and finally to the navel where this extra energy can be stored.

When the energy finally goes up into your head, it will produce a very distinct warm and tingling sensation. The usual immediate response is that it feels good and amazingly refreshing. Some people claim they can think more clearly and are more creative. This is possible once they have reached the stage where they can easily convert the Ching CHI into expanded consciousness automatically. As previously emphasized, this sexual energy is later converted into original CHI, the pure life-force, during the spiritual levels of the Taoist practice.

Remember that all the organs and glands are activated as a result of this massage.

5. Learn to Use your Mind to Direct the Aroused Organs' and Glands' CHI

Practice the Orgasmic Draw until you can pull the sexual energy up from the ovaries to the pineal gland in one draw of the "straw." In the beginning simply move from one station to another. Later this back channel, the Governor Channel, will feel more open. Eventually you will be able to settle your mind on the ovaries and the pineal gland at the crown of the head, and bring the sexual energy from the ovaries all the way up to the brain through what has been previously described as the Thrusting Channel, using only the power of the mind and all the senses. Up to this point in your practice, you had incorporated the assistance of muscle power to direct the sexual energy upward. At this stage, through practice, the muscles have become well developed and are responding automatically. This allows you the freedom to eventually use only the power of your mind and senses to direct the aroused organs' and glands' CHI upward.

You must take time to really feel the sexual energy when you practice. Do not rush, and always maintain that pumping action after the exercise as you breathe in and out. Gradually use your mind more and your body less as you practice. Let the feeling of the energy be your guide.

A. GOLDEN NECTAR

Since this sexual energy, compared to other sexual energy, is cooler and more creative, it cannot harm you if left in the head. When you feel that the energy has filled the brain, you will feel a honey-like fluid flow from the pituitary gland down to the nose, palate and tongue. The taste will vary with different people and on different days. It is called "Golden Nectar" and can taste delicate, like champagne, honey, coconut juice, or perhaps slightly metallic. It can feel like a warm tingling sensation on your tongue. For some people the energy flows from the brain into the pituitary gland, down the nose, palate and mouth, to the throat, heart, solar plexus, and finally to the navel. As your practice grows, the ovaries' energy will flow thicker, eventually feeling like honey flowing from a jar (the brain) into a cauldron (the navel).

B. CIRCULATING THE ENERGY DURING LOVEMAKING

During lovemaking we need to move the energy in a circle, and not just store it in the brain, in order to direct the excess energy to re-vitalize the organs and glands. This circulation is aided by the internal pressures you create during the Orgasmic Draw as you squeeze the perineum and buttocks. As you press the lower trunk energy into and up the spine, press the energy in your upper body downward, and hold the contraction as long as you can. When you exhale completely, relax the entire body. The natural direction of the CHI is to continue in a circle up the back of your body and down the front to the navel.

Continue cycling the sexual energy in this way until your orgasm travels upward into the organs, glands and higher center. In the begin-ning this might take three to nine such cycles, but after you have prac-ticed for a while, one such round is enough.

6. Organs' Orgasm

A. THE CHARACTERISTICS OF EACH ORGAN

In the Tao system we believe the organs and glands are the creation and storage places of the positive and negative emotions of our life. Each organ and gland stores and accumulates different kinds of emo-tional energy. Once the organ is depleted and weak, the negative emo-tions easily settle in, or the organ is influenced by the other organs of the body. If we become aware of the source of unwanted energy, we will have a way to correct it. Each organ's characteristics (i.e., associ-ated organ, element, etc.) are as follows:

(1) THE LUNGS

Associated organ: large intestine. Element: metal. Season: au-tumn—dryness. Negative emotions: sadness, grief, sorrow. Positive emotions: righteousness, surrender, letting-go, emptiness. Parts of the body: chest, inner arms, thumbs. Senses: nose—smell, mucous, skin, touch.

(2) THE KIDNEYS

Associated organ: bladder. Element: water. Season: winter. Negative emotion: fear. Positive emotions: gentleness, alertness, stillness. Parts of the body: side of foot, inner legs, chest. Senses: ears—hearing, bones.

(3) THE LIVER

Associated organ: gall bladder. Element: wood. Season: spring. Negative emotions: anger, aggression. Positive emotions: kindness, self-expansion, identity. Parts of the body: inner legs, groin, diaphragm, ribs. Senses: eyes—sight, tears.

(4) THE HEART

Associated organ: small intestine. Element: fire. Season: summer. Negative emotions: impatience, arrogance, hastiness, cruelty, violence. Positive emotions: joy, honor, sincerity, creativity, enthusiasm, spirit, radiance, light. Parts of the body: armpits, inner arms. Senses: tongue—taste, speech.

(5) THE SPLEEN

Associated organs: pancreas, stomach. Element: earth. Season: Indian summer. Negative emotions: worry, sympathy, pity. Positive emotions: fairness, compassion, centering, music-making. Parts of the body: neck. Senses: mouth—taste, appetite.

(6) THE TRIPLE WARMER (CIRCULATION SEX)

There is no element, season or emotion associated with the Triple Warmer. The Triple Warmer refers to the three energy centers of the body:

The upper level: brain, heart, lungs. Property: hot.

The middle level: liver, kidneys, stomach, pancreas, spleen. Property: warm.

The lower level: large and small intestines, bladder, sexual organs. Property: cool.

The main goal of the organs' orgasm is to strengthen, satisfy and restore the organs to their natural state in order to generate good virtue and healing for ourselves and others.

B. ORGANS' ORGASM PRACTICE STEP-BY-STEP

Once you have practiced the steps above and have become successful in moving the aroused sexual CHI in the Microcosmic Orbit, you can begin to move this orgasm energy into the organs. Remember, as you follow the steps below, always move the CHI in the Microcosmic Orbit first before continuing.

(1) Once the sexual energy is aroused, inhale and pull up the left and right anus to draw the energy to the left and right ovaries. Circulate the energy in the Microcosmic Orbit, and then drop the sexual CHI into the ovaries.

(2) When you begin to feel the sexual energy in the ovaries, move it to the left and right kidneys. Wrap the orgasmic energy, now highly refined by all of the organs and glands, with all of the combined virtues of those organs into compassion energy. Feel the kidneys bathe in this healing, creative and revitalizing energy. The actual sensation of a kidneys' orgasm is different from anything else. In fact, as you bring the compassion energy to each organ, each will have a different type of orgasmic feeling that is beyond words. It is greater than anything you have ever experienced. The organs' orgasms have a longer-lasting orgasmic feeling, bringing good health, fulfillment, joy and happiness. This kind of joy and fulfillment comes only from the sexual, creative, and generative qualities of the compassion energy that fills the organs.

Every time you move the orgasmic energy in the Microcosmic Orbit, pull it up to the ovaries, then to the left and right kidneys, and proceed, moving the energy up to:

(3) the spleen (on the left) and the liver (on the right);

(4) the left and right lungs; and

(5) the left and right sides of the brain.

(6) When you have become proficient in the Microcosmic Orbit and moving the energy to the left and right organs, contract the middle anus to bring the sexual energy to the cervix;

(7) the aorta and venacava;

(8) the pancreas; and

(9) the heart. Be very careful moving the energy to the heart because problems can be created here. Be careful in the beginning not to draw too much sexual CHI into the heart.

(10) Next take the energy to the thymus gland. This is very important for women because when this center is rejuvenated, the sexual energy will be able to increase a great deal with the assistance of that gland, thereby increasing the assistance of the other glands.

(11) Next bring the energy to the thyroid and parathyroid glands;

(12) then to the pituitary gland;

(13) to the pineal gland; and

(14) up to the crown.

(15) A final refinement to remember is that the lower contraction is not centered in the stomach or abdominal region. You must not tighten your stomach muscles during the Orgasmic Draw as this will draw CHI away from the Microcosmic Orbit. We must concentrate on the front of the undertrunk, i.e., the vagina, perineum, and urogenital diaphragm. Our goal is to so train these muscles that by using them we can flood the body with restorative energy. Directing power from the lower trunk toward the center of the body pours energy into the navel region. Since ovary and egg energy, like the blood, tend to follow the CHI energy, the navel, in effect, grips the ovary and egg energy and pulls it up into the body through the spine. Therefore, if you contract the urogenital diaphragm as if you were holding in a bladderful of urine, you will lock the passages so tightly that no internal urge can burst through the sealing rings of muscle. Make sure that there is no infection in the urinary tract which can cause infection in the bladder when you stop the urine.

C. DAILY PRACTICE

Nothing will come of nothing. You must spend time in practice to reap the benefits. An ounce of practice is worth a ton of theory. Modern life, it seems, affords little time for anything but acquiring and spending. You must be willing to surrender some time to advance. The practice must become part of your daily routine. You will make some progress if you do the exercise more often than not. If, however, you practice as regularly as getting out of bed in the morning, progress will be swift, CHI will begin to build in your upper body, and you will be able to collect it at your navel.

Once you have mastered this technique, it requires only a few minutes each day to bring the sexual CHI to all the organs and glands with simply a few Orgasmic Draws. After a while when you do the Orgasmic Draw a few times you will feel, all at once, the sexual energy filling the organs and glands quickly.

If you can, practice six or nine complete contractions of the Orgasmic Draw, with each complete draw consisting of nine hard contractions. If possible, practice both in the morning and at night, and you will progress quickly. Once you have mastered the technique, eighteen to thirty-six repetitions performed morning and night should not be unduly strenuous. If you become extremely aroused, do fewer repetitions. With such intensity of training, you will easily develop the muscle tone required within a month or two. How quickly you progress is not important; what is essential is that you progress steadily. Rock bottom minimum should be one round per day, just to maintain the practice.

The preferred times for these exercises are from eleven a.m. until one p.m., and eleven p.m. until one a.m. During these periods the tide of Yin energy changes to Yang, and vice versa. At these times the power flows very well. If it is impossible to practice during these hours, do not be discouraged because as long as you exercise daily, you will definitely advance.

D. MASSAGE

After each practice session of the Orgasmic Draw, be sure to massage your breasts and genitals. This will disperse any energy that did not get drawn up and will alleviate any feelings of congestion or fullness.

Use your hands or a silk or taffeta scarf. Briskly rub your breasts in a circular motion, pressing them against your ribs. Then massage the mons and outer lips of the vagina, the perineum and the sacrum. This active massage should be done until you feel a cleanliness in your breasts and genitals. (Figure 6-14)

One woman reported that she stopped the massaging step because she did not think it was important, and then noticed an increase in breast congestion right before her period. When she resumed the massage practice, she did not have any more problems pre-menstrually.

E. Safety Points for Ovarian Breathing, Ovarian Compression, and the Orgasmic Draw

1. Never lie flat on your back during these exercises. The CHI power may stick in your chest, causing considerable irritability and undue pressure on your heart.

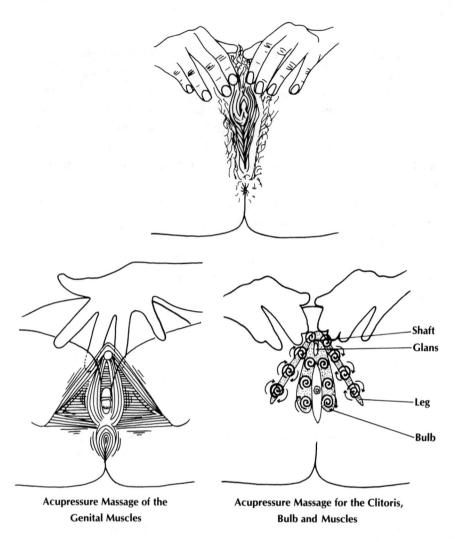

Acupressure Massage of the
Genital Muscles

Acupressure Massage for the Clitoris,
Bulb and Muscles

Shaft
Glans
Leg
Bulb

FIGURE 6-14

Massaging the Genitals after Practice

2. Never lie on your left side when practicing. This also stresses the heart and overfills it with energy.

3. Never place any objects under your side while in the lying position. This will bend the channel of energy and may cause back pain.

If any of the problems mentioned in points 1 to 3 arise, release the energy safely by using the venting exercise described in Chapter 5. Any pain or discomfort should disappear within one week of beginning to vent.

4. Practice on an empty, but not hungry, stomach whenever possible. Always wait at least one hour after eating.

5. Wear loose clothes or wrap yourself in a light blanket during this practice. You will perspire if the exercises are done properly, and will suffer a chill if you are not covered. After practice, change your clothes so that you are removed from the moisture of the fabric. There should be a gentle flow of clean air in the room. Avoid any drafts or wind. Wind tends to blow the CHI power away. It might cause your energy to become cold easily.

6. As you advance, beads of sweat may accumulate on your brow. Rub this sweat into the skin—it has desirable properties which should be returned to the body.

7. Do not breathe through the mouth during these exercises. It is easier to control the flow of air when breathing through the nose. Inhalation through the nose charges the air with energy and invigorates the brain.

8. Do not be concerned if you feel little effect during the first days or weeks of practice. Each person needs a varying amount of time before heat flows from her ovaries.

9. You must develop intense concentration. Keep your mind from wandering. Allow thoughts and images to leave without following them. Empty the vessel of the mind of thoughts, and powerful energy will stream into the void. Your power of concentration will develop greatly if you persist in this discipline. Learn the Microcosmic Orbit meditation, and carry it out immediately after practicing the Orgasmic Draw.

10. During the resting period close the eyes and follow the energy's path. The mind should not stray to thoughts or fantasies, but should flow with the course of the energy. This may sound very difficult. You will be amazed at how quickly you can become sensitive to your own energy. When you experience these energies within yourself, you will know exactly what we mean. Since the energy flows along natural courses, it guides your mind even as your mind guides the energy.

11. Those who suffer from constipation should practice in the morning. These exercises will help greatly to remedy the problem.

12. If you are infected with venereal disease, thoroughly cure yourself before engaging in this exercise. Otherwise the pain will be quite severe when you draw so much blood and power to the pubic region.

F. Cleansing Side Effects

Although they may appear elementary, the exercises in this and the preceding chapter are highly refined techniques for increasing vital power. They are like sharp swords which must be used with care to perform their functions without harming oneself. If you follow the instructions closely, you will not suffer any distressing side effects. Study the methods with seriousness, assimilate every line of the text, and persist until you have succeeded.

1. It has been our experience that many students of this method soon begin to move their bowels with unaccustomed ease. Some will pass an unusual amount of gas for a time and move the bowels two or three times per day. In this way the body uses its new resources thoroughly to cleanse and purify itself by completely natural means. The unusual number of evacuations and gas decreases within one or two months.

2. This purgative detoxification is followed by regular bowel movements and a deep sense of bodily purity and strength. The saliva becomes lighter and sweeter. Improvement in bowel function arises from the increased flow of vital energy into the entrails. This energizes the involuntary muscles and allows them to function with ease. There may also be a noticeable increase in burping, which is a healthy exhalation of impurities and noxious gas within the body. Burping also lessens after a time, as the body becomes more refreshed.

3. The Orgasmic Draw is excellent for improvement of hemorrhoids. Hemorrhoids are caused by sedentary life styles, accumulated heavy toxins, gravitational pooling of blood, stressful bowel movements, and depressed levels of CHI energy in the Hui-Yin. In already existing hemorrhoids the Orgasmic Draw may cause increased hemorrhoidal bleeding for two to four weeks. If the bleeding is not excessive, perform the exercise at half-strength. You will gradually be cured. The exercise remedies specific causes of hemorrhoids by evacuating stagnant blood from the anal blood vessels. While performing the Orgasmic Draw as a cure for hemorrhoids, you may use medication to speed the healing process. Horsetail Grass (Equisetum Narvensis) is an excellent remedy used as a tea and in sitz baths. People who have serious hemorrhoid problems should consult a doctor.

G. SUMMARY of the Orgasmic Draw Exercise

1. Sit with your feet flat on the floor. Use the stimulation of a hard object against your vagina and clitoris, if necessary. Rub your breasts to stimulate yourself. Direct the sexual energy from the nipples down to the ovaries, and expand the energy in the ovaries and genitals, finally concentrating it in the Ovarian Palace.

2. Inhale deeply through your nose when you are near or in the midst of orgasm while simultaneously clenching both fists, clawing your feet, clenching your jaws, tightening the Cranial Pump at the back of your neck, and pressing your tongue firmly to the roof of your mouth.

3. Inhale once more, drawing up the entire genital-anus region, especially concentrating on the front part of the Hui-Yin (perineum) and the urogenital diaphragm. Pull the energy from the Ovarian Palace downward to the perineum by squeezing the vagina's outer and inner lips as tightly as possible, thereby squeezing the clitoris. Hold your breath for a while, inhale again, contract and pull down the front part of the anus, again holding your breath. Feel the sexual energy collect at the perineum. With all muscles flexed, inhale without exhaling, clench, and pull up your sexual region nine times, holding the energy at the front part of the perineum. Retention of the energy here is very important. When out of breath exhale and release all the muscles in the body. Rest. Use your mind to guide the energy from the Ovarian Palace to the front part of the perineum.

4. Arouse the breasts again, and with an inhalation clench the fists, feet, neck and jaws. Draw up the entire genital area, urogenital diaphragm, anus, and especially the vagina, squeezing the energy tightly to the clitoris and pulling it up to the perineum. Rest for a while, inhale again and contract the front part of the anus, pulling the sexual energy down from the ovaries to the perineum. Hold your breath for awhile and inhale again, contract the middle part of the anus and then the back part of the anus, pull the sexual energy up through the perineum, and continue to draw it up to your coccyx to enter the hiatus in the sacrum.

Arch the sacrum back and outward, straightening it, to activate the Sacral Pump. Hold the energy here and continue to inhale three to nine times, pulling the sexual energy in from the Ovarian Palace and sexual organs, with increasingly harder contractions if necessary, until the energy in your clitoris and your vagina subsides. Squeezing the buttocks more tightly may be helpful. When you are out of breath, exhale; then relax and let your sacrum and neck return to their normal positions, and rest to induce the activation of the Sacral and Cranial Pumps as the CHI enters the spinal cord through the sacrum.

5. To draw the energy to T-11, repeat the same procedure described in 1. through 4. above. Bow your spine outward and straighten your spine to accommodate the dense sexual energy and increase the pumping action. Retain the energy at T-11 until this point fills with energy. Bring the energy from the Ovarian Palace to T-11 nine times with hard contractions, inhaling each time without exhaling. Exhale and relax every part of your body, mentally guiding the CHI to flow from the Ovarian Palace to T-11.

6. To draw the energy to C-7, practice in the same manner as described above. As you bring the energy to C-7, inhale and push the top of the sternum back toward the base of the neck to straighten the entire spine, increase the pumping-up of the energy, activate the thymus gland, and join the thoracic and cervical vertebrae.

7. To draw the energy to your Jade Pillow, practice in the same manner as previously described. Inhale and pull up to the Jade Pillow, pushing the chin in toward the back and base of the skull to activate the Cranial Pump. Clench the teeth, squeeze the muscles at the back of the skull, and press your tongue hard to the palate to increase the pumping action.

8. Next draw the energy to the Pai-Hui, or crown of the head. Repeat the same process, maintaining a straight upper spine. Turn your eyes and all your senses up to the top of the crown. Press your tongue firmly to the palate to help activate the Cranial Pump. Continue to pull the energy to the top of your head until you feel the aroused energy at the lower center subside. Practice nine hard contractions and continue to inhale, each time pulling the energy from the Ovarian Palace up to the crown. Use your mind, eyes and all your senses to spiral the sexual creative energy nine, eighteen, or thirty-six times, first in a clockwise, and then in a counterclockwise direction. When the spiraling has finished, rest for a while and feel the energy enter the brain. Eventually by settling your mind on the ovaries and the pineal gland at

the crown of the head, you will bring the sexual energy from the ovaries to the brain by using only the power of the mind and all the senses.

9. The cool energy can be left in the brain or, when you feel the brain is full, let the extra energy (Golden Nectar) flow down the Functional (front) Channel to the third eye, nose, throat, heart center, solar plexus, and finally to the navel where it can be stored.

10. During lovemaking do not store the energy in the brain, but circulate it to direct the excess energy to revitalize the organs and glands. Squeeze your buttocks and perineum, and press the lower-trunk energy into and up the spine. At the same time press the energy in your upper body downward, holding the contraction as long as possible. Then exhale completely and relax the entire body. The CHI will continue to circle up the back and down the front of your body to the navel. Continue cycling the sexual energy in this way until your orgasm travels upward into the organs, glands and higher center.

H. The Orgasmic Draw is the Basis for Alchemical Sex

To make full use of the CHI Ching gathered at the navel requires study of the Taoist methods of meditation. Slightly behind or below the navel is the lower Tan Tien center, the lower field of energy in the body within which the Taoists store CHI before refining it back upward. The CHI moves in circles among the lower, middle, and upper Tan Tiens. Each time it spirals past it is refined into a higher quality of CHI. The process of refining and balancing the energy is taught in the Microcosmic Orbit, the Fusion of Five Elements, and the Lesser Enlightenment of Kan and Li courses.

It is not unlike taking crude honey mixed with wax, dirt and dead bees, and methodically refining it into the sweetest of nectars. Taoists treat the ovaries like raw honey. The Orgasmic Draw is the step of preventing the raw honey from leaking out of an old bucket and storing it in a new and well-sealed "jar." In this "jar" or "cauldron," placed at the level of the navel about two-thirds of the way back toward the spine, the ancient Masters mixed and cooked the different CHI energies of the body in a process they called "alchemy"—the precursor of modern chemistry. (Figure 6-15)

177

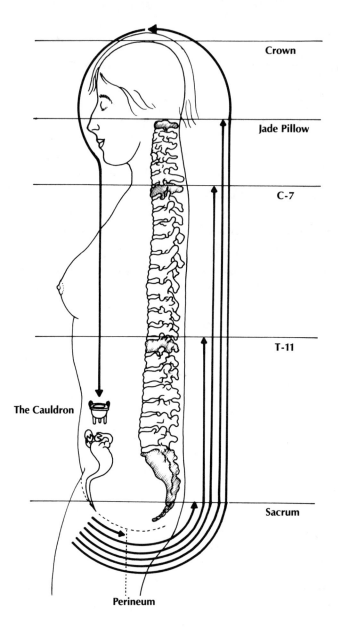

FIGURE 6-15

Internal Alchemy Begins at the Cauldron

The secret alchemical agent they used was nothing more than ordinary sexual "essence," i.e., Ching. Without it, however, none of the
higher levels of alchemical meditation would work. The Sexual Kung
Fu exercises of Ovarian Breathing, Ovarian Compression, and the

178

Orgasmic Draw may seem simple and too rudimentary to affect spiritual development, but their proper mastery is essential before you can move on to a loving relationship in full command of your sexual and spiritual powers. Your sexual essence is an elixir of life and the fountain of your youth, and is well worth training vigorously to safeguard.

7. EGG EXERCISES AND OTHER TIPS FOR WOMEN TO INCREASE SEXUAL ENERGY

A. An Introduction to Egg Exercises and Vaginal Weight Lifting

The use of a stone egg to strengthen the vagina is a practice which evolved in ancient China. As time went on, the secret of this practice remained in the Royal Palace and was taught only to the queen and concubines. Many who mastered the technique experienced very good health, remaining young and bountiful with sexual organs in old age as tight and resilient as those of a young, unmarried lady. Some believe that the queen and concubines practiced the technique in order to please the king while making love. Originally, however, the Egg Exercise and Vaginal Weight Lifting were implemented for improving health, both physically and spiritually, since these exercises provide more power to the Chi Muscle to lift the sexual energy inward and upward where it will be transformed into higher spiritual energy.

The egg is a marvelous way to strengthen and control the Chi Muscle. It is easier to practice control of this muscle with an egg in the vagina since, as the egg moves, you can feel the direction in which the Chi Muscle moves more distinctly. Controlling this voluntary muscle means control of the many involuntary muscles in this area as well. Also, as you master the use of this muscle of the vagina and perineum, you simultaneously tone up the lower abdomen. Thus, your performance of Ovarian Breathing, the Orgasmic Draw, and the Organs' Orgasm greatly improves, and the flow of sexual hormones increases.

Vaginal Weight Lifting is a very powerful practice to strengthen, in addition to the Chi Muscle, the urogenital and pelvic diaphragms. The strength of these two diaphragms is very important since these diaphragms serve as floors to the sexual organs and all vital organs.

When the Chi Muscle and diaphragms are loose, CHI pressure will leak out from the organs as they stack upon each other, dropping all their weight to rest upon the perineum. When strong, the muscle and the diaphragm function as seals, preventing leakage of life-force and sexual energies.

1. Selection of your Egg

Gem and mineral shops generally have a large selection of sizes and materials as well as prices. We researched and tested several different materials and found a volcanic rock called obsidian carved into egg shapes which contained the properties that we are looking for: embracing the Yang power of the volcano, but originating from the Yin power of the center of the Earth. These characteristics attract and concentrate the Yin essence of a woman. Further details, as well as the eggs themselves, can be obtained from the Healing Tao Center.

When you look at the eggs you will have to decide what size looks like it might feel comfortable in your vagina. The eggs range in size from that of a quail egg to jumbo supermarket eggs. Most women choose a medium-sized one, that is, an egg approximately one inch in diameter, made of either stone or wood. Wooden eggs can be easily drilled for the attachment of weights, and are therefore suited for the Vaginal Weight Lifting practice. We prefer to use stone eggs, such as obsidian, for the internal sucking exercise because of their smooth, non-porous nature. The smaller the egg, the more work your muscles will have to do because they will have to contract more strongly to cause any movement of the egg. Select an egg with a smooth surface.

2. Care for the Egg

Proper attention and care to one's feminine hygiene is an absolute necessity prior to beginning this practice. Cleanliness of the vaginal canal and the eggs are equally important. Wooden eggs should be boiled or cleaned every one to two months with a diluted vinegar solution (one tablespoon per quart of water) and allowed to dry for at least one hour, since the wooden egg easily absorbs vaginal fluid and can be a culture for germs if permitted to remain wet. A stone egg should be boiled by bringing it to the boiling point, and then allowing it to cool down. Boiling the stone egg is necessary prior to its first use. After that, simply wash it with water after each time you use it. A word of caution about using soap or detergent: some people are allergic to certain chemicals that are found in soap and detergent, especially when inserted into the channel where the membranes are very sensitive. Also, many women are unknowingly allergic to alcohol (isopropyl or rubbing type), therefore its use should be avoided for cleansing purposes.

3. Caution in Practicing the Egg Exercises

a. Before practicing the egg exercises, you must first master Ovarian Breathing.

b. You must be fully aroused before inserting the egg. If you produce very little fluid naturally, use a lubricant.

c. Married women should use a smaller egg.

d. Do not practice lying down.

e. If a problem arises and the egg becomes stuck, do not panic. Lie down and relax and the egg will come out.

4. Using the Egg

A. BEGINNING THE EXERCISE

The first time you use the egg, you will probably want to, and should, exercise all precaution until you become accustomed to it. Each time before practicing the egg exercise, you must warm yourself by massaging the breasts, making sure the vagina is expanded and some lubricating fluid is being emitted. In this chapter we provide you with a simple breast massage to warm you up. If you decide to practice immediately after the Orgasmic Draw, there is no need to try this simple version of massage because you have already massaged the breasts before the Orgasmic Draw. Once you master the Egg Exercise you can practice it in conjunction with the Orgasmic Draw or Ovarian Breathing by placing the egg in the vagina while practicing. However, it is important that you separate every exercise at first, and then join them at a later time when you become more proficient.

To assist you in inserting the egg easily, if necessary, use a lubricating jelly, any spermicidal jelly or cream that is not petroleum based, any natural lubricating oil, such as a raw cooking oil, that you know is safe, or any lubricant that you have used that you do not have a chemical reaction to. Always insert the wider end of the egg first. Once inserted, assume the standard Horse Stance posture (feet shoulders' width apart and firmly grounded; ankles and knees bent; groin folded; spine and neck in alignment). Elevate your arms in front of you to a 45-degree angle with your palms facing upward. Assume a clenched fist position. It is from this basic rooting stance that each of the Egg Exercises is performed. (Figure 7-1(a) and (b))

FIGURE 7-1

The Horse Stance for the Egg Exercise

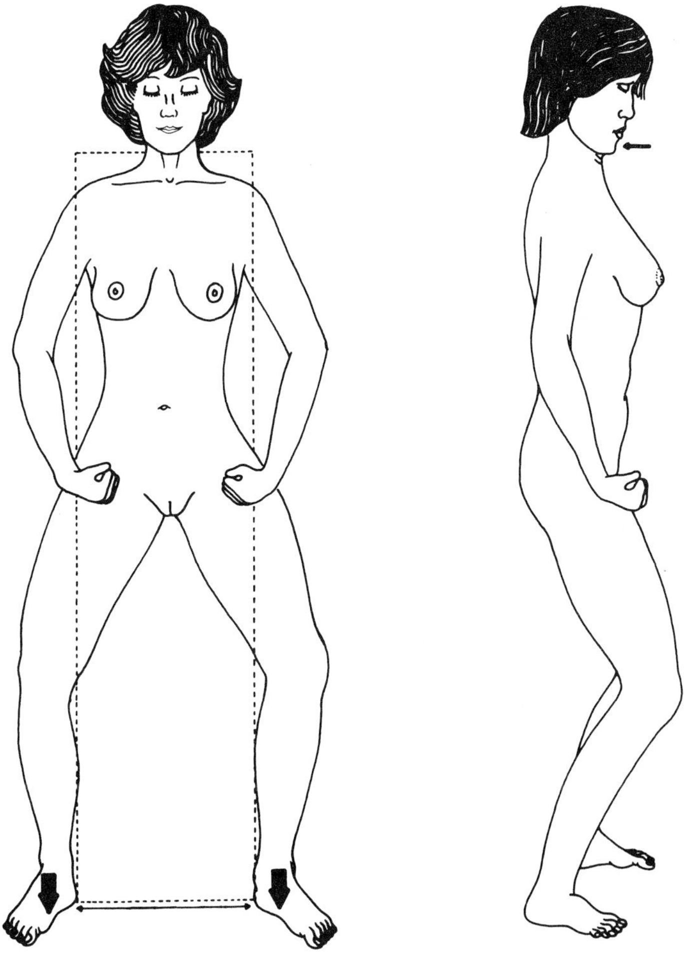

(a) Feet shoulder's width apart and firmly grounded

(b) Side View

183

The cervix represents the back limit of the vagina. Squeezing the muscles the way you would to have a bowel movement will expel the egg. In the beginning make sure not to practice on a cement floor so that if the egg drops out, it will not break. You can also place a towel under your feet.

B. THE THREE SECTIONS OF THE VAGINAL CANAL (FIGURE 7-2)

With the practices of Ovarian Breathing and the Orgasmic Draw, you began to gain control of your Chi Muscle. To gain further control

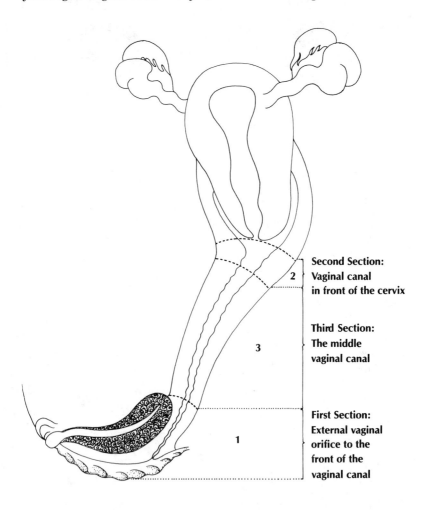

Second Section:
Vaginal canal
in front of the cervix

Third Section:
The middle
vaginal canal

First Section:
External vaginal
orifice to the
front of the
vaginal canal

FIGURE 7-2

The Three Sections of the Vagina

through the Egg Exercise, we divide the vaginal canal into three sections.

(1) THE EXTERNAL VAGINAL ORIFICE AND FRONT OF THE VAGINAL CANAL

The first section includes the muscles of the external vaginal orifice and the front part of the vaginal canal. When the egg is inserted, you will contract the uterus, closing the orifice tightly so that the egg cannot drop out.

(2) THE ANTERIOR OF THE CERVIX

The second section to be contracted consists of the muscles of the vaginal canal immediately in front of the cervix.

(3) THE MIDDLE OF THE VAGINAL CANAL

The third section encompasses the muscles of the middle of the vaginal canal. These are the muscles that will move the egg up and down, left and right, and tilt it in different directions. (Figure 7-3) You

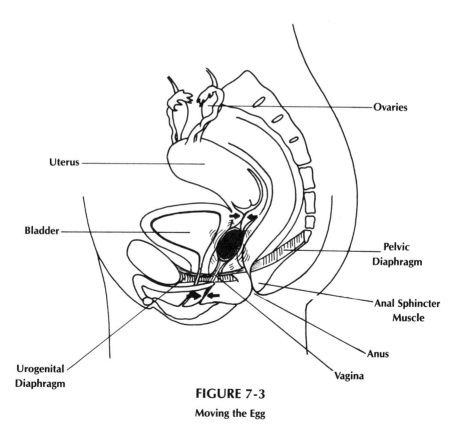

FIGURE 7-3

Moving the Egg

185

will practice moving and using these muscles until you master their movement as easily as using your hand. As you play with the direction you will learn to differentiate each movement of these muscles. If you have a male partner, he will soon notice the results of this practice. Practice for a few minutes at a time, as often as you like. Insert the egg before practicing Tai Chi, Iron Shirt, or any of the other physical practices. Gradually, increase the length of time you retain it. Just remember that it is there, since laughing, sneezing, or coughing can sometimes cause the egg to blast out of the vagina quite unexpectedly.

5. Two Eggs Technique

You can upgrade the practice by using two eggs in the vagina at the same time, moving them up and down, in different directions, or banging them together to achieve a vibration that will stimulate the inside organs. (Figure 7-4) Two eggs are more difficult to manage, quite like drawing a square and circle simultaneously using both hands. It is important to know how to manage one egg well first.

Once you are well trained and are master of the Chi Muscle, you can dispense with the eggs, using your mind and the appropriate muscles to move the sexual energy as you wish.

B. Breast Massage Techniques Preliminary to the Egg Exercise

The importance of a preliminary massage before practicing the Egg Exercise and Vaginal Weight Lifting cannot be overlooked. Its purpose is to stimulate hormone secretion from the breasts and ovaries. Once ejected from their glandular source, these hormones become available for transformation into higher energy as they travel along the pathway of the Orgasmic Draw. Performing the massage with a silk or taffeta cloth creates a certain friction which is more conducive to hormonal stimulation, and is, therefore, more efficient in obtaining results.

Begin the massage by gently, but firmly, pushing the fatty tissue of the mound of each breast against the rib cage, moving two or three fingers of each hand in small circular movements. Start at the central

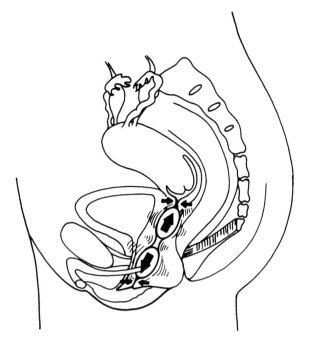

Squeezing Two Eggs Apart

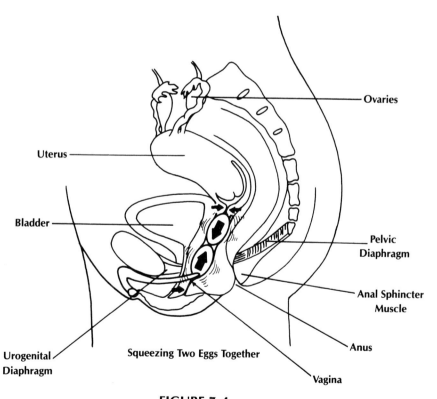

Ovaries

Uterus

Bladder

Pelvic
Diaphragm

Anal Sphincter
Muscle

Anus

Urogenital
Diaphragm

Squeezing Two Eggs Together

Vagina

FIGURE 7-4

nipple areas and work your way around and outward until each entire breast has been massaged. When using a cloth both sides can be worked simultaneously if a long enough piece of cloth is used (three feet by ten feet is a good size to work with).

Be observant of the body's signals that the hormone secreting process has begun: erect nipples and a subtle filling or hardness of the breast are two positive indicators. Breast massage will increase the energy flow to the breasts, thereby helping to break down congestion which, over a long period of time, can contribute to the development of cancer.

Breast cancer is the leading cause of cancer death in women. If discovered early enough, it can be cured. In the interest of broadening our awareness of the body's ever-changing state of health, we suggest that once a month, ideally after each menstrual period, women regularly incorporate into their practice a simple technique of breast self-examination for early detection of breast cancer. Always look thoroughly for any changes that your breasts may have undergone since your last checkup. Stand in front of a mirror and become familiar with their appearance. Is there any unusual dimpling or puckering of the skin, discoloration, ulceration, hardening or lump? Have the superficial blood vessels grown larger or increased in number? Has the size, shape or contour of your breasts changed? Next, elevate your hands above your head and ask yourself the same questions.

After completing the breast massage, the genital area should be massaged. Using the same cloth and fingertip circular motions, cover the entire mons and labial area inch by inch. After having sufficiently stimulated the clitoris, warm, moist vaginal secretions will mark the body's readiness for the egg's insertion. (For a more detailed approach to breast massage, return to Chapter 6.)

C. SUMMARY of Egg Exercises Step-By-Step

1. Insert the Egg

When you feel you are ready, insert the egg into the vagina, large end first.

2. Horse Stance Alignment

Align your body in the basic Horse Stance described earlier.

3. Contract the First Section

Isolate and contract the muscle groups responsible for closing the external vaginal orifice tightly. This will help to keep the egg in the vaginal canal.

4. Contract the Second Section

Inhale and contract the vaginal canal muscles immediately in front of the cervix so that you are now contracting two sections at the same time. Keep both points closed. There is no need to use hard muscle contractions. The strength required depends a great deal on the control of these muscles you have gained by practicing the Ovarian exercises of Chapters 5 and 6.

5. Squeeze the Third Section

Slightly squeeze the egg from the middle of the vaginal canal until you feel that you have a good grip on it. Inhale and squeeze again, gradually increasing the squeeze, and then inhale more and squeeze harder. (Figure 7-5) Once you feel you have a good grip on the egg, slowly move it up and down. Start with a slow motion, gradually increasing to a fast motion. When you are out of breath, exhale and rest. The resting period is very important. It is at this time that you will feel CHI build up in this area. Try to master each movement before continuing to the next step.

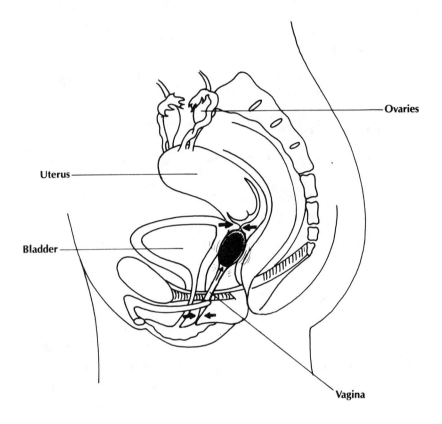

FIGURE 7-5

Moving the Egg Up

6. Use the Second Section to Move the Egg Left and Right

Next move the egg left and right using the top, or second, section. Practice until you master this action. (Figure 7-6)

7. Use the First Section to Move the Egg Left and Right

Next move the egg left and right from the bottom, or first, section. Using the mind and some muscle movement are important since you cannot move the egg with hard muscle contractions alone. There are many involuntary muscles within the vaginal canal which the mind and Chi Muscle help to move.

190

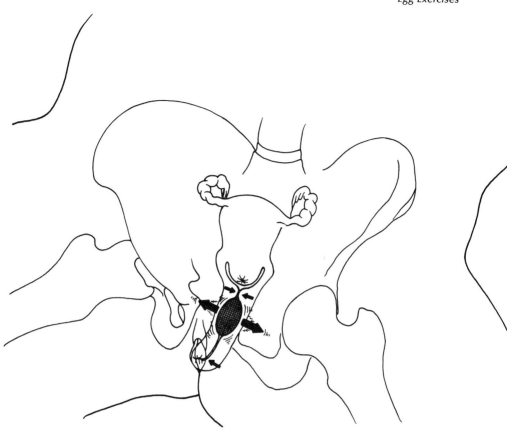

FIGURE 7-6
Using the Second Section to Move the Egg
Sideways

8. Use Both Sections to Move the Egg Left and Right

Now move the egg left and right as you wish, holding it by the top and bottom muscles. Master this step before continuing to the next exercise. (Figure 7-7)

9. Use Both Sections to Tilt the Egg

Next tilt the egg up and down, from the top and the bottom. Master this action.

191

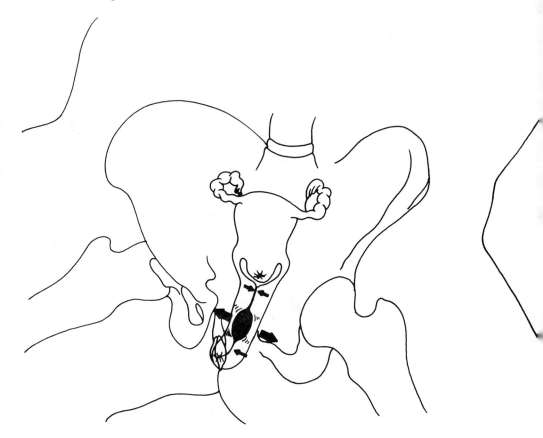

FIGURE 7-7

Using Both Sections to Move the Egg Sideways

10. Combine all Movements

Combine all of these movements, moving the egg left and right, tilting it up and down, moving it up to touch the cervix, and then down to the external vaginal orifice. Rest. All during the Egg Exercise the contraction of the vaginal canal in the area in front of the cervix and the external orifice is to remain constant until you have finished moving the egg.

This particular Egg Exercise should be practiced two to three times per week. You may, and should, perform this very same exercise daily without actually inserting the egg by following the same sequence using the contractile strength of the vaginal muscles to suck in an imaginary egg and move it up, down, left and right.

To enhance your development you should begin using a smaller egg. Later, the larger eggs may be used to mark the progress in your "sucking" abilities. Eventually, the practice of egg-sucking will become so mastered that you will be able to suck the egg into the vagina from the outside with a vacuum-like force. Such a powerful sucking activity enhances experiences in your life such as childbearing or lovemaking. Imagine the intense pleasure of your lover as you demonstrate to him your power and skill.

D. Egg Exercise during Ovarian Breathing and the Orgasmic Draw

Once you master the Egg Exercise described above, you can combine the practice with Ovarian Breathing and the Orgasmic Draw. Each will enhance the other's practice.

1. Prepare with the Breast Massage

Prepare with the breast massage until you feel yourself ready, and insert the egg into your vagina.

2. Align Yourself in the Horse Stance

Align your body in the basic Horse Stance described earlier.

3. Close the External Vaginal Orifice

Isolate and contract the individual muscle groups responsible for tightly closing the external vaginal orifice.

4. Gather the Energy at the Ovarian Palace

Gather the energy from the ovaries and the breasts at the Ovarian Palace. Inhale slowly and deeply. Draw the sexual energy down through the uterus to the clitoris and hold it there.

5. Grip and Move the Egg

Contract and hold the lower, then middle and upper vaginal muscles and feel your grip on the egg. Then push the egg deeply up into the vaginal canal. Move it up and down and feel the increasing sexual energy.

6. Begin Ovarian Breathing and the Orgasmic Draw

As you feel more energy gather at the vaginal canal, follow the procedures of Ovarian Breathing and the Orgasmic Draw. Pull the energy to the front part of the perineum, to the sacrum, T-11, C-7, C-1, Jade Pillow, and crown. Circulate the energy in the brain and bring it down the front channel to the third eye, tongue, throat, heart center, solar plexus and navel. Collect the energy at the navel. Please review the details of the practice of Ovarian Breathing and the Orgasmic Draw in Chapters 5 and 6.

E. Vaginal Weight Lifting (Figure 7-8)

The only difference between the Egg Exercise and Vaginal Weight Lifting procedure is the addition of a weight to the specially drilled egg. As mentioned earlier, in weight lifting we use wooden eggs. Usually an egg is chosen of approximately a one-inch diameter with holes drilled in it through which a string can be threaded for attachment to a weight. Use a sturdy string that can sustain at least ten to twenty pounds of weight, or use three strands of string. Begin with a one-half pound weight. You can buy a half-pound plate that has a hole through which the string can be tied, or use a small cotton or plastic bag into which a weight can be placed and the bag easily attached to the egg's string and hung.

Suspending weights from the egg is a most effective way to increase the strength of the pelvic and urogenital diaphragms and the vaginal muscles. This is also a tremendous exercise for the cervix, the ovaries, and the organs and glands. With the increase in weight the vagina alone does not have enough strength to lift the weight, making it necessary for all the internal organs and glands to join in contributing to the strength. The heavier the weight the more counterpressure must be exerted by the vagina, the cervix, the ovaries, the diaphragm, the organs and glands. This extended effort will result in increased CHI pressure and hormone production. Make sure you can handle the weight well before adding more to it.

The exact sequence of steps is then followed as described in the Egg Exercise above. This time, however, do not move the egg up and down. Hold it by tightening and squeezing the external and middle sections of the vaginal canal around the egg and pulling the egg up. Do not release it. This exercise is to be performed one time only, two to three times per week, with the weight gradually increasing in one-half pound increments, and not exceeding ten pounds.

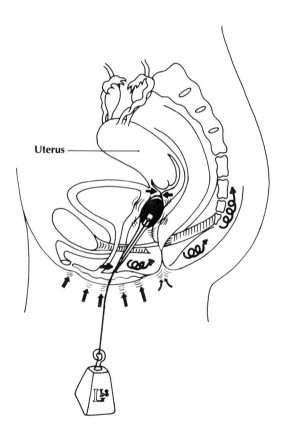

FIGURE 7-8
Vaginal Weight Lifting

1. Practical Exercise Step-By-Step

A. INSERT THE EGG WHILE HOLDING THE STRING AND WEIGHT

Place a chair in front of you and then place the weight on the chair. If you are not already prepared, start with the breast massage, followed by massaging the mons, the perineum, and the coccyx. When you feel the CHI is ready, insert the wooden egg with the string attached into the vagina, always attempting to increase the force of suction used to draw it in. Use the other hand to hold the string with the weight.

B. ASSUME THE HORSE STANCE

Align your body in the basic Horse Stance described earlier.

C. GRIP THE EGG USING THE MUSCLES OF THE VAGINAL CANAL AND RELEASE THE STRING AND WEIGHT

Inhale, closing the external and internal vagina tightly. At the same time contract the uterus so that the vaginal canal has been closed on both ends. Inhale, squeeze the egg tightly, and pull it up until you feel you have gripped the egg firmly, then slowly release the string with the weight attached. Do not remove your hand in case you did not grip the egg firmly enough. If the egg with the weight attached falls out, it might hurt you.

D. USE THE CERVIX TO PULL THE WEIGHT UP

Hold your breath and contract harder. Inhale and start to pull from the cervix and feel the force of the cervix helping to pull up the weight. When you feel you are holding the egg with the weight securely, start to rock the pelvis, thus rocking the weight, 30 to 60 times. (Figure 7-9) This will generate a tremendous energy. When you feel the energy build up, inhale slowly and deeply down to the ovaries, gathering your sexual energy, and carry it through the uterus and down to the clitoris. Hold it there.

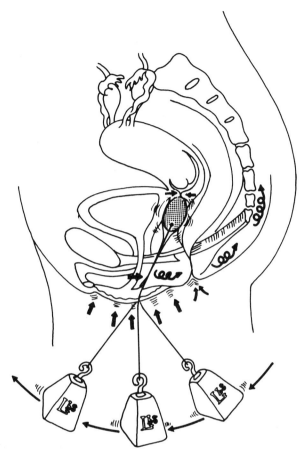

FIGURE 7-9
Swinging the Weight Back and Forth

E. EMPLOY ALL THE MUSCLES OF THE VAGINAL CANAL

Contract and hold the lower, then the middle and upper vaginal muscles, so that the egg pushes deeply up into the vaginal canal and the weight will not pull the egg out.

F. BRING THE ENERGY INTO THE HEAD

Now draw all the energy you have just gathered up the spine and into the head, as you continue to hold the egg deeply inside of you.

197

G. CONTINUE PULLING THE ENERGY INTO THE BRAIN

Still holding the same breath, continue gathering and pulling the sexual energy up into the head, where the brain can now be bathed in this wondrous nourishment.

H. HOLD THE ENERGY IN THE BRAIN

Hold this energy in your brain, initially for 30 to 45 seconds, and gradually increase this time period.

I. BRING THE ENERGY TO THE NAVEL

Finally, stick the tongue up to the palate, exhale, bring the energy down, and collect it in the navel point.

J. REST THE WEIGHT ON THE CHAIR AND EXPEL THE EGG

Grip the string on the weight and place the weight on the chair. Let the egg go, utilizing the contractile strength of the vaginal muscles to expel it.

K. THE OVARIES PULL AND LIFT THE EGG AND WEIGHT UPWARD

When you feel you can pull from the cervix well, begin to use the force of the ovaries. You will try only the left side first, then the right ovary, and finally both sides together. When you feel you can once again secure the egg in the vaginal canal, use your mind and start to contract the left ovary, wrap the CHI around that ovary, and then pull from the left ovary toward the cervix and the vaginal canal, pulling the egg and attached weight upward. Do the same on the right side, and then both sides together.

L. THE KIDNEYS PULL THE EGG AND WEIGHT

Next move to the kidneys and the adrenal glands situated on top of them. Practice using the force of each kidney separately first in order to identify the feeling. Inhale and use the contraction of both kidneys to help pull the weight up. Then, starting with the left kidney and making sure you feel the force coming from there, use your mind to contract the muscles around the left kidney even more, and wrap it with CHI. Then pull the left kidney down again, pulling it toward the left ovary and the bladder. The ovary, in turn, will pull on the cervix; the cervix will pull on the vaginal canal; the vaginal canal will pull on the egg; and the egg will pull on the weight. In other words, once you have secured the egg in the vaginal canal, you will pull with the higher organs and glands which, in turn, will pull on the lower organs and glands, and they, in their turn, will pull on the egg and weight. Practice the same procedure with the right kidney. Once you have mastered the left and right kidneys, combine both kidneys in the practice. This will give you a great deal of internal force to pull an even heavier weight.

M. THE SPLEEN AND LIVER PULL THE EGG AND WEIGHT

Next move up to the spleen and liver. Start again on the left side, contracting the muscles around the spleen, situated beneath the left side of the rib cage. Contract and wrap the CHI around and into the spleen. Pull the spleen toward the left kidney, pull the kidney to the bladder and left ovary, the left ovary to the cervix, the cervix to the vaginal canal, and the vaginal canal to the egg and weight. Practice the same procedure on the liver, which lies under the right side of the rib cage. Pack, wrap and pull the liver up and toward the right kidney, to the bladder and right ovary, to the cervix, to the vaginal canal, and to the egg and weight.

N. THE LUNGS ARE EMPLOYED NEXT

Moving to the lungs, start with the left lung first. Practice contracting the left lung and wrapping CHI around it until you actually feel the lung contracting. When you have again secured the egg in the vagina, begin to contract the lung with more force and pull from the lung to the spleen, then to the kidney, bladder and left ovary, cervix, vaginal canal, and egg and weight. Practice in the same manner on the right side beginning with the right lung.

O. BE CAUTIOUS WITH THE HEART AS IT PULLS ON THE EGG AND WEIGHT

As you move on to the next organ, the heart, be cautious, making sure that you are well in control of the other organs first. The heart and lungs can easily become congested with energy and can cause chest pain and difficulty in breathing. If you have this problem, tap the area around the heart and practice the healing sound of the heart (as described in the book *Taoist Ways to Transform Stress into Vitality*). Practice until you can control the contraction of the heart muscle and wrap the CHI around the heart. Again secure the egg in the vaginal canal, contract the heart and lungs and pull up toward the spleen, liver, adrenal glands and kidneys, bladder and ovaries, cervix, vaginal canal, egg and weight.

P. THE THYMUS GLAND IS DIFFICULT TO CONTRACT

The thymus gland is difficult to contract because of its location under the sternum. The only way to do this is to sink the chest and sternum down, press the sternum to the back, and contract and wrap it with CHI. Mastering this contraction and wrapping the heart and lungs with CHI will help greatly in contracting the thymus gland. Once again, secure the egg in the vaginal canal, sink the sternum to the back and contract the lungs, from left to right, toward the thymus under the sternum, then contract the heart to the thymus which is in close proximity. Pressing and contracting the heart will greatly increase the force of the thymus. Feel all three organs and the gland create the force to pull the spleen, liver, kidneys, bladder, ovaries, cervix, vaginal canal, egg and weight.

Q. PULLING FROM THE PITUITARY AND PINEAL GLANDS ALL THE WAY TO THE BRAIN

The pituitary and pineal glands are the most difficult to master. If, however, you master all the other organs, these glands will be easier to learn to control. The tongue and eyes act as major tools in exerting force on the pituitary and pineal glands. Practice first, by pressing the tongue to the palate and turning the eyes upward. Contract the eye muscles toward the middle of the brain to the pituitary gland. Contract the muscles of the skull and squeeze the brain into itself toward the pituitary gland, located in the middle of the brain. Concentrate on and contract the middle part of the anus and pull all the way up into the brain. Contract the lungs, heart and thymus gland and push up toward the middle of the brain. Now secure the egg in the vaginal canal, press your tongue firmly to the palate with the tip of the tongue, touching the lower jaw behind the teeth and the flat part of the tongue touching the middle of the palate. Turn your eyes up toward the middle of the brain, and squeeze the head muscles toward the brain's middle area. Contract the lungs, heart, and thymus gland, and press upward to the middle section of the brain. The pituitary gland, together with all of the other glands and organs pull up the spleen, liver, kidneys, bladder, ovaries, cervix, vaginal canal, egg and weight. Repeat the practice, now focusing on the pineal gland.

When finished with all of these steps, make sure that you circulate the energy for a few rounds in the Microcosmic Orbit, finally collecting it in the navel. Since all the steps of this exercise are very important and extremely powerful, you must use caution. Gradually you will feel all the organs and glands contributing to the internal force that will pull the weight. If you have already mastered the organs' orgasm, you will handle this exercise with ease.

R. CLEANSE THE EGG THOROUGHLY

Since the mucous secretions on the egg are an ideal medium for bacterial growth, be sure to cleanse the egg thoroughly after each use.

S. MASSAGE YOURSELF

Massage the Hui-Yin point in the perineum. Massage the mons and the coccyx. This massaging after each exercise is very important. It will help you clear the remaining energy so that the body can absorb it easily.

T. CHANNEL THE ENERGY IN THE MICROCOSMIC ORBIT

Gently tap the lower abdomen with your palm to remove the excess energy from the ovaries, vagina and clitoris. Sit down quietly and channel the excess energy in the Microcosmic Orbit, so that all your organs will benefit.

F. Herbs to Tone Your Ovaries—Maneewan's Special Recipes for Women

Women who experience any weakness of their sexual organs will find it quite to their advantage to follow two of Maneewan Chia's simple and delicious recipes.

1. Maneewan's Ovaries' Strengthening Tonic

To gradually increase the energy flow in the ovaries, sample this mixture.

1 cup whiskey

1 cup honey

1 cup lemon juice

Stir the mixture well until the honey dissolves. Store the mixture in a previously sterilized jar. Shake the jar well before each use. Drink one to two tablespoons daily.

Caution: If you are experiencing a very heavy menstrual flow, refrain from taking the mixture for a few days until you have normalized. This recipe will last several months, and the more it ages, the better it becomes. Store it in a cool dry place.

2. Don Quai—Chicken Soup

As an herb containing numerous invaluable properties, Don Quai should become an integral component of a woman's health care regimen.

Loaded with good nutrition for the ovaries and hormones, this herb is essentially required by a woman's body throughout her lifetime. It is especially good as a blood tonic, being quite rich in iron, and it is great for alleviating a variety of menstrual problems. Don Quai is taken only one to two times per month and only after the menstrual cycle has ended, never during the cycle.

This herb can be obtained in Chinese herb stores located in every Chinatown. Many of these stores have mail order services.

Simply place one to two heads of the herb (about one inch in size) in chicken broth or soup, and season as desired. Simmer in a slow cooker for approximately three to five hours.

Vegetarians can make Don Quai in the same manner using the slow cooker and a meatless broth.

After using Don Quai on a regular basis for a one- or two-month period, you will notice a definite increase in your strength.

G. Sunning (Figure 7-10)

If you are lucky enough to have a sunny area with some privacy, you will probably enjoy this practice.

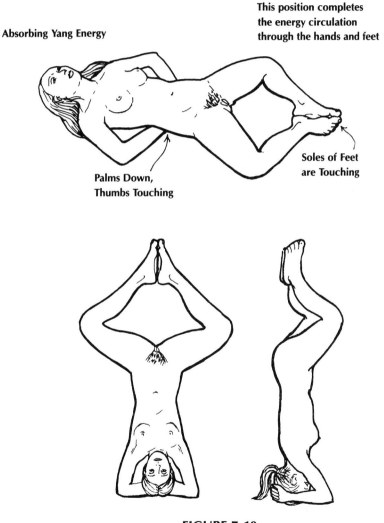

Absorbing Yang Energy

This position completes the energy circulation through the hands and feet

Soles of Feet are Touching

Palms Down, Thumbs Touching

FIGURE 7-10

Sunning

The sun's energy is very healing and soothing to the genitals and can be absorbed by the ovaries through the genitals. The best time of day is in the early morning (between seven a.m. and nine a.m.) and in the late afternoon (between three p.m. and five p.m.). Sunning should be done no more than five minutes in the beginning, eventually working up to ten minutes.

Massage the mons area and alongside the outer lips. Open the labia to the sun and use your mind to draw the solar energy into your ovaries. Let this energy mix with your own energy as you circulate it in the Microcosmic Orbit.

8. DUAL CULTIVATION

A. An Introduction to Dual Cultivation

1. Opening the Healing Love Energy Channel

Most people would agree that sex is enjoyable. In this book you are learning how to utilize the normal sexual energy that you create and how to multiply it. By now you should be aware of the fact that if you do not transform the sexual energy that you produce, but let it drain out, you lessen your vitality. This is accompanied by more and more psychologically draining effects, such as tiredness or depression, or actual physical suffering, such as pain in the back or kidney areas. If you continue to deplete yourself, eventually you will drain the vitality from all the organs and glands, making the body weak, sick and old.

As previous chapters have indicated, in order to transform the sexual energy, you must direct it upward to a higher energy center. Doing this requires channeling the flow of this energy. We have stressed the need and importance of opening the channels of the Microcosmic Orbit, the main route through which the energy begins to travel.

In ancient times, the ways to develop CHI flow were regarded as top secret, especially the way to channel sexual healing energy. Sexual energy is extremely powerful as a means to attain rejuvenation and a higher spiritual energy. There are textbooks, such as the *Plain Lady* book, a sexology book written thousands of years ago in ancient China by an unknown author, demonstrating various traditional positions for having sex and promoting healing. But these books do not show how to channel the energy. At the time this book became available, the Taoist system of channeling energy was not available to the general public, but remained a secret taught only verbally to the Emperor and a few others who were not permitted to put it into writing.

We feel today that the time is right to teach people how to benefit from this transformed energy, or Healing Love, because many people misuse their sexual energy, hurting themselves and others. Our purpose in writing this book is to help people benefit from the channeling of this energy.

2. The Sexual Organs are the Roots of Life

The Taoist system regards the sexual organs as the roots of life, connected to all other glands and organs. Once you begin to practice the methods taught in this book, you will begin to feel the close relationship of the glands and organs, especially the pineal and pituitary glands, kidneys, liver, lungs, and heart.

3. Energizing all the Organs and Glands

The ovaries have a close connection with the sexual organs, and by properly channeling their energy using certain lovemaking and hand positions, we can learn to use sexual healing energy to vitalize our entire systems. There are hundreds of lovemaking positions and hand gestures. The purpose of a position is to stimulate, according to reflexes, and to energize all the internal organs. These positions help only if the energy channel through which you move the energy upward is open; otherwise, the lovemaking positions and hand gestures will not have much meaning.

The exercises described in this book are part of the Healing Love practice; however, to a certain extent, they can also stand alone as guidelines to your own sexual practice. In particular, the Anus Chi Muscle exercise and the Breast Massage will help you get in touch with your organs' and glands' energy.

4. Exchanging Energy with your Partner

Many couples have used the techniques described here; they are no longer mysterious and they are no longer only in the province of Taoist Masters. These techniques can increase the possibility that you will experience Beyond Orgasm (Valley Orgasm) whenever you have the desire. This is one of the goals of this book.

Synchronizing your breathing with your partner's and then harmonizing your breathing seems to come quite naturally to many people. Lying with noses in proximity, you begin to feel the two breaths become one. Breathing in and out together is the principal way to begin to build up CHI in both you and your partner. This buildup of CHI can be a relaxing time, or it can be arousing, depending upon your intention.

No doubt you and your partner are both eager to enjoy your sexual pleasures together. Use this book as a tool in learning how to practice and use the Orgasmic Draw in order to multiply your orgasms and bring you both to the point of Valley Orgasm. As you practice the Orgasmic Draw, your partner practices the Big Draw as taught in the companion book *Taoist Secrets of Love: Cultivating Male Sexual Energy*. These practices will give you both a great deal of energy to share. This energy can be transferred back and forth between you and your partner through your tongues or genitals—each organ acting as a switch to transfer energy between the two channels that complete each one's Microcosmic Orbit. In fact, with practice you will be able to exchange energy in a variety of ways, including over physical distance. Some people will actually feel the energy circulate in their own Microcosmic Orbit and will feel that energy transfer into their partner. Some couples have described the feeling of the energy as a cocoon surrounding them, and some feel the energy between them or above them.

5. Valley Orgasm and How to Get There

Difficult to explain in words, a person must reach a certain level in lovemaking to understand what is meant by Valley Orgasm (Beyond Orgasm). The major sensation is the atmosphere between you and your lover. If you are both in a low mood, or one of you is in a low energy cycle, it becomes difficult to reach this point. Meditating to move the energy in the Microcosmic Orbit will help bring each of you to the same energy level and is most important to the initiation of sexual pleasure. The more you and your partner can meditate and practice the Orgasmic and Big Draw together, the more both of you will harmonically tune in to each other.

Practicing such techniques as Tongue Kung Fu, as described in the book *Taoist Secrets of Love: Cultivating Male Sexual Energy*, will greatly contribute to foreplay and sexual arousal. When you feel you are ready to engage in lovemaking, and have built up sexual arousal substantially, you can begin to use the Orgasmic Draw, while your partner

207

uses the Big Draw. After each Orgasmic or Big Draw, the energy starts to move between you, fusing you into an energetic or meditative state that can make you both feel connected and simultaneously experience a cosmic tranquility. You can understand how difficult it is to describe this state; it is similar to describing what meditation feels like. You must experience it yourself. In order for you and your partner to experience the energy, you must begin with the basic training described in this chapter, initially using some external help (i.e., breathing techniques, muscle locks, placing of hands, etc.) to guide you into the internal practice (mind control). We will elaborate on a few lovemaking and hand positions to help you and your partner open the channels faster, so that the exchange of Valley Orgasms will be easier.

6. Sexual Organs' Exercise Positions

There are a few basic positions that we use in lovemaking, and from these basic few come hundreds of others. Many simply alter the positions of the legs: one leg up and one leg down, or both legs up, etc. This slight differential accounts for many positions, but as we have emphasized, although certain positions help you to reach a certain area of the sexual organs to stimulate certain reflexes, it is the channeling of the sexual healing energy that is most important. If you cannot channel the energy, these positions and hands gestures are meaningless. The nine basic positions are as follows:

A. FACE TO FACE

(1) The woman lies on her back with the man on top. (Figure 8-1(a))

(2) The woman lies on her side with her hips twisted so that her pelvis is facing upward. (Figure 8-1(b))

(3) The man lies on his back with the woman on top. (Figure 8-1(c))

(4) The man is in a sitting position and the woman sits on his lap. (Figure 8-1(d))

(5) The man and woman lie on their sides facing each other. (Figure 8-1(e))

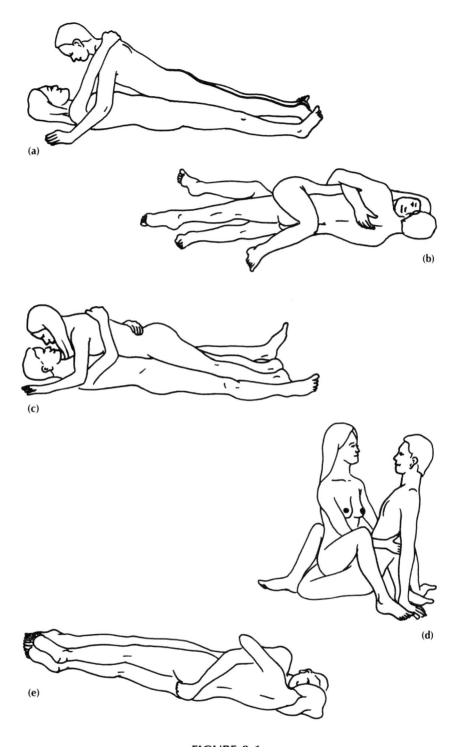

FIGURE 8-1

Face-to-Face Positions

B. BACK-FACING

(1) The woman bends over, supporting herself with her hands and knees, and the man kneels behind her. (Figure 8-2(a))

(2) The man lies on his back, while the woman is on her knees facing his feet. (Figure 8-2(b))

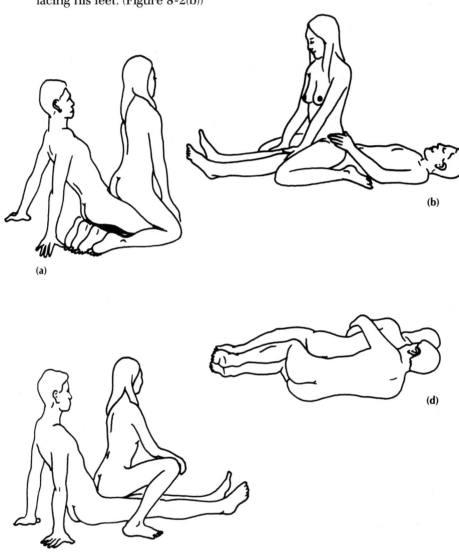

(b)

(d)

(a)

(c)

FIGURE 8-2

Back-Facing

(3) The man sits up, and the woman sits on his lap facing his feet. (Figure 8-2(c))

(4) The man and woman lie on their sides with the man facing the woman's back. (Figure 8-2(d))

The basic principle is that the one who moves is the one who brings healing to the other, while the one who does not move receives the healing. The inactive person can easily concentrate. When the mind is quiet, this partner will be able to feel his or her partner's sexual healing energy.

7. Hand Gestures Link the Meridians of the Fingers and Toes with their Corresponding Organs

The hands and feet are the outer extremities of the body, and they are linked to the organs, glands and nervous system through a system of meridians, or energy routes, through which the energy of the organs and glands flows. Finger gestures have been used frequently in the ritual Taoist practices and are most useful to join the circuit and channel the energy through the meridians.

In lovemaking we stimulate and increase the sexual healing energy to flow through the subtle meridian channels. If we do not direct the energy back from the extremities, the energy can leak out through the hands and feet. Knowing the fingers' and toes' corresponding meridians can help to develop the ability to channel the outward flow of energy back through the meridians to the area you choose to direct it.

There are hundreds of hand gestures used in various other systems. If you are not trained and familiar with their usage, you will not be able to discern their power, although many people claim to have such ability. Some people spend a lot of time learning many gestures which in actuality have similar uses or only one use. When careful study is made, there are only a few basic hand positions that are effective. The simplest ones are the most useful; however, the most important factor is the energy flow, not the simplicity.

A. THE FINGERS AND THEIR CORRESPONDING ORGANS

The fingers correspond to certain organs as described below and this connection influences bodily functions.

211

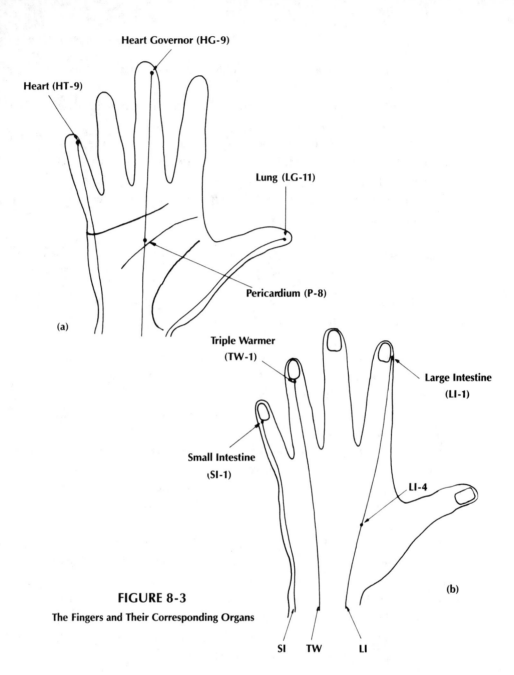

Heart Governor (HG-9)

Heart (HT-9)

Lung (LG-11)

Pericardium (P-8)

(a)

Triple Warmer
(TW-1)

Large Intestine
(LI-1)

Small Intestine
(SI-1)

LI-4

(b)

FIGURE 8-3

The Fingers and Their Corresponding Organs

SI   TW   LI

(1) The thumbs correspond to the lungs meridian (Figure 8-3(a));

(2) the index fingers correspond to the large intestine meridian (Figure 8-3(b));

(3) the middle fingers correspond to the pericardium meridian (Figure 8-3(b));

212

(4) the ring fingers correspond to the triple warmer meridian (Figure 8-3(b)); and

(5) the pinkie fingers correspond to the heart and small intestine meridian. (Figure 8-3(a) and (b)).

B. THE TOES CORRESPOND TO SPECIFIC ORGANS

The toes also correspond to specific organs, thereby affecting the body's functions. (Figure 8-4)

(1) The big toes correspond to the liver and spleen meridian;

(2) the second toes correspond to the stomach meridian;

(3) the fourth toes correspond to the gall bladder meridian; and

(4) the small toes correspond to the bladder meridian.

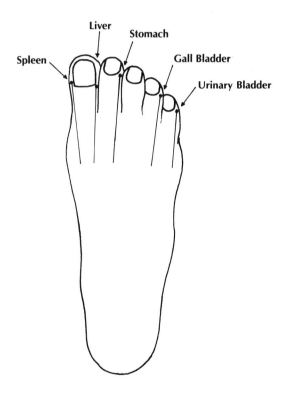

FIGURE 8-4

Energy Meridians in the Toes

B. Descriptions of Positions and Hand Gestures for Healing Love

1. Lovemaking Positions

According to the *Plain Lady* book mentioned above (also called *Shu Nu Ching*, or *White Madame*), there are eight healing positions for men and seven for women. All these positions are helpful to heighten the lovemaking experience, but their most important function is healing through the use of the energy that is generated. Since the *Plain Lady* book does not teach moving energy, a process which requires meditation practice, all the positions described in that book for healing have to be practiced many times a day for many days to reap any benefits. In the sexual healing energy practice we are describing here, we began with such energy practices as Ovarian Breathing, the Orgasmic Upward Draw, the Egg Exercise, etc., all of which assist you in gaining control of your sexual energy and directing the energy to the place that you designate without merely depending upon reflexes and the positions used.

Although we will describe in detail only two positions, these two positions can be used to benefit both partners. As both partners alternately move, they alternately bring CHI to the area, gland or organ of his or her partner. Remember, the basic principle is that the one who moves is the one who brings healing to the other, while the one who does not move can easily quiet the mind and concentrate to feel and receive the partner's sexual healing energy.

Onc you master the energy and can direct the energy as you wish using the mind and some muscles, the positions and gestures will not be very important.

A. MAN ON TOP POSITION (FIGURE 8-5)

This is the most common of the lovemaking positions. The woman lies on her back with her legs spread. She may have a pillow under her buttocks to raise her pelvis. The man lies flat on top of the woman or supports some or all of his weight on his elbows, hands or knees. Remember the Taoist theory that men are like fire and women are like water. Fire is easy to light, or is activated faster, and burns easily, as most men usually become active sexually initially and seem ag-

214

gressive. A woman, like water, may be passive in the beginning, and usually needs to be moved to lovemaking by a man. So in the beginning of lovemaking, it is beneficial for the woman to lie on her back and the man to use foreplay to bring the woman to the boiling point. Once a woman is active and aroused, she should play an active, or aggressive, part also by such activities as kissing him, playing with his tongue and ears, and holding and massaging his penis. All these activities will create a sense of harmony. Ordinarily the couple will then first move into the basic position, and then continue with other positions, most likely ending up in the basic man on top position again.

FIGURE 8-5
Man on Top Position

B. BENEFITS OF THE MAN ON TOP POSITION

There are benefits to this position.

(1) First, the entire systems of both the woman and man become energized. The *Plain Lady* book recommends practicing three sets of nine shallow penetrations and one deep penetration three times a day for twenty days. (The nine shallow thrusts stimulate the plexus of nerves surrounding the woman's G-Spot and are best for exchanging sexual energies, while the deep thrust forces air out of the vagina, creating a vacuum inside the woman during the nine shallow thrusts that follow. This has a very stimulating effect on the woman.) In many years of experience in teaching and practice, we have found that both partners can be energized in one extended lovemaking session in which sexual healing energy is brought directly to the organs and glands. We stress the importance of the man not ejaculating and thus losing the energy. In this more passive position it is easy for the woman to draw and direct the healing energy up the spine, as she learned to do in Single Cultivation practicing the Orgasmic Upward Draw, and then down the front channel. In this way she will be able to guide the sexual healing energy to her organs and eventually through her partner's Orbit to his organs.

(2) Secondly, the face to face position is greatly satisfying to the senses and emotions. It permits all five sensory organs of both part-ners to come in contact: the tongues, ears, eyes, mouths, noses, and all hair and skin. These senses, especially the tongues and eyes, are the major carriers of life-force energy. We have mentioned that the tongue works like a switch. Once you have completed the Microcosmic Orbit by using the connective tongue, the CHI flows through the tongue. As you kiss and move your tongue to touch your partner, or his tongue touches your sensory organs, you can feel those senses become stimu-lated which, in turn, stimulate the flow of energy from your corre-sponding organs.

(3) In this position it is easy for the woman and man to help each other open or clear their Microcosmic Orbit channels easily by moving a hand to the point that needs the energy flow.

(4) This position also gives a woman the greatest stimulation. Her clitoris is stimulated, and the man is able to reach her G-Spot. The weight of the man on top gives pressure to the woman's pubic bone, as

well as to her breasts, and these pressures will help the woman become stimulated much faster.

(5) The woman can follow rhythmically by wriggling her hips, bumping and grinding in response to the pressure of the man as he presses down and thrusts inside. These movements create a certain kind of CHI pressure in the organs and glands, doubling the CHI in the cavities of the body, thereby permitting the energy to circulate much faster, and exchange more easily.

(6) In this position, the farther up in the air the woman legs are, the deeper the penetration the man can accomplish in his thrusting, making this a particularly good position for a couple trying for a pregnancy. It is important, however, to make sure that the uterus is not penetrated.

C. WOMAN ON TOP POSITION (FIGURE 8-6)

Known as the sixth position in the *Plain Lady* book, the position with the woman on top will help to increase blood circulation.

As we live our modern lives, we have a tendency to overeat fatty foods which cause the blood to clot and settle in certain parts of the organs. This clotting causes a slow-down of the blood flow and creates a situation in which heat cannot be released or circulated to a cooler part of the body where the temperatures can be exchanged. The temperature of the whole body rises, resulting in an overheating of the organs. During lovemaking when we generate sexual, organ, and gland energy and fuse them into a very special kind of energy, which we call Love's Special Energy, a harmonic fusion occurs which helps to dissolve these blood clots. The kidneys and liver play the major role in this work.

In this position, the man can easily pull sexual energy to the kidneys and liver. When the woman is on top, the woman is freer to be active and so it is easy for her to direct the stimulation of the vagina and clitoris and maintain a certain angle to her sexual organs in a way that only she knows will stimulate her. Therefore, this position can help a woman with menstrual problems, such as cramps, most of which are caused by insufficient blood circulation in the ovaries and cervix. By directly stimulating the sexual glands, the clitoris, and the

FIGURE 8-6

Woman on Top Position

G-Spot, and pulling the sexual healing energy directly to the ovaries and cervix, the problem can be alleviated.

To attain this position the man lies on his back and the woman, on her knees and facing him, lowers herself onto his erect penis. Either the man or woman can guide the penis into the vagina. Couples may start in this position or arrive at it by rolling over from the man on top or the side by side position. Begin with the man in motion in order for the woman to receive the healing energy and reach the boiling point. Embrace each other, making sure you do not bend the penis or let it slip out of the vagina.

218

D. BENEFITS AND DRAWBACKS OF THE WOMAN ON TOP POSITION

There are both good and bad points to this position.

(1) The woman on top makes the woman experience a more active role, a sense of superiority, a free feeling of movement, and a sense of doing whatever she wishes. This helps to make the woman more open to the world and able to better understand men. Some women become tense when they consider that men try to rule the world in every respect. However, it is the rule of nature that Yin and Yang must be balanced. In every situation women play an equally important role. In Taoism we regard timing as very important. When the Yang is too extreme, the Yin takes over. When the Yin is too extreme, the Yang takes over. Likewise, during the beginning of sex the man is on top to arouse the woman, because he, like fire, is aroused more easily than the woman. Once the woman is aroused, she will assume the top position to arouse the man. In this way the roles are interchangeable.

In the top position the woman can experience putting the penis into her vagina, and can take as long as she desires to insert it to give the feeling of prolonged genital sensitivity. Both will feel the gentleness of the slowly spreading vagina as the penis is inserted.

(2) The woman can direct the glans of the penis to stimulate it in the most sensitive way by placing it only in the two inches that form the outer vagina. It is difficult for a man to remain in only the first two inches. The man tends to want to plunge deeper into the tighter area which alleviates his anticipation, but which also, because of its tightness, makes him finish fast.

The woman receives the sexual healing energy by permitting the man to do the thrusting as she guides his penis to the area she would like to have stimulated. In this position the man or woman can use their hands to stimulate the clitoris which will help the woman reach the boiling point faster.

(3) The man can enjoy the stimulation of liver energy by using his eyes to watch the expression of the aroused woman, her face and her breasts, and see the sexual organs in contact, moving in and out of each other. Once the eyes are stimulated, the man can bring the sexual energy to the liver by slightly contracting the right side of the anus. The woman can use her free hand to arouse her nipples, or her part-

ner's nipples. This will greatly stimulate both partners' organs and glands.

(4) The woman on top is a good position for the later months of pregnancy since it allows intercourse without her growing belly getting in the way. It is also good for the man who has a big stomach in relieving the pressure since, during the sexual act, the stomachs will meet first rather than the sex organs. Older men, and men who have heart problems, are also helped by this position since the man does not expend vigorous energy. Because the man can be less active, he can easily guide the energy to strengthen the heart.

(5) The woman on top has to be very careful that she does not move too vigorously which may bend and hurt the erect penis. This type of injury takes a long time to heal. Make sure that the penis has a full erection. If the penis becomes soft, start with slow movements to build up again to the high energy point. When the penis is soft, or during vigorous thrusting, the penis can slip out or half-way out of the vagina, and this is when it can get hurt easily.

2. Traditional Lovemaking Positions and Healing

The following are a few classic lovemaking and healing positions as outlined in the *Plain Lady* book. We list these positions for your reference only. With a properly opened energy channel you can guide the energy to heal yourself as you wish at any time and in any position, so it does not matter at all how many positions you use. For the most part you can use the few basic positions as outlined and change them into hundreds of positions. We want you to concentrate on the energy, not on the positions or gestures. Practice will help you to understand the energy. Many people like to read and listen to philosophy, but if they do not practice and experience it, they find it very difficult to understand. Working on the energy is the best way to experience the higher spiritual work.

There are several positions of healing for men and women. Remember that when the man is more active, he gives the healing. The woman lies still to receive it, quieting her mind to feel the energy, and using her concentration to guide the energy only for the purpose and to the place she needs healing. When the man lies still, the woman does the healing.

A. THE FIRST POSITION IS FOR HEALING (FIGURE 8-7)

The first position is for healing, supplying energy for women who are experiencing any kind of menstrual problem, such as cramps or excessive bleeding, loss of feeling in the vagina, or any other female problem. The woman, lying on either side or on her back with her legs spread wide open, has the task simply to maintain that position and receive the healing energy of the man who is accommodating her position with his own and is penetrating. Practice up to two sets of nine penetrations in this position per day for fifteen days.

For menstrual problems, loss of feeling in the vagina and other complications in the female sexual organs, the woman lies on the side, toward the back with the legs wide open

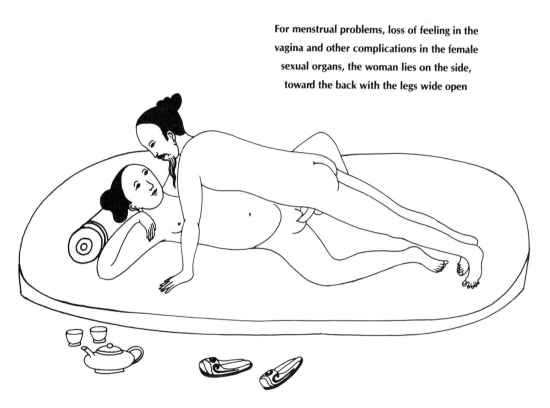

FIGURE 8-7

The First Position is for Healing

221

B. THE SECOND POSITION IS FOR ENERGIZING THE BODY AND HEALING THE SEXUAL ORGANS (FIGURE 8-8)

Position number two is for energizing the body, and is especially beneficial to those who suffer from low energy. By healing the female sexual organs, the basic energizing organs of the body, general weakness and lack of energy will be improved. To achieve this position, the woman lies on her back with her head and shoulders supported by a big pillow, and the legs spread wide apart. This position tilts the head forward and tends to curve the vaginal channel. The man enters from the front, penetrating in three sets of nine, three times a day for twenty days.

FIGURE 8-8

The Second Position is for Energizing the Body
and Healing the Sexual Organs

C. POSITION THREE IS FOR STRENGTHENING ALL THE INTERNAL ORGANS (FIGURE 8- 9)

The third position is for healing and strengthening all the internal organs. The woman lies on either side with both legs held together and bent backward from the knees. The man, lying in front of her, penetrates from the front, performing four sets of nine penetrations up to four times a day for twenty days.

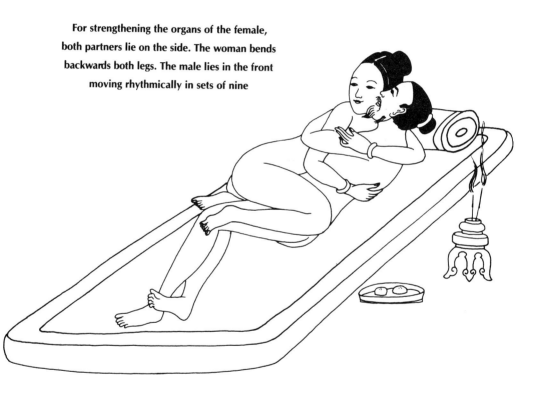

For strengthening the organs of the female, both partners lie on the side. The woman bends backwards both legs. The male lies in the front moving rhythmically in sets of nine

FIGURE 8-9

The Third Position is for Strengthening all the
Internal Organs

D. POSITION FOUR IS FOR HEALING BONE PROBLEMS (FIGURE 8-10)

The fourth position is for healing any kind of bone problems, such as bone weakness. In addition to helping speed up the healing process of broken bones, this position also alleviates circulatory system problems and heals arthritis. (One cause of arthritis, according to Chinese medicine, is bad circulation.) By increasing metabolism and thereby circulation, the risk of disease of the bone marrow, or leukemia, is also lessened. To attain this position, the woman lies on her left side with the left leg bent backward as far as possible, and her right leg stretched out straight and free. The man faces the woman to penetrate, practicing five sets of nine penetrations, up to five times a day for ten days.

For weakness in the bones and joints and circulation problems, the woman lies on the left side with the left leg bent backwards as far as possible. The right leg should be straight. The man lies on his right side facing the woman, penetrating gently in a rhythm of nine

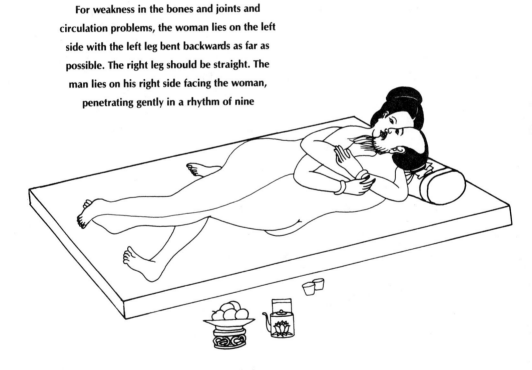

FIGURE 8-10
The Fourth Position is for Healing Bone
Problems

E. THE FIFTH POSITION HEALS BLOOD VESSEL PROBLEMS (FIGURE 8-11)

Position number five is for any kind of blood vessel problem, such as varicose veins, hardening of the arteries, high or low blood pressure, or blood clots. Excessive blood clotting, practically ignored in Western medicine, is a very important part of the theory of pathology in Chinese medicine, and is treated as a kind of blood disease. The position is the same as the fourth position, except it is executed with the woman on her right side in six sets of nine penetrations, up to six times a day for ten days.

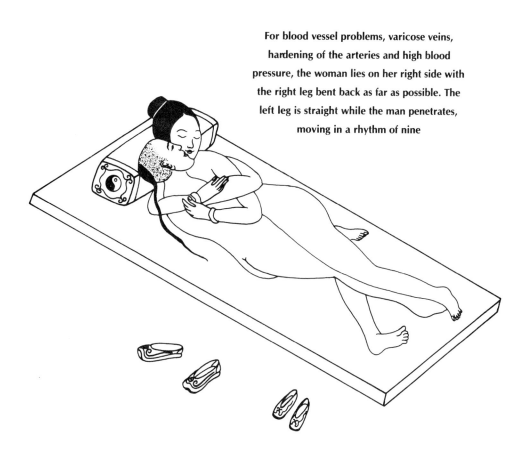

For blood vessel problems, varicose veins, hardening of the arteries and high blood pressure, the woman lies on her right side with the right leg bent back as far as possible. The left leg is straight while the man penetrates, moving in a rhythm of nine

FIGURE 8-11
The Fifth Position Heals Blood Vessel Problems

F. POSITION SIX INCREASES BLOOD COUNT (FIGURE 8-12)

This position is for generating and building more blood, especially in those who lack the capacity for generating new blood, such as a woman who bleeds excessively or is anemic. It is also beneficial in stabilizing blood pressure. For this position the man is on his back in a relaxed position and the woman is upright, facing him, on her knees and on top of him. She does not move; it is the man who moves up and down beneath her. The woman must spread her legs appropriately to be able to hold this position properly.

For increasing blood production, high blood pressure or other blood-related problems, the man lies on his back while the woman sits on top facing him. The woman remains passive while the man moves

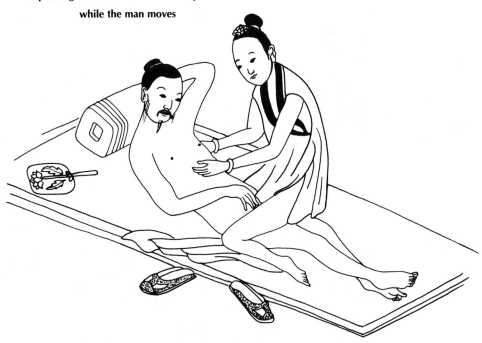

FIGURE 8-12

The Sixth Position Increases Blood Count

G. POSITION SEVEN IS FOR LYMPHATIC SYSTEM PROBLEMS (FIGURE 8-13)

This position improves the functioning of the lymphatic system. The man again lies on his back and relaxes while the woman kneels over him facing toward his feet on her hands and knees. The man penetrates and moves in this position. The woman can move slightly if she chooses, but basically it is the man who is giving the healing.

For problems related to the lymphatic system, the man lies on his back, the woman over him on her knees. The woman remains still, while the man moves in sets of nine

FIGURE 8-13
The Seventh Position is for Lymphatic System
Problems

H. POSITION EIGHT IS TO TONE THE ENTIRE BODY (FIGURE 8-14)

This position is for healing the body in general. It is a difficult position. The woman is on her knees and bending all the way over backwards, as far back as she can go. The farther she can bend and the closer she comes to a backbend, the more ideal. If it is impossible to go very far, use a pillow to prop yourself up, and bend as far back as you can without hurting yourself, spreading the legs wide enough so that the man can penetrate from the front. He performs most of the movement.

For all-purpose healing the woman should lie on her back with the legs bent at the knees and the back flat on the bed. The man penetrates from the front, moving in sets of nine

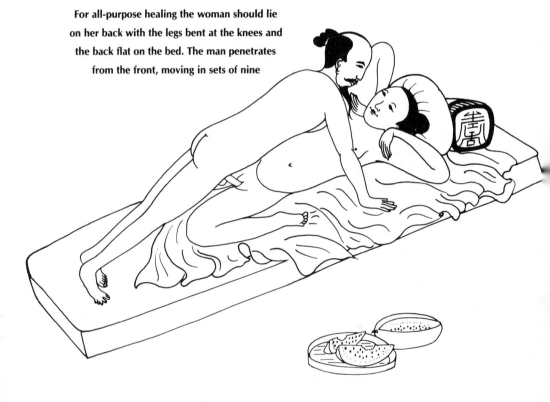

FIGURE 8-14

The Eighth Position is to Tone the Entire Body

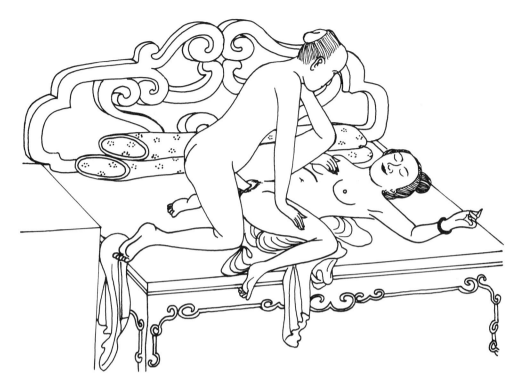

FIGURE 8-15
The Ninth Position is for Lack of Energy

I. POSITION NINE IS FOR LACK OF ENERGY (FIGURE 8-15)

This position is for those who feel weak all the time, have blurry eyes, perspire frequently and profusely, often feel faint, experience fast heartbeats, or any similar symptoms. During contact in this position, the woman is basically the one who moves, rotating her hips in a circular pattern, and it is she who does the healing. If the man becomes too excited and in danger of ejaculating, the woman has to rest for a while. The man can perform the Big Draw to regain control or rest so that he does not ejaculate. The woman is on her back, and the man, leaning on his hands so as not to put all of his weight on her, penetrates from the front as deeply as possible. This will allow enough room for the woman to rotate, first nine times in a clockwise direction, resting, rotating nine times in a counterclockwise direction, and then

FIGURE 8-16

The Tenth Position Heals the Sexual Glands and
Organs, the Endocrine Glands, and the
Pancreas and Liver

resting again. If it is comfortable, she can rotate all the way around. She is doing the work, and should continue to do so until she feels she has generated enough energy. This can be practiced nine times a day for ten days.

J. POSITION TEN HEALS THE SEXUAL GLANDS AND ORGANS, THE ENDOCRINE GLANDS, THE PANCREAS AND LIVER (FIGURE 8-16)

This position helps to heal and improve the functioning of the sexual glands, sexual organs, endocrine glands and liver. It is particularly good for those suffering from diabetes. For this position the woman lies on her back and wraps her legs around the man's thighs, not his buttocks or back. The man penetrates shallowly an inch and a half using only the head of the penis. The woman rotates her hips both clockwise and counterclockwise for nine times and then rests. Initially, she can rotate nine times in one direction and then rest, and then return nine times in the opposite direction and rest.

230

3. Basic Hand Positions to Energize the Body (Figure 8-17)

Using hands to assist in the circulation of sexual healing energy in the Microcosmic Orbit to energize the system is one of the most important aids in this Taoist practice. During lovemaking the more you can extend and draw an orgasm upward rather than outward, by performing the Orgasmic Draw while your male partner uses the Big Draw to draw in his own sexual healing and control the loss of semen, the more the sexual energy can be increased. At this point if we can guide the energy flow into the proper channels, the benefit will be tremendous.

There are distinctions among our different energy centers which expand as our awareness expands. As we open ourselves up and discover these distinctions, we open ourselves to their possibilities. It is important to realize that even when you keep yourself open to recognize the distinctions as they exist in you, others may recognize some you may not be aware of. Do not let your ego limit you. As your awareness expands, it is the quality of your maturing awareness that makes the distinctions. Working at something to develop awareness of it and being able to make distinctions are what opens up a subject for us.

The first area in which you begin to feel the energy is in the sex centers, which, as you have learned, are located differently in men and women. In males it is found at the base of the penis and the pubic bone area, while in females, in the Ovarian Palace. When the sex center is not activated and becomes "closed," many different sexual difficulties arise, as well as feelings of self-destructiveness, self-hatred, a negative attitude and orientation toward life, low or no energy or enthusiasm, and listlessness. The feeling is agitated and lazy at the same time. This all promotes violent behavior. Bring your attention to this area and radiate, like the sun radiates, your sexual energy from your organs. When energy begins to move and the sex center begins to open up, the sense is one of creative and personal power, with the ability to get things done. There is an appreciation for fun and pleasure in life, and vitality.

The perineum area has the characteristics of being grounded, solid, and peaceful when it is open, resulting in a certainty and a security within ourselves and a security within change. When it is closed, there is paranoia, or fear, of change. Feeling insecure, wishy-washy, fickle, upset or lonely are the sensations experienced. During the process of your practice, when energy is stuck there, you can feel shaking, jerking or chills. Radiate your sexual energy down into the perineum and create a star or sun glowing there that is beautiful. Feel grounded, solid, peaceful, filled with certainty and the ability to be secure within change. You are now ready to bring the sexual energy to the first energizing point.

A. THE SACRAL PUMP ENERGY POINT

As you or your partner approach orgasm and you practice your respective Draws, exchange the excess Yin and Yang energies and feel the orgasm move upward. Lie still and quiet for a moment, embracing each other, and put both of your palms on your partner's buttocks, with the fingers touching the crest of the buttocks, and the palms covering the buttocks toward the sacrum. (Figure 8-17) The man should do the same to the woman in each of these exercises. Feel the sexual healing energy from your partner's hands pass to your buttocks and give you assistance in raising your own sexual healing energy up the spine. At the same time slightly pull up the vagina and the front part of the anus, and then pull up the middle and back part of the anus to draw up the sexual healing energy to the Sacral Pump. Feel a warmth and tingling in the sacrum, or other sensations as this point opens up.

Enjoy this moment of peace. Feel the tension and stress begin to melt away in the legs, hips, pelvis, chest and head as you radiate this point. Think of this point as the place containing rootedness to past

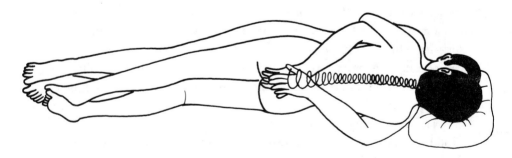

FIGURE 8-17
The Sacral Pump Energy Point

and present that goes down into the legs, connecting with the nerves there. When it is closed, the past seems a prison, housing unconscious fears and hopelessness that things will remain as they always have been, never improving. Sense and radiate at this point all the treasures in your past that will become your resource, and the blossoming of all your deep potentials as they become part of your daily living, balancing you in time and space. The feeling is often wide because the energy is awake everywhere. Here is the place where we can blend the earth energy, sexual energy and refined energy. Take as long as you wish to enjoy this point.

B. THE KIDNEYS' ENERGY POINT

When the feeling in the sexual organs subsides, the energy flow is low and you can resume lovemaking, building up to the height of sexual healing energy. Perform the Orgasmic and Big Draw again, exchange the excess Yin and Yang energies, and embrace again in stillness. Both partners should now place their hands and palms on the other's left and right hips with the fingers touching each other on the hips, and the palms covering the hips and facing toward the kidneys and adrenal glands. (Figure 8-18) These points are key energy sources. At the same time slightly pull up the front, middle, and back parts of the anus and bring the sexual-healing energy up to the Door of Life point (located opposite the navel between Lumbar 2 and Lumbar 3). Hold the energy at this point for a while, then slightly pull up the left and right part of the anus, bringing more energy directly to the kidneys. Wrap the sexual energy around the kidneys like a cocoon, and then pack the energy into the kidneys.

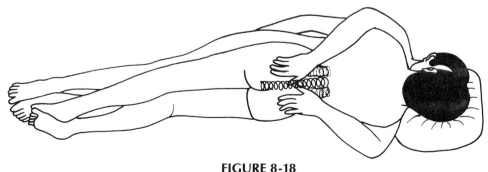

FIGURE 8-18
The Kidneys' Energy Point

The Taoist system regards the kidneys as transformers. When the kidneys are strong, they fill with CHI pressure, enabling them to perform the very important task of cleaning out the toxins and waste materials which have become embedded in the cells. Once the toxins are cleaned out, the cells will energize. Taoists also regard the kidneys and each kidney's surrounding area as the places where prenatal energy (our principal energy) and sexual essences are stored. The refined foods, pollution, toxins, etc., of modern life gradually deplete the kidneys as a source of energy. Energy depletion from the kidneys, blockage of energy flow, or a closing of the kidney point are believed to be major causes of many disturbances, such as back pain, imbalance, depression, the feeling of being taken advantage of and fear.

(1) EXCESSIVE LOSS OF SEMEN CREATES FEAR

Excessive loss of sperm energy drains the kidneys. This depletion is the major reason for fear in men, causing them to lose confidence in sex and in life, not an uncommon situation for men in today's world. Using sexual stimulants creates a speedy depletion of a man's sexual energy, similar to trying to pour gasoline onto old half-burned wood: you only speed up and use up the vital energy stored in the body that is so necessary to life. If your partner ejaculates, holding him at these specific kidney points will be the most important way to revitalize him, thereby helping him to recover lost energy much faster than any kind of drug or sexual stimulant.

Holding your partner's little fingers can also help to overcome this fear. The little fingers are the beginning and ending of the heart and small intestine meridian. When the kidneys generate fear, this fear will first affect the adrenal glands, and these glands will stimulate hormones that affect the heart, thereby increasing the meridian energy, a condition that can tilt the whole system off balance. Holding the little fingers will regulate the flow and balance of energy. In this way your partner can recover his confidence, and give his heart to you. Remember that lovemaking is caring about each other. If he cares about you, you must care about him.

When the kidney point is open and radiating, there is a sense of openness, generosity, abundance and balance. All fears are outshone in that radiance.

C. THE ADRENAL GLANDS POINT AT T-11

When you feel that the sexual energy is low, resume lovemaking to the point of high energy. Next move the energy up to the rejuvenation energy center, or Thoracic-11 (T-11), located at the spinal joint of the two lowest floating ribs. You and your partner should put the heel of both palms on each of these lowest ribs with the palms covering between the second and third lumbar vertebrae. (Figure 8-19) These areas are where the kidneys are located, above which the adrenals rest. The adrenal glands, located on a long muscular band which can be felt along the entire back in this area, secrete certain hormones to increase the growth and vital force of the trillions of cells of the body. It is the adrenal glands that will make cells last longer and stay younger.

Our modern lives abound with tremendous stress. We are fearful on the streets, in planes, and in the working place. We are burdened with all kinds of excitement, such as the stimulation of television or radio commercials constantly trying to sell more things to us. All of this stress depletes the adrenal glands' function, and this depletion locks the adrenal glands' point and becomes the main cause of hypertension, listlessness, depression, sadness, frustration, insomnia and low-key performance.

To bring the sexual energy to the adrenal glands, slightly pull up the front, middle, and back of the anus, and thus the Chi Muscle. Pull the sexual energy up to T-11 and feel the energy there. Then contract the left and right anus and pull up more energy to the kidneys and the adrenal glands. Wrap and pack the energy there, and feel the warm sexual energy vitalize the glands. Remember that these exercises can be performed simultaneously by both partners.

When the adrenal glands' point is open, you will feel energetic, confident, filled with a sense of vitality, and the ability to get things accomplished.

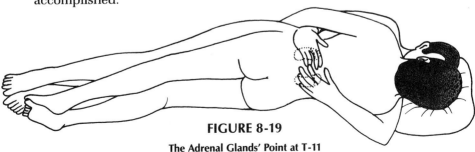

FIGURE 8-19

The Adrenal Glands' Point at T-11

FIGURE 8-20

The Liver and Spleen Point

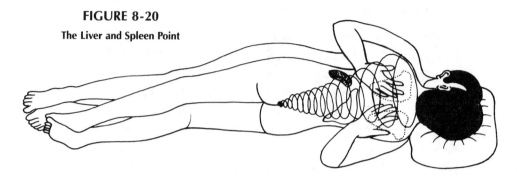

D. THE LIVER AND SPLEEN ENERGY POINT

The fourth Upward Draw (or Big Draw for your partner) energizing point is the liver and spleen point, situated at the ninth and tenth ribs and on the muscular band just below the scapulae. Put your fingers on the scapulae with the middle of the palms immediately below the lower tip of the scapulae. (Figure 8-20) As you cover this area, feel your CHI energy activate your partner's energy. Slightly contract the front, middle, back and then the left and right sides of the anus, and bring your own energy up to the liver and spleen, continuing up to the point between the scapulae. The liver is the main storage house of energy and contains the capacity for natural beauty. The liver and spleen energy point, when open, provides a sense of freedom and the ability to take risks for ourselves and others. Opening this energy point and radiating energy there can also help to relieve anger, panic, worry and anxiety, fears of the past, back pain, release the tension of the diaphragm, generate deeper breaths, and improve digestion. You might release gas and begin to yawn a great deal as your digestive system is clearing itself. You sense an opening to the present moment.

In the beginning you can practice drawing upward to one or two points only. When you are more advanced, all of these upward contractions will become more automatic, and eventually you will be able to energize the whole line of points at once. Do not, however, confuse the points with the actual organs. These points simply correspond to the organs.

E. THE HEART AND LUNGS' POINT

The fifth Upward Draw (or Big Draw) point is the heart and lungs'

236

energizing point, located between the fourth and fifth ribs. Feel the crest of the scapulae and follow each scapula down to the center point between them at the spinal cord, opposite the heart center. Use your palms to cover the area between the scapulae and the spinal cord. (Figure 8-21) Feel your energy pass to your partner and your partner's energy pass to you. Slightly contract the front, middle, back, left and right parts of the anus, and bring the sexual energy to the lungs and heart. Be very careful in pulling the energy to the heart and lungs since excess energy at these points can cause pain in the chest. The completion of the Microcosmic Orbit is very helpful in preventing such congestion. The Healing Sounds of the heart and lungs are also helpful in relieving congestion, as are brushing-down with the palms or stroking or tapping the chest. (See the book *Taoist Ways to Transform Stress into Vitality* for an elaboration of the Six Healing Sounds.)

In addition to chest pains the heart center, when closed, leaves us with a feeling of ignorance of our real relationship to things. We may feel sorry for ourselves, unloved, and incapable of love. We often feel under attack. We can feel overwhelmed, rushed, cruel, arrogant and lonely. Usually the worst feeling is one of unworthiness or lack of deserving. When that heart center is open, we feel sunshine from the inside. We have a sense of joy and love that is sometimes a floating sensation. In all of our meditations it is important to fill our hearts with loving, smiling energy, because when we feel love, we are truly related to all things. There is a sense of honor and respect. When open this point will also help to increase circulation and improve respiration, which will quickly energize the entire body. It can help to relieve

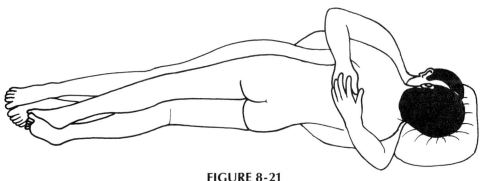

FIGURE 8-21
The Heart and Lungs' Point

upper back pain, shoulder, neck and arm tensions and pains, and provide a way to recover from tiredness. Allow this energy to circulate through your being to create the feeling of gratitude that will be the catalyst for all your spiritual work and enlightenment.

F. THE C-7 POINT

The sixth energizing point is the C-7 point, the largest protrusion of the spinal column located at the junction of the shoulder and the base of the neck. This point controls all the tendons of the body. The Taoists regard this as the great union point of the CHI flow connecting the hands, head and spine. Opening and connecting this point is very important to the practices of Healing Hand Kung Fu, Iron Shirt Chi Kung, and Tai Chi Chi Kung. (A description of these practices can be found in the last chapter of this book entitled *The Healing Tao System: Courses Given in Various Centers*.) Place your left hand on C-7 and the right hand on the sacrum. (Figure 8-22) Contract and bring the sexual energy up to this point.

The C-7 energy point, when it is closed, stirs within us the feeling of denial of our connectedness, as if we stand as individuals against the rest of the world. It also creates the feeling of being inappropriate and ill-fitting, or not being in the right place. It is demonstrated in a stubborn viewpoint, while at the same time being burdened by our inappropriateness. As the point opens up and radiates the energy, the experience is as though a mantle is being draped from our necks down onto our arms, giving us the ability to embrace each other in our humanity, opening our viewpoints and flexibility, our appropriateness, manifested in the feeling of connectedness. As the feeling spreads far-

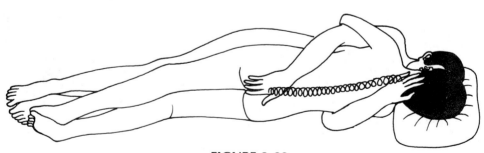

FIGURE 8-22
The C-7 Point

ther down our arms to our hands, we become more aware of the healing ability in our palms.

G. THE NECK POINT

The seventh energizing point is located at the middle of the back of the neck, between the third and fourth cervical vertebrae. Use your left palm to cover this point and the right palm to cover the sacrum as you slightly contract the front, middle, and back parts of the anus. (Figure 8-23) (There is no need to contract the left and right parts.) Bring the energy to the neck and feel the neck energize. The neck is the busiest traffic area in the body. All the controls of the body, including all emotions, are signaled from the brain and pass through this "bottleneck." When under stress and emotional strain, the neck begins to accumulate and jam with tension.

The neck is the passageway of many meridians channeling the organs' CHI energy to and from higher centers. In the middle of the neck runs the Governor Channel, while the bladder, triple warmer and large intestine meridians travel along the sides of the neck. Emotions, generating from the organs (anger from the liver, fear from the kidneys and bladder, grief from the lungs and large intestine, hastiness from the heart and the small intestine, and worry from the spleen, stomach, and pancreas) "jam" in the neck causing the neck to be stiff.

Oftentimes when your partner has lost too much sexual energy, it will result in an increase in tension, creating a greater emotional "jamming" in the neck. As a result your partner will be easily angered, fearful, and frustrated. The neck point is a marvelous place to release the tensions and emotions of your partner. Hold this point gently.

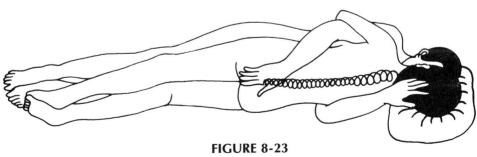

FIGURE 8-23
The Neck Point

There is no need to contract the anus, just hold your partner and mentally guide the sexual healing energy to melt the tensions and emotions away. You can lightly massage to help release the tension. This will increase your partner's relaxation tremendously.

H. THE JADE PILLOW ENERGIZING POINT

The eighth energizing point, the Jade Pillow, is located between C-1 and the base of the skull (the occipital bone) in a little hollow between two muscle bands and outside of the spinal column. Embrace your partner quietly and place your left palm over the base of the skull on the hollow place, with the right palm over his sacrum. (Figure 8-24) Feel the heat that is generated as the sexual healing energy passes to your partner while your partner's energy passes to you. There is no need to contract the anus. Use your concentration to direct your energy to melt tension and clear the mind.

Radiating the energy in the Jade Pillow will impart to you a sense of being able to draw inspiration in. This point is connected very much with our breathing, as well as a part of the brain that is located there. When it is blocked, the sensation is of a burden that is suffocating you. As you guide sexual energy to this point, and the energy accumulates there, you can work out this block. The brain revitalizes, the mind clears, consciousness increases, and memory improves. There is a limitless feeling as of a sky. As it opens, breathing becomes easier and an inspirational sensation occurs, as if something beyond our imagination can enter and operate through us. Rest your attention at this point, quieting the mind, and look into the spaciousness and luminosity. This point also influences the eyes, ears, nose, and mouth.

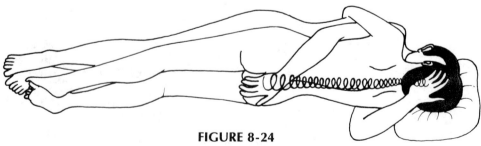

FIGURE 8-24

The Base of The Skull (Jade Pillow) Energizing
Point

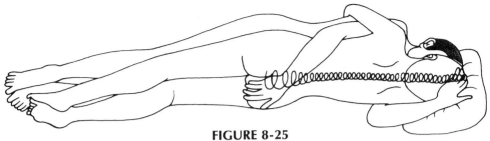

FIGURE 8-25

The Crown Energizing Point

I. THE CROWN ENERGIZING POINT

The ninth point, at the top of the head above the mid-brain, is called the crown point (the Pai-Hui, or GO-20), and is the seat of the pineal body. Its functions are related to sensitivity and the sexual cycle. The crown point governs hearing, body rhythms, equilibrium, the perception of light through the eyes and skin, and is the superior countersupport of the brain and spinal cord. In Chinese it is called the "Hundred Point Joint."

When the crown energy point is closed, we do not feel in charge of our lives, but rather out of control and reckless. We are filled with delusions and pride, and experience eratic mood swings and headaches. When the crown is open, we are guided by higher forces. We radiate happiness, blossoming like a flower giving off a fragrance. We rule over our own expression and experience.

In the latter part of the higher Taoist practice, this point serves as a compass directing a person's soul and spirit to the place where he or she is eventually supposed to go. Once this point is fully developed, you will see a clear, creative light, giving direction and sustenance to your spirit body.

Once you reach this higher level of sexual healing energy, very slightly pull up the front, middle and back of the anus and the Chi Muscle, and bring the CHI to the top of the head. (Figure 8-25) Assist this movement by looking up with your eyes while concentrating on the highest point. In the beginning you might feel pressure or a sense of expansion in the middle of the head. This is an indication of energy reaching this point. Use your mind, your eyes and all the senses to move the energy in a clockwise motion, circulating it nine, eighteen, twenty-four, or thirty-six times, depending upon how you feel.

Again it is important to emphasize the opening of the Microcosmic Orbit. With the Orbit open, you will easily be able to guide the sexual healing energy up to the top of the head, and when energy has filled this point, it will overflow, pouring down to the middle of the eyebrows where the pituitary gland is housed. The Taoists regard this point as the "Original Cavity of the Spirit." The crown energizing point houses the master endocrine control gland, the pineal gland, regulating growth, gonadal, adrenal and thyroid functions.

J. THE THIRD EYE POINT

The third eye point, located between the eyes in the center of the forehead, radiates like sunshine, or the opening of a flower, as the sexual energy flows down from the top of the head to this area. When the forehead is open there is a sense of purpose, a direct and simple knowledge, an intuitive wisdom and sense of direction in life. A sense of your own personal being emerges. As the positive energy accumulates there and ripens, you smell fragrances, taste the nectar trickling down onto the tongue, or see a beautiful, blue pearl. When closed, the feeling is of the mind wandering and indecisive, fickle, and often agitated. An internal dialogue of self-criticism and invalidation continues endlessly. When this center is closed, you feel you have no direct knowledge or perception.

K. THE THROAT CENTER

From the third eye point, the energy will continue to flow down to the nasal passages, the palate, the tongue, the throat center. The throat center is located at the notch at the base of the throat and top of the sternum. It is a place of communication and change. When open, our expressions flow, both verbal and non-verbal. This point has the power of the word: what you say and what you ask for come about. Openness in that center promotes speech, so that the sentences we use are the ones we live out. An open throat center also brings about lucidity in dreams, the expressions between our souls and our other selves. When the center is closed, you can feel choked up, as with guilt, and you may have difficulty swallowing, as if there were a lump in the throat. You may feel an unwillingness to change. Feel the energy radiate into the throat, as though you are sunbathing there. Let go of all things and all memories of that closed feeling. Feel the throat open and blossom with the power of speech. Be aware of the lucidity in your dreams and a flexibility manifested in your ability to express yourself.

The energy continues to flow down to the heart center again, at the middle of the breast, one inch from the lower end of the sternum. This heart center point is a very important point in the woman's practice. It is the seat of energy transformation, and thus the seat of healing and loving energy in a woman. From the heart point the energy will flow down to the solar plexus, and then down to the navel.

L. THE NAVEL CENTER

As the navel center opens, we feel a sense of balance, equanimity and centeredness, of allowing ourselves to be as we are, and everything else to be as it is, which takes no effort. The experience is one of mindfulness. An open navel center allows us to let things be, put a value on everything, and feel true abundance. When it is closed, there is a lack of balance and centering. The navel center is a storage place for excess energy, and so is a storage place for the energy of our work. As we continue to bring the energy to the navel center, the navel naturally centers and opens. As you feel the energy accumulating in the navel, you will find it to be the place of value, the original connection you had with your mother, and the place of nourishment as you came into this world. Here we feel the natural abundance of all things.

Try to practice holding one point at a time, and move up one by one in sequence. Do not practice all the points in one session in the beginning. Once you feel that all your partner's channels are open, you can choose the appropriate points to use at that time. Judge by the needs of your partner. Discuss the hand positions ahead of time with your partner, describing what you would like to accomplish, and share the entire book with him so that he can understand the practice. Your mutual understanding and working together on the practices described here will result in harmony.

Once you have completely opened your partner's back channel with the help of your hands, you can use the hands to help speed up the flow of sexual energy.

C. Step-By-Step Practice to Balance and Harmonize the Total System

While your sexual organs are in contact with your partner, you are joining with his or her front channel, the Functional Channel. The energy flowing through each one's Functional Channel is more easily joined when there is sexual arousal. At this time a lot of energy is generated from the organs and glands, and it all flows down to the sexual region. Remember that if you do not redirect it up, the most vital force that your body creates will be lost to the universe, with no benefit to you at all unless your intention is to bear a child.

1. Guide the Aroused Sexual Energy up the Spine

Begin by guiding the aroused sexual healing energy up the spinal column to the points listed below one at a time with the assistance of the hands. As you become more advanced in the practice, you can put your hands on different points, thereby causing the energy to jump faster.

A. THE KIDNEYS' POINT

Start with foreplay to bring your partner, or your partner to bring you, up to the boiling point. Remember that if the organs, glands and sexual energy are not ready when you engage in lovemaking, there will be less energy to exchange. This can be harmful to the organs, glands, and sex organs. When you feel the sexual healing energy is activated, embrace each other for a while. Then both of you can begin to use your hands simultaneously, or one can singularly touch the other if you both choose. Put your right hand on the sacrum with the middle finger touching the tip of the coccyx and the palm covering the sacrum, especially the opening of the sacral hiatus. (Figure 8- 26) Feel the heat being absorbed into the spinal cord as it helps to activate the Sacral Pump which moves the energy upward. Place your left hand on the Door of Life, opposite the navel and between Lumbar 2 and Lumbar 3. Feel the sexual energy moving upward from the sexual region, past the sacrum and up to the kidneys' point. Use the anus muscle to hold and guide the energy up, if necessary. At this time you can inhale to pack and wrap the sexual healing energy, bathing the kidneys with healing, creative and generative energy.

244

FIGURE 8-26

Move the Energy to the Kidney Point

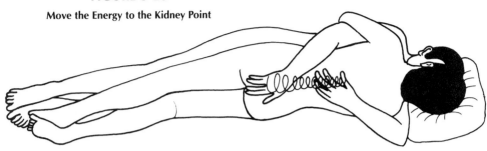

B. THE T-11 POINT

When you feel the sexual energy level is low, your partner or you should resume a three shallow—one deep, a six shallow—one deep, or a nine shallow—one deep series of penetrations. Taoist Masters discovered the G-Spot many thousands of years ago. In all their manuals on sex they always advised shallow thrusts because the glans, or head, of the man's penis will stimulate the glans, or clitoris, of the woman, and fit right behind the pelvic bone where the G-Spot is. Build the energy to the point in which both of you can exchange the energy. Embrace quietly for a while with the right hand still holding the sacrum, and move the left hand to the T-11, the point of the adrenal glands. (Figure 8-27) Hold this position until both of you feel the energy move.

FIGURE 8-27

Move the Energy to the T-11 Point

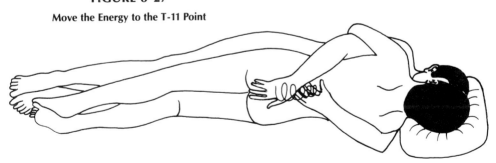

C. THE LIVER AND SPLEEN POINT

Repeat the above step, but this time move the left hand to your partner's liver and the spleen point, below and between the scapulae. (Figure 8-28)

FIGURE 8-28

Move the Energy to the Liver and Spleen Point

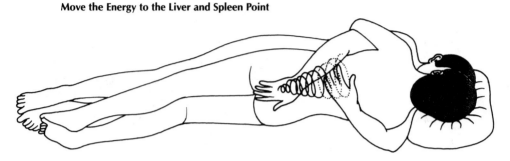

D. THE HEART POINT

Repeat step (b) again. After both of you have built up to the height of sexual-healing energy, embrace again. The right hand remains at the sacrum and the left hand moves to the heart point, located opposite the heart center and between the fourth and fifth ribs. (Figure 8-29)

FIGURE 8-29

Move the Energy to the Heart Point

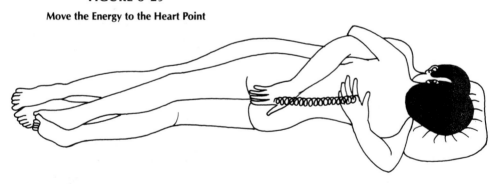

E. THE C-7 POINT

Build the sexual energy to its highest point again and embrace. Maintain the position of the right hand and move the left hand to the C-7 point at the base of the neck. (Figure 8-30) Feel the sexual energy being drawn up, activated by your partner's palms, the anus Chi Muscle, and the eyes-mind concentration.

246

FIGURE 8-30

Move the Energy to the C-7 Point

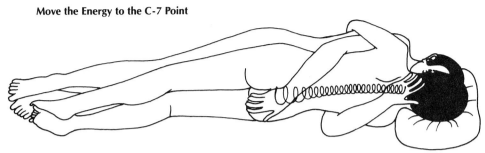

F. THE JADE PILLOW POINT

Build up the sexual energy and embrace. The right hand remains on the sacrum. The left hand is moved to the base of the skull. (Figure 8-31) When you join this point with the sacrum point, you will activate the Sacral Pump and Cranial Pump, and so will greatly feel the flow of sexual energy. The consistent increase in the activity of these pumps is very important to your health, and mental and spiritual practice.

FIGURE 8-31

Move the Energy to the Jade Pillow Point

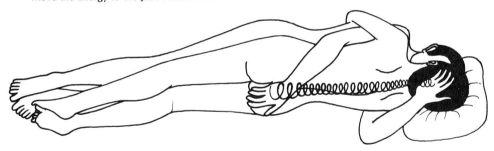

G. THE CROWN POINT

Build up to the highest point of sexual energy arousal and embrace, with the right hand remaining on the sacrum. Move the left hand to the top of the crown. (Figure 8-32) If the channels are well open, you will gradually feel energy flow like a fountain of youth up to the head, and then a sprinkling of the energy in the brain. Once it fills

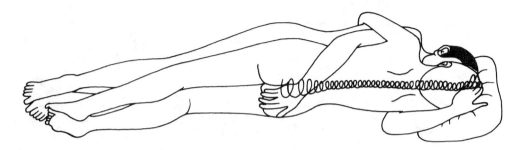

FIGURE 8-32

Move the Energy to the Crown Point

the brain, the energy will shower down the front channel to the tongue, the heart, and then down to the navel.

H. EXCHANGE THE ENERGY USING THE EYES, NOSE AND TONGUE

Now look into your partner's eyes. At this point there is a lot of energy in the eyes that can be exchanged. You can feel that you are looking into your partner's soul. His and your eyes, like magnets, draw and pull from each other. At this moment the energy exchange through the eyes and tongue is very deep.

Rub your nose against your partner's nose. Feel a spark of energy jump from one to the other.

Move your tongue into your partner's mouth. Touch his tongue and massage it with your tongue. Feel the sparkling energy pass from your tongue to your partner's tongue. The fragrance of the energy flowing from mouth to mouth, from palate to palate, is beyond words.

The eyes, nose and tongue of each of you help to join and encourage the flow of sexual energy down the front channels. If you and your partner now have a lot of saliva, be sure that you both are in good health before swallowing it.

I. CERTAIN TIMES OF THE DAY HEIGHTEN THE HEALING EFFECT (FIGURE 8-33)

The Taoists believe that the organs of the body and their corresponding meridians are activated and stimulated during certain times

248

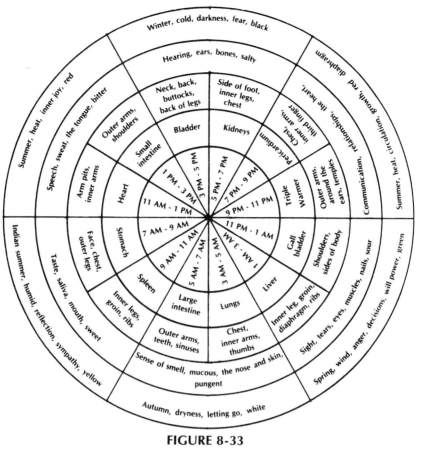

FIGURE 8-33
The Body Clock Chart

of the day. Since good health exists when there is a complete balance of energy within the organs and meridians of the body, sexual activity, being stimulating and energizing when properly done, can further deplete a body that is suffering from an energy imbalance when practiced at a low energy time. Since the sex act leaves a person open and vulnerable to universal energies, it is wise to choose a time when the universal energy will be beneficial.

The best time for sex is in the early morning when your body is well rested. A particularly bad time for sex is in the late evening, especially when you are tired or under emotional stress, because the organs' energy is not strong enough to handle the sexual energy. A nap or rest beforehand is recommended if this is the only time convenient for you.

The hand positions described in this chapter are used in most of

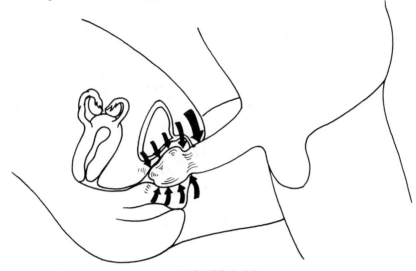

FIGURE 8-34

To help the man delay or stop ejaculation, the
woman grips tightly with her vagina the head
and shaft of the penis

the positions that we described previously in this chapter. These positions can help you and your partner stimulate each other in one particular area of the sexual organs to initiate a greater reflex of the organs. But the most important part of the practice is to open the channels so that the sexual energy can abundantly flow directly to the organs and glands to stimulate them as well. Once you master the opening of the channels, you can direct the sexual energy more with your mind and less with your hands, or without using the hands entirely.

Try to practice one position at a time to make sure you both feel the opening of the channels. If you are quite sure you are open, make sure that your partner is also open. If you cannot open your partner's channel, you can send some more of your sexual energy to him, or if you cannot open your channel, your partner can send his sexual energy to you. When a woman sends her sexual energy at this time, as well as during the time of exchanging energy, she enhances the lovemaking and helps her partner by squeezing his penis tightly. First she must be sure that her partner is in a safe stage of arousal, or he may ejaculate. Squeeze and hold for a while, then release. (Figure 8-34)

Exhale and mentally send the sexual energy to the point where your partner needs help, covering it with your palms. With practice you will feel your energy pass more easily through your hands to reach the point that you intended. You will sense the energy, even taste it.

D. The Valley Orgasm

A Valley Orgasm is the means to attaining more pleasure, more healing energy, and more energy to transform into a higher spiritual energy. A Valley Orgasm in a man occurs when he is 99 percent of the way to ejaculation. At this point he pulls out of the vagina and practices the Big Draw to milk his prostate gland of semen, and rather than release it outwardly, send it in an inward and upward direction where the energy will be transformed. He relaxes, allowing the sexual organs to settle down to approximately a 60 percent arousal, and then he begins again by practicing sets of nine shallow-one deep penetrations to bring him again 99 percent of the way to ejaculation. Again he does the Big Draw, the exchange, and then relaxes, settling down a bit and then coming back up again. Each time he draws back and sends the energy upward, he doubles and triples his sexual energy. He can continue to multiply it in this way and draw the energy to higher centers as long as he does not let the sexual energy escape. Sexual energy is the one energy that can be multiplied without end and can continue increasing. Each time the orgasmic feeling will come up higher than the last time; each time it is brought through the Microcosmic Orbit to all the organs and glands. This kind of higher center organs' and glands' orgasm is very different from the lower orgasm which is confined to the genitals, very brief and leads to vital energy loss.

Do not confuse the orgasm with ejaculation; they are two different things. An orgasm can last as long as you want, and can travel as high as you want. Once the man has ejaculated, however, the orgasm is gone. The most pleasurable time is the peak of the orgasm right before ejaculation. Many people want to go beyond that point, however, and if they have not been trained to control it, the point beyond ejaculation will be the end of the orgasm, and thus the end of the buildup of sexual energy at that time.

The Valley Orgasm in women is more intense than in men. Women

251

can achieve almost as high an orgasm as they desire, and can cultivate their orgasm higher and higher. In an earlier chapter we stated that women do not lose much energy in normal sex, and that most of their energy is lost during menstruation. Even though women can have an ejaculation during sexual intercourse as men do, they lose only fluid and not an egg. Men during ejaculation lose about 200 million sperm. Women can arrive 99 percent of the way to the point of orgasm, perform the Orgasmic Draw to bring the orgasm higher in the Microcosmic Orbit, exchange energy with the organs, rest, and begin again to achieve a higher orgasm. Each time the woman holds back, the sexual energy doubles, triples and keeps on growing as long as she holds back, drawing the energy upward and inward.

Compared with men, women have a much easier time learning the sexual draw exercise, since women do not have to control ejaculation. Also, the emotional hookup that ties men to their ejaculations is not true for women and their periods. The notion of reducing menstrual tension does not threaten most women's view of their femininity.

1. Increasing Sexual Energy through Several Upward Draws

As we have described, in a Valley Orgasm we use several upward draws to bring the energy inward and upward. It seems that the more that is drawn up, the more energy is produced again in inexhaustible amounts, provided the energy is not released outward. This drawing up or holding back consists of one round of both partners approaching 99 percent of orgasm, drawing the sexual energy up, and controlling the sexual organs to return them to 60 percent orgasm. Each time you perform the upward draw you will increase internal energy significantly, and it will become more and more internal. Instead of losing all that energy as in ordinary sex, and feeling depressed and exhausted afterwards, after an upward draw you will have more energy than before and feel refreshed and filled with healing energy.

In some cases people have so much tension and anger that when they allow their sexual energy to release outward, they feel they have released the tension too. However, in actuality, the tension is building up again and now they have no other way to handle it. The only way to rid themselves of it is to dump out their life-force, mixing their sexual energy with anger and other negative emotions.

The ancient Taoist System described the benefits of these methods in detail as follows:

A. THE FIRST UPWARD DRAW

After you or your partner have reached the 99 percent of orgasm point and have first used the Orgasmic or Big Draw to draw the sexual orgasm energy upward, this sexual energy will rise to increase the energy of the entire body.

B. THE SECOND UPWARD DRAW

The second upward draw will strengthen the senses and rejuvenate the entire body.

C. THE THIRD UPWARD DRAW

With the third upward draw the body stats to improve the immune system to resist disease, illness, flus and colds. Many of my students have used this system to help them overcome a cold or the flu.

D. THE FOURTH UPWARD DRAW

The fourth upward draw will help to stabilize and balance the internal organs. Many people are born with misplaced or unstabilized organs. One person's ears are lower while another's are higher or of a different shape. The same thing holds true for internal anatomy as for external anatomy. In some the kidneys may be too far back, or too far forward. The stomach may be in a dropped position, the pancreas too high, or the lungs too high, too low, too big, or too small. These unstabilized organs can cause all kinds of physical problems for us. Chronic problems, unbeknownst to the afflicted individual, could be caused by a mislocation of his or her organs. A dropped stomach or uterus, for example, can be improved by the power of sexual energy. Once you can increase the internal CHI pressure, it will start to stabilize the organs.

E. THE FIFTH UPWARD DRAW

The fifth upward draw improves blood vessel problems or high blood pressure, and, in an anemic's case, increases blood production.

F. THE SIXTH UPWARD DRAW

The sixth upward draw can help to strengthen lower back problems.

G. THE SEVENTH UPWARD DRAW

The seventh upward draw strengthens the extremities, bones and bone marrow.

H. THE EIGHTH UPWARD DRAW

The eighth upward draw can help to strengthen the spleen and the body's aura. This will help to protect the person from bad emotions being thrust upon him or her externally.

I. THE NINTH UPWARD DRAW

The ninth upward draw will help to build and strengthen the spiritualized body, and serves as spiritual food.

J. THE TENTH UPWARD DRAW

The tenth upward draw is a completely spiritualized or psychic state, not limited by time and space.

2. Dual Cultivation of the Valley Orgasm

A. SOLO PRACTICE AS PREPARATION

Initially the Orgasmic Draw is physically demanding. However, with solo practice the orgasm is moved more smoothly from the genital area up to the brain by internal control and eventually is directed solely by the mind. It is important to do a lot of solo practice before attempting this with a partner, mainly to avoid discouragement. According to Shere Hite, author of *The Hite Report*, most women who masturbate achieve orgasm within a few minutes. However, with a partner a woman can prolong the arousal period and often become distinctly more aroused. The precision and timing of the Orgasmic and Big Draw come with practice. With a cooperative partner there is yet another world to experience.

B. EXCHANGING ENERGY

When you approach orgasm and do the Orgasmic Draw, the aroused ovary energy goes up to the brain. As you pump it up, this cool energy accumulates in the head. If you have practiced the Microcosmic Orbit you know that the tongue acts as a switch in your own body, uniting the two acupuncture meridians that make up the Orbit. The genitals also are a switch, and thus, no matter what your position, energy that has been built up can now be funneled into your partner's Microcosmic Orbit and vice versa.

The energy can travel in a variety of routes. One route can be from your tongue to your partner's tongue, down your partner's Functional Channel to the navel, then down to his genitals, switching over to your genitals, up your spine and round and round. It can circulate through both of your Microcosmic Orbits simultaneously, or you both might experience the energy outside of your bodies, feeling like a cocoon around you both, or a presence above your heads, etc. Since a woman's aroused energy is not as hot as a man's, your partner might perceive the cool energy from you, or you may notice warm energy from him entering your body.

Each woman's perception can be different. Some might feel cold energy, like a draft, traveling through her head. Some might feel like permitting the pulsation to go out, and then pulling it in and drawing it up.

C. SEXUAL VAMPIRISM

The issue of one partner draining the other's sexual/life-force energy is an old one in Taoist circles. Legend has it that old men in China would seek out young women who did not have any children—women who, in the old man's frame of reference, had a maximum of Yin energy. Then, without letting the woman know what they were doing, they would do the Big Draw while their penis was in the vagina, and drain out the women's Yin energy, thereby increasing their own energy at the woman's expense. A woman who masters this system can be more powerful than a man. Woman can drain a man's energy many times faster than man can drain woman's. There are many stories existing about people who have used the system in the wrong way and with the wrong intention, and who have become too powerful in an evil way. Using the system in a selfish way tends to lead to an evil energy, which will eventually destroy the practitioner. However, the same sexual energy properly used can help you achieve good health and higher spiritual attainment.

According to the Taoists, even assuming no evil intentions, the draining of a partner's energy can happen unintentionally, especially if only one partner knows the practice. The safeguard against this is the circulation of the energy through both partners' bodies. This exchange of energy eliminates the possibility of one partner gaining energy while the other one loses.

3. Transforming Sexual Energy into Spiritual Love: Cultivating the Valley Orgasm

A. YIN AND YANG EXCHANGE

"Yang can function only with the cooperation of Yin, Yin can grow only in the presence of Yang."—Yellow Emperor's Female Consultant on Sex.

Our universe changes perpetually because of the eternal flow of Yin and Yang energies. The very essence of Yin-Yang exchange is the cyclical alternation of day and night. Due to this alternating energy flow, or respiration of the heavens, living things can grow. Were there only day and no night, all would be burnt; or if there were only night and no day, nothing would have strength to grow. As living things, humans are also subject to the law of Yin and Yang exchange.

The human being can live happily only if he or she is in harmony with the principles of life. If one violates the law of the Yin and Yang interchange, by forbidding the sexual communion of Yin and Yang energy, energy will not flow in the body. The life-force will slowly stagnate and leak out. Life will become a long slide into depression, interspersed by spasms of enslavement to the passions.

If you have learned to increase your orgasm through the Orgasmic Upward Draw, you are on the threshold of a new experience. That experience will alter your perceptions of your own body and mind. It will change the way you see your lover and change your understanding of sex and love.

"Drawing Nectar up to the Golden Flower" is incomplete without the exchange of Yin and Yang energy. (Figure 8-35) The Golden Flower is the light at the crown of the head. The Orgasmic Draw pulls up and conserves your nectar, or sexual essence. It is the exchange of your Ching with your lover's that transforms it, and in the process gives you an experience of sex which is deeply shared as love. Your orgasm will be totally unlike that known as a simple, local, outward-pouring and

FIGURE 8-35
"Drawing Nectar Up to the Golden Flower"

short orgasm. As you make love over a period of time, the pleasure spreads, filling the Microcosmic Orbit and the entire body. Unlike the ordinary quick orgasm, or peak orgasm, whose thrilling moment is confined primarily to the genital area, this orgasm will deliver to you a new sense of equilibrium that will be stored in your body long after your pleasure has become a fleeting memory.

Taoists advocate the Valley Orgasm as a continual rolling expansion of the orgasm throughout the whole body, prolonging inward orgasm to a half-hour, one hour, two hours, or longer in a gradual, but ultimately greatly heightened ecstasy. You can enjoy this form of sexual love indefinitely without paying for your pleasure with your life-force.

During the Valley Orgasm, lovers can relax and have all the time in the world to share their tenderness. There is no frenzied explosion, only wave after wave of higher subtle energies bathing the entwined man and woman. The Valley Orgasm is not a technique, but rather a certain kind of experience that the lovers allow to happen to themselves, encouraged by a time-tested process.

The Valley Orgasm is made up of all the methods you have learned thus far: the Orgasmic Draw for women, the Big Draw for men, the healing positions, the hand-energized positions, and increasing sexual energy through the upward draw. All this combines to make the best orgasm you can have. Yin and Yang exchange is one of the major parts of the Valley Orgasm.

4. The Valley Orgasm Step-By-Step

A. FIRST UPWARD DRAW

(1) TIMING

Bear in mind that when the woman is active, she can control the thrusting of nine shallow-one deep in order to stimulate the glans of the clitoris and the G-Spot, with the shallow thrusts entering only approximately two inches into the vaginal orifice, thereby touching the G-Spot. When you become stimulated, start to amplify the orgasm to a higher, more intense sensation. Use the Ovarian Breathing technique, gently open and close the vagina, and slightly pull the Chi Muscle up to bring the orgasm higher. When you reach the point of orgasm, rest with the glans of your partner's penis touching the G-Spot. If it is in the proper spot, it will feel as though fitting in a slot. Rest here and exchange the sexual energy.

You must take care that your partner does not reach the point of no return. When he is near ejaculation, pull his penis out to the point of your G-Spot where the energy can be exchanged. Rest at this point. If you are good at helping your partner to stop or control the ejaculation, you can squeeze the base, not the head, of the glans of the penis, and this will block the urge to ejaculate. (Figure 8-36) There is danger in bad timing; therefore, if you do not master this firm gripping technique, your partner can lose his semen. This means that you must use this grip before the urge to ejaculate occurs, and not right at the moment of ejaculation. A firm grip accounts for the success of this technique. Important to developing this grip are the Orgasmic Draw and the Egg and Vaginal Weight Lifting exercises. Delaying ejaculation will

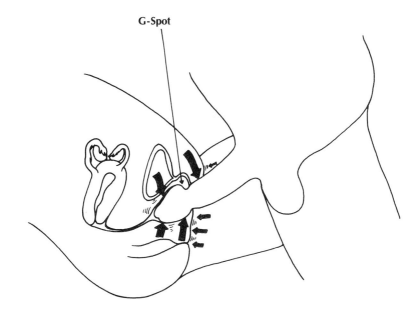

FIGURE 8-36

The woman holds tightly the head of the penis
in the area of the G-Spot. Through muscular
pressure she massages the penis

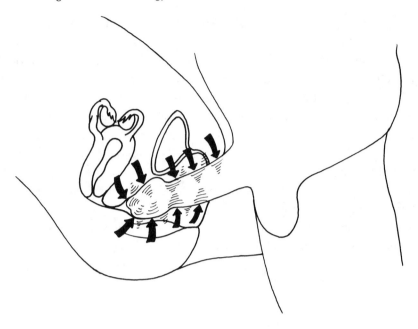

FIGURE 8-37

**The woman presses on the penis to prevent loss
of erection**

also help your partner to maintain his erection, enabling you both to proceed to the next exchange faster. (Figure 8-37) For additional information on delaying ejaculation in men, please read the section entitled "The Secrets of Semen Retention" in the book *Taoist Secrets of Love: Cultivating Male Sexual Energy*.

Relax and exchange the energy. At this point, it would be good for your partner to practice the hard contractions of the Big Draw first until he is able to move his Yang sexual energy upward and gain control of it. Once he learns and masters this, you will not have to grip the glans of his penis to assist him in this control. Feel his hot, male, Yang energy begin to pass to you. This hot energy is unlike your energy. Once you feel it, inhale and take your turn to practice the Orgasmic Draw, drawing your Yin sexual energy plus his Yang sexual energy up to the higher center. First permit the energy to flow into your Microcosmic Orbit. Then exhale, and let the cool, female Yin energy flow into your partner. (Figure 8-38) At this point your partner can use the

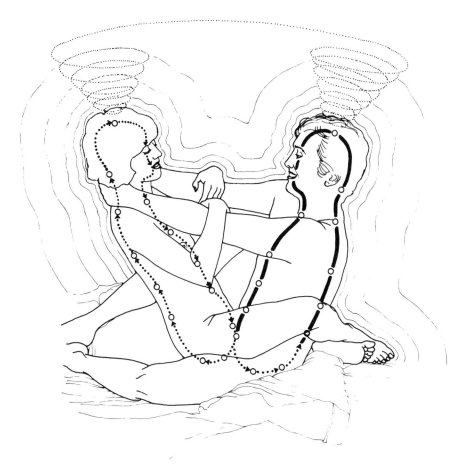

FIGURE 8-38

Exhale and let your cool, woman's, Yin energy
flow into your partner

gentleness of Testicle Breathing (as described later in this chapter) to
absorb the cold Yin testicle energy into his system.

Remember you cannot receive his power without giving freely of
your own. The exchange heals both partners. Man needs the soft re-
ceptive energies a woman provides to achieve perfect balance. Similarly, woman needs the expanding male energies to attain her own
higher harmony. This is nature's underlying reason for attraction between the sexes.

If the man has been inactive, he will now perform the thrusting. When he approaches the point of orgasm, again he should withdraw the penis to the area of the G-Spot and execute the hard contractions of the Big Draw until he gains control again, exhaling his excess Yang energy to you. You will follow with the Orgasmic Draw to draw your energy plus his upward, and send him your excess Yin energy.

(2) EMBRACING AFTER LOVEMAKING

When you cease active lovemaking, begin your embrace in any pleasing position. If the man is heavy, the woman is usually on top. If the woman is stronger than the man, she is usually on the bottom so that he can draw the power more readily. If the woman is weak, she may be on top where she can draw easily. In any case, make sure it is a position you can rest in for a long while. You should keep two extra pillows handy for this purpose.

(3) COORDINATE YOUR BREATHING WITH YOUR LOVER'S

Remember that "CHI" means "air" or "breath" in Chinese. Life is breath. All living activity has the quality of inhalation, exhalation, or some combination of the two. This is why Chinese philosophy classifies everything as Yin (exhalation) or Yang (inhalation) to a greater or lesser degree. The act of love is essentially an act of respiration. You breathe your Ching into your lover's body and soul. You inhale this life energy by drawing it up to the head, and exhale it by venting it to your partner.

It follows that after both of you have exchanged the sexual energy and embraced, you will coordinate your breathing. In a chest to chest position, each partner places an ear near the other's nose. In this position you can easily feel the other's breathing. In the act of love the breathing cycles stimulate and harmonize all of life's processes. Physically breathing together unifies the two partners and focuses the rhythm of all of their energies so that together they may contact the source of their own life current. You should become so sensitive to the presence of your partner's breathing that each deep, strong breath is as powerful as the feeling of your partner pushing his penis into your vagina.

To coordinate your breathing you will exhale deeply first and feel the Yin essence of breath penetrate into your partner. Wait for your partner to inhale and absorb this Yin essence, and then exhale, send-

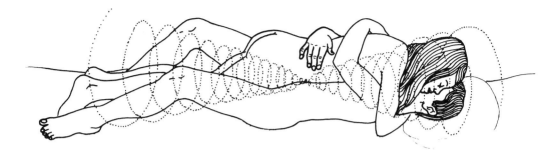

FIGURE 8-39

Absorb Yin and Yang after lovemaking

ing the Yang essence of his breath to you. (Figure 8-39) Continue to coordinate the breathing until both of you feel in balance.

(4) INHALE POWER UP THE SPINE TO THE HEAD; EXHALE OUT THE G-SPOT AND PENIS

After you breathe together for a time, gradually draw the power up to the crown of the head. Upon inhalation the man mentally conceives the Yin power moving from the vagina into the penis; the woman uses her mind to bring the Yang power from the penis into the G-Spot and clitoris. Both draw the power back to the perineum, or Hui-Yin, and the coccyx, or Chang-Chiang, and bring it up to T-11, C-7, C-1, the Jade Pillow and up to the crown, or Pai-Hui. From there the energy travels through the tongue which, throughout the entire exercise, is to be raised to the top of the mouth. The goal is not to use muscular force, as in the Orgasmic Draw or Big Draw, but simply to use the power of thought to direct the sexual energy. "Think" the energy up to the crown point. Although this instruction seems incomprehensible at first, those who have begun the practice of Sexual Kung Fu will begin to feel the power and will understand intuitively what is meant. The power will rise to the head eventually as your mind learns how to direct its own CHI energy to connect mind and body.

In the beginning you can accelerate the exchange of Yin and Yang power with the help of the hands' energizing points and long, deep, muscular contractions. When you feel the expansion and heat from the glans of your partner and your vagina fills with fluids, inhale

263

slowly and deeply through the nostrils. While you inhale, contract the vagina, perineum, anus and buttocks, and as you slightly tighten this contraction, "think" the energy into the clitoris and G-Spot, past the Hui-Yin, into the Chang-Chiang and up the spine to the crown of the head. When you have finished the inhalation, hold the breath and contraction for as long as possible. Keep drawing the power up to the head until you can hold the breath no longer.

When your partner releases his breath, consciously giving you his excess hot, Yang energy, you must exhale deeply to bestow the Yin energy upon him. Release all tension by relaxing the head, throat, chest, abdomen and pelvis. Let the relaxation spread from the top to the bottom of the body in a wave. When the gentle wave reaches the pelvic region, send the Yin energy into your partner through the clitoris and G-Spot. This contraction and relaxation should be executed gently, creating a feeling of pulsation traveling between your body and his.

Lovingly offer him the essential energy. This surrender shall carry with it all the emotions of love and devotion. This is not sentimentality. It will inspire him to surrender his nourishing Yang essence and to totally embrace the Yin within Yang. This is the nature of a woman's fulfillment. If you attempt to withhold your energy, he will sense, consciously or unconsciously, your feeling of separateness, even though it may be nothing more than an obstruction in the energy flow (usually in the heart). Allow him to absorb the Yin energy he needs as you surrender the excess. The Yang energy will flood your entire body while the Yin floods his.

If you are just beginning to practice, you may be so overwhelmed by the sensation of sexual love that it will seem impossible to distinguish his Yang energy from your Yin. Everything may seem hot and explosive and as though comprised of a single energy. As you build up your nervous system to handle higher charges of energy using the healing and meditative techniques, the exchange of Yin and Yang energy will gradually evolve into awareness. If you build energy at successive points in the body, greater powers of exchange will be available to you and your partner. Begin by drawing the power to the Hui-Yin, or perineum, and meditating there.

In this first upward draw of the Valley Orgasm, if both of you have an open Microcosmic Orbit and can circulate the healing and energizing sexual energy, the Orbits will fill with energy, passing it through all the organs and glands, thereby helping to energize the entire body system.

(5) HELPING YOUR PARTNER TO CLEAR AND OPEN A BLOCKAGE

If you have more power than your partner, help him now to open his centers by directing your power to his unopened centers. Both must concentrate on these points. The CHI will flow to whatever place the mind focuses on. Proceed one point at a time. Both can use the palm-energizing method and concentration to help open the blockage.

Remember that you cannot open all the points in one sexual embrace. To open one point may take many exchanges of Yin and Yang. If your partner ejaculates there will be no energy to exchange since most of it will be lost and little will remain to be transferred.

The resting periods are most important since it is at this time that you can actually feel the energy exchange. This is the time that you and your partner can assist each other in clearing blockages, or you can help him to open his Microcosmic Orbit.

(a) Embrace each other and then put your right hand on your partner's sacrum with the middle finger touching the tip of the coccyx and the palm covering the sacrum, especially the opening of the hiatus. Feel the heat being absorbed into the spinal column and helping to activate the Sacral Pump, which will be instrumental in moving the energy upward. Place your left palm on his Door of Life, opposite the navel and between Lumbar 2 and Lumbar 3. This will help your partner move the sexual energy up to the kidneys' area. Your partner does the same to you. Once you become adept at this and feel the point opening, move up to the next point.

(b) Move the left hand to the T-11, the adrenal glands' point, with your right hand remaining on the sacrum.

(c) Next move the left hand up to the liver and spleen point, below and between the scapulae, maintaining the right hand on the sacrum.

(d) The next point is the heart and lung point, located between the fourth and fifth ribs and opposite the heart center. Again, place the left hand on this point, leaving the right hand on the sacrum.

(e) Progress upward through the remaining points: the C-7, the middle of the back of the neck, the Jade Pillow near the base of the skull, and the top of the crown. Move onto each point gradually to make sure it is open. For more details on the hands' energizing points, refer to earlier descriptions in this chapter.

It is also possible to jump over a point if you feel you need more energy at another moment in time. If both of you are fairly open, you can both simply place your right hands on your sacrums, and your left hands on the bases of the skulls or the tops of the crowns.

(6) RETURN TO LOVEMAKING

Decide on who is to be the active one and return to lovemaking. After another round of 81 shallow and 9 deep thrusts, as you again approach orgasm or your partner ejaculation, you will gradually feel the orgasm move up the spine a little bit. It can spread to the entire back, or climb higher than the normal orgasms you have had before. With the first Valley Orgasm, feel the orgasm climb, approaching the organs. Rest, drop down into the valley again, and this time climb higher. Rest again, drop down into the next valley and climb even higher. You will find that each valley will have a different orgasmic sensation, and you will not always return to the same old valley.

B. SECOND UPWARD DRAW

Resume lovemaking, build up the sexual energy to the limit that you can tolerate. Rest with the penis glans touching the G-Spot. Permit your partner to perform the Big Draw a second time to prevent ejaculation in order for the orgasm to rise higher. When your partner releases his Yang energy, you can perform the Orgasmic Draw, bringing the energy all the way up to the head and the senses by means of the sacrum and the spine. This upward draw can help to strengthen the senses.

Using gentle contractions and pull-ups of the Chi Muscle are very important in directing the energy to the senses.

(1) BRING THE SEXUAL ENERGY TO BOTH EYES

Pull up the left and right perineum to bring the sexual energy to both eyes. When you feel either hot or cold energy at the eyes, move them around beginning with a clockwise direction (Figure 8-40(a)) and returning in a counterclockwise direction in order to absorb the energy inward. (Figure 8-40(b))

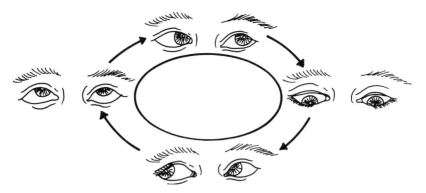

(a) Use the mind and eyes to help circulate the energy nine times,

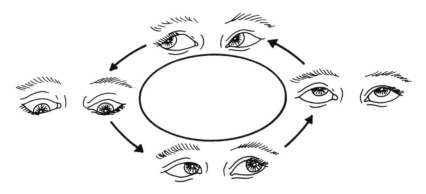

(b) and counterclockwise nine times

FIGURE 8-40

(2) BRING THE HEALING ENERGY TO BOTH EARS

Bring the healing energy to both ears by pulling up the left and right sides of the perineum and moving your ears around if possible. If this is impossible, mentally move the energy around the ears.

(3) BRING THE HEALING ENERGY TO THE TONGUE

Contract and pull up the middle part of the perineum, and bring the healing energy to the tongue. Move the tongue around.

(4) BRING THE ENERGY TO THE NOSE

Contract and pull up the front part of the perineum, and bring the energy to the nose. When finished, exchange the energy with your partner.

267

C. THIRD UPWARD DRAW

It requires practice for you to control the sexual energy well enough to proceed to the third upward draw. Proceed gradually, making certain that as you continue along each step, you have firm control over your sexual energy first. Meanwhile, your partner also plays a big part since he must control his own sexual energy.

(1) BRING THE ENERGY UP THE SPINE TO THE CROWN

Resume lovemaking, building up the sexual energy to the limit that you can take. Rest the penis glans at the G-Spot. Let your partner perform the Big Draw a third time to prevent ejaculation so that the Orgasm can be raised higher. When your partner releases his Yang energy, you can perform the Orgasmic Draw, bringing the energy through the sacrum all the way up the spine to the crown. Remember that the third upward draw helps to improve the immune system's resistance to disease. The glands, especially the thymus gland, and the bone marrow play a substantial role in a healthy immune system.

(2) USE YOUR EYES AND MIND TO MOVE THE ENERGY

When the energy reaches the brain, turn your eyes, ears, and tongue up to the pineal and pituitary glands, moving the eyes and using the mind to move the generative sexual energy for the purpose of revitalizing the glands.

(3) THE FLOW OF NECTAR TO THE THYMUS GLAND

When the pineal and pituitary glands are filled with the sexual energy, they will produce a certain kind of fluid that we have been describing as nectar. This nectar is a mixture of sexual energy and hormones released from the glands. The property of this very special kind of hormone has special life-giving and healing energy. It will flow down through the palate to the throat and thymus gland. Creative sexual energy has a very close relationship with the thymus gland, with each one enhancing the other. When there is an excessive loss of sexual or ovaries' energy, the first to be affected are the pineal, pituitary and thymus glands.

As the fluid and the energy flow into the thymus gland, you gradually will feel the gland blossom like a flower. (Figure 8-41) This will be manifested in a sensation of fullness underneath the sternum. The

268

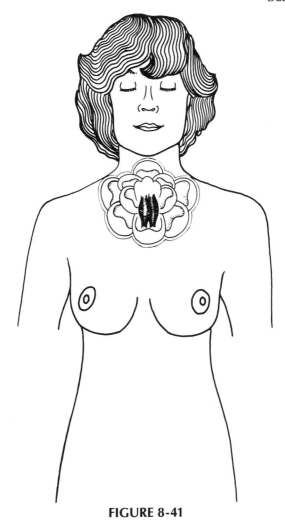

FIGURE 8-41

The Blossoming of the Thymus Gland

thymus gland is regarded by Taoists as the seat of greater enlightenment, the seat of love and the seat of life-force, or CHI, energy.

(4) THE RIBS ABSORB THE OVERFLOW OF NECTAR

Once the nectar has filled the thymus gland, the overflow of energy
will be absorbed into the ribs, thereby helping to increase bone marrow in which is produced white blood cells, which help protect the
body against foreign substances and infection. The flat chest bones
are the major producers of white blood cells.

269

D. THE FOURTH UPWARD DRAW WILL HELP TO STABILIZE THE INTERNAL ORGANS

Once you can master the third upward draw, and have filled the glands with the energy, you can begin to bring the sexual energy to the organs. Again you will employ the assistance of the Chi Muscle in the perineum region as an important aid. You will use gentle contractions and slight pull-ups to help. By the time you have reached this level of practice, your body has become more adept at controlling the sexual energy. You will now bring the sexual energy directly to the organs to transform it into a higher energy, otherwise the system can become allergic to its own raw sexual energy. The Taoist Masters discovered that all the energizing points of the spine (the sacrum, T-11, C-7, C-1, Jade Pillow, etc.) can help to transform the raw sexual energy into what will be the primary stage of life-force energy.

(1) BRING THE SEXUAL ENERGY AND THE ORGASMIC VIBRATION TO THE OVARIES AND KIDNEYS (FIGURE 8-42)

Proceed as before, approach the high point of orgasm, rest and exchange the energy. After the exchange begin to bring the energy to the ovaries and then to the kidneys. Using gentle contractions and slight pull-ups, left and right, of the Chi Muscle as an aid, bring the sexual energy and the vibration of the orgasm to the ovaries. Start with the left side first, and wrap the energy around the left ovary. Then bring the vibration of the orgasm and the sexual energy to wrap the left kidney. Gradually you will feel the energy start to vitalize the glands and organs. This orgasmic vibration felt at the ovary and kidney has a very different sensation than genital orgasm. It can feel gentle, cool, and clean, filling you with the sensational fulfillment of a true orgasm. Each organ and gland will create a different kind of orgasm from the other, but all will be different and more fulfilling than genital orgasm. Once you have mastered bringing the sexual energy and orgasmic vibration to the left ovary and kidney, begin to bring the energy to the right side. When you feel the fulfillment on the right side, bring this fulfillment to both sides simultaneously. You will gradually feel the kidneys' and ovaries' region as stronger, warmer, and filled with life-force.

You should master each organ, then gradually move on to the next one, continuing one at a time.

270

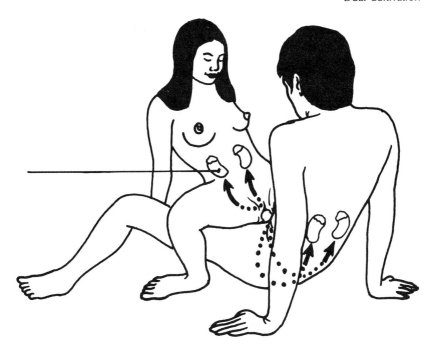

FIGURE 8-42

Bringing Sexual Energy to the Kidneys

(2) BRING THE SEXUAL ENERGY AND ORGASMIC VIBRATION TO THE SPLEEN AND LIVER

The next organs to bring the energy to are the spleen and liver. Using gentle contractions again and slightly pulling up the left and right sides of the Chi Muscle, bring the sexual energy and its orgasmic vibration up to the left ovary. Pause for a while. Bring it up to the left kidney; pause and wrap the energy and the orgasm around this kidney, inhaling and pulling it up to the left side underneath the rib cage to the spleen. Wrap the sexual energy and the orgasmic vibration around the spleen, gradually increasing the orgasmic sensation which, again, will feel very different from the other organs' orgasm, and more fulfilling than a genital orgasm. Next, bring the energy and orgasm to the right side and the right ovary, the right kidney, and then the liver. Giving a more intense orgasm than any other organ, the liver can generate the sensations of warmth, expansion, energy, loveliness, kindness, and a very euphoric and satisfying kind of feeling.

271

(3) BRING THE ORGASM AND SEXUAL ENERGY TO THE LUNGS

Next bring the orgasm and the sexual energy to the left lung, first passing through the left ovary, left kidney, spleen, and finally to the lung. Once you master the left side, begin to bring the energy to the right side, and then both sides together. Each person can have a different orgasmic feeling.

E. THE FIFTH UPWARD DRAW INCREASES THE AMOUNT OF BLOOD VESSELS AND BLOOD CIRCULATION

(1) WRAP AND ENERGIZE THE CERVIX WITH THE SEXUAL ENERGY

After the fifth exchange of energy, pull the middle part of the Chi Muscle at the perineum up toward the cervix, which has a great supply of blood flowing through it. When strong, it will help tremendously in increasing blood circulation as it is wrapped and energized with the orgasmic feeling.

(2) PULL THE ENERGY UP TO THE AORTA AND VENA CAVA

Next pull up to the aorta and vena cava, the main arteries and veins leading from and to the heart, respectively. When these are strong, the flow of blood will increase. Bringing the orgasmic vibration and sexual energy to these vessels will help increase the flow of blood through the heart. In the later practice of the higher levels of the Healing Tao, the mind is used to amplify the orgasmic vibrations in these vessels to create an even greater flow of blood.

(3) PULL UP THE SEXUAL ENERGY TO THE HEART

Next pull up sexual energy to the heart, the organ responsible for pumping the blood. Wrap and energize the heart, bring the orgasmic vibration there, and feel the heart unfold like a blossoming flower.

Remember that in attempting to bring the energy to the heart you must be very cautious, since the heart easily becomes congested with excess energy causing pain and breathing difficulties. As previously indicated, if you experience these problems, practice the Heart Sound, gently tap the chest around the heart, and brush down your chest with your hands to try to force the excess energy out of this area. Then do not practice the heart upward draw for several days. Instead, return to the fourth upward draw until you master that.

F. SIXTH UPWARD DRAW, THE PLATEAU PHASE: CIRCULATE YOUR MICROCOSMIC ORBIT INTO YOUR LOVER'S ORBIT

Depending upon the level of vital energy and the spiritual development of the individual lovers, a couple over time will experience new "openings" that occur during their lovemaking. This means you will suddenly find you have made a quantum leap in your feelings and awareness. This usually happens during the plateau phase of the Yin-Yang exchange. The period of lovemaking when you are not thrusting passionately is referred to as the "plateau" phase, as opposed to the "peaks," the moments prior to the orgasm that is averted by doing the Orgasmic Draw and Big Draw. The plateau is the physically passive exchange of energy that occurs between the peaks.

The subtle energies within your resting bodies are not passive at all, but are moving dynamically between partners, building to a new level of sexual-electromagnetic tension. It is an internal wave of energy building up, similar to an ocean wave that gathers momentum and crashes, only to be replaced by the next wave. After the sexual energy has been raised to a high intensity by thrusting and drawing it up the spine on the route of the Microcosmic Orbit with the Orgasmic Draw and the Big Draw, the Yin-Yang exchange can begin to happen in many different ways.

(1) JOINING THE TWO MICROCOSMIC ORBITS

In the beginning the energy exchange between lovers may seem to be chaotic and occurring between any two points of bodily contact. As you grow more accustomed to the energy gained by stopping the man's ejaculation, you will begin to discriminate the clearly defined channels of the Microcosmic Orbit rising up the spine and descending the front of the body. During the plateau phase of lovemaking you may feel a warm flowing current passing between your vagina and his penis and between your lips.

These are two individual Microcosmic Orbits joined into one larger flow circling your two bodies. (Figure 8-43) This experience will greatly enhance the balance of energy in both lovers and deepen the bond of loving in their life. The CHI flow is increased in amplitude: you may even feel like a warm electric current is passing between you. This effect often occurs in lovers in good health, who have practiced the

Orgasmic Draw and the Big Draw, after only a few lovemaking sessions.

Both the man's and woman's Microcosmic circuits can be joined in a number of different ways. The most common is the intersection of their two circular Orbits at the mouths and genitals, forming a figure eight. The figure eight can cross as the Microcosmic energy drawn by the man up his spine is passed into the woman through his tongue, which acts like an electrical switch. The male energy then enters her Microcosmic Orbit and travels down her front, or Functional Channel, and down through her vagina, into his penis and back up his spine.

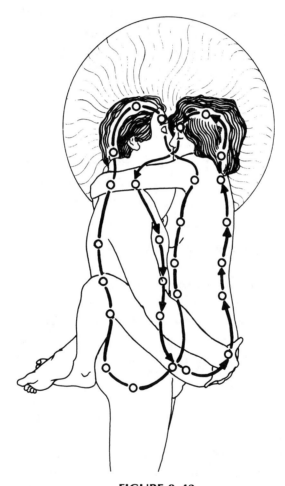

FIGURE 8-43

The Fusion of the Microcosmic Orbits

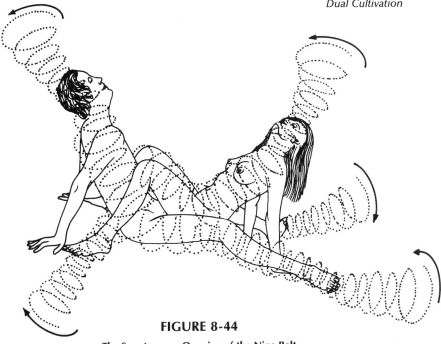

FIGURE 8-44

The Spontaneous Opening of the Nine Belt
Routes during Heightened States of Energy
Arousal

The woman circulates her Orbit in a parallel fashion, up her back channel and down his front channel, before it reenters her body at the vagina and proceeds back to her perineum and spine. This is the simplest way to direct this level of exchange of Yin and Yang energy.

Each couple can play with different figure eight patterns of exchange. At first you may verbally tell your lover what you are concentrating on. Later, as you become more sensitive to your own and your lover's energy, the CHI exchange itself will become a silent language, punctuated by the pleasure of sending a tingling warm current into your lover. The figure eight may cross at your mouths only, or at your genitals. It may snake around your Governor Channels, up your spine and down his, or vice versa.

At this level many couples experience spontaneous openings of some of the eight special psychic channels taught in the Fusion of the Five Elements Meditation of the Healing Tao. (Figure 8-44) These channels include the positive and negative arm and leg routes, the Belt Routes spiraling around the body, and the Thrusting Route up the center of the body. Do not be alarmed if your energy begins moving in ways you are not accustomed to. Many lovers experience a column of energy rising on a line midway between their bodies. If this is your experience, simply relax and enjoy the interplay of these subtle energies. Some couples report the CHI shooting up to the top of their heads and showering down a fountain of "nectar." Others feel as though wrapped in a cocoon with their lover, with lines of invisible energy being spun around them.

When you have opened all your psychic channels and you know what is possible in terms of energy exchanges, you will then be free to choose the path of expressing your love at will. It is interesting that lovers who know nothing of these esoteric methods sometimes have similar experiences during normal sex. Although unable to exchange energy at will, they do know the sensations first-hand from the spontaneous opening of their subtle energy channels. The Taoist practices of Healing Love are designed to focus your awareness on the infinite possibilities that lie within you. This concentrated awareness is what spontaneously sparks these experiences of divine energy exchange. In this sense love is universally the path to the greatest freedom; thus, the more you share with your lover, the more choices are open to you.

5. Cultivating the Valley Orgasm

The Valley Orgasm is a true fusion of two lovers' beings, shared in an intensified and balanced way. As an even higher experience of Yin-Yang exchange that goes beyond the Microcosmic, it may occur spontaneously in any couple dedicated to expanding their love and spiritual awareness. No technique can guarantee it will happen, but the methods taught here vastly increase the probability of a couple enjoying regular Valley Orgasms during lovemaking. It is a state of prolonged orgasm, the balancing of Yin and Yang, a function of opposites, a melting. However, do not be disappointed if you learn to block ejaculation and master the Orgasmic Draw and Big Draw, but do not soon have a Valley Orgasm. This happens frequently and should be expected, especially in a stressful urban setting where there are so many distracting forces working against the sustained balance of subtle energies.

A. CULTIVATION IN THE THREE TAN TIENS

During a Valley Orgasm the lovers simultaneously experience an

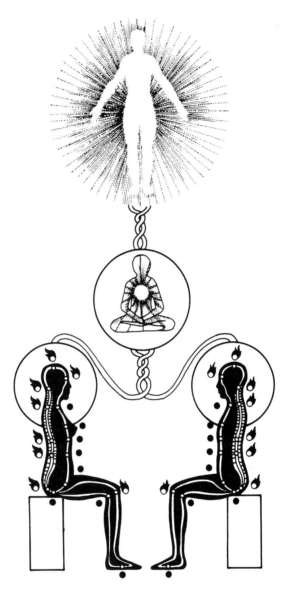

FIGURE 8-45

The Taoist Practices of Healing Love Open the
Way to Experience the Greatest Freedom

opening of a specific energy center. This releases a tremendous energy
that is truly thrilling as it radiates to fill every cell of your body and
joins you with your lover. The Hindus call these centers "chakras." The
Taoists refer to them as lower, middle and upper Tan Tiens, and locate
them in the abdomen, heart, and head. (Figure 8-45)

FIGURE 8-46

The Spontaneous Opening of the Three Tan

Tiens in High States of Arousal

In truth, the entire body is one Tan Tien, or energy center, but in practice it is easier to learn with smaller vortexes of energy until you can handle the greater power. The sequence of opening them is generally to start with the lowest center and move up. If the higher centers open before the lower ones, the energy may be unstable and short-lived. In that case the lovers should direct their higher energy into the lower centers to create a more grounded polarity. Filling the lower body with higher energies will lend greater fullness to the feeling of intimacy and create a greater foundation for future exploration of the spiritual world of the two lovers.

By opening these energy centers you transform your sexual essence into spirit. The Valley Orgasm is actually a fusion of Ching, CHI and Shen (sexual, life-force and spiritual energy) in two lovers. (Figure 8-46) All three are normally present in everyone, but in a divided and

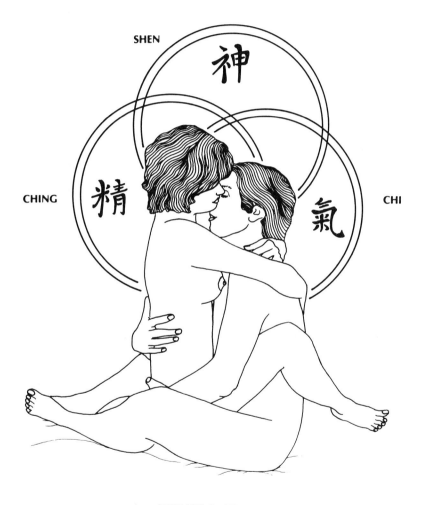

FIGURE 8-47

The Valley Orgasm is actually the fusion of
CHING (Essential Energy), SHEN (Spirit) and
CHI (Vital Energy)

279

weakened state. The two lovers can supply energies missing in their partner and bring out recessive energies with the simple presence of the opposite subtle polar energy. When you open a new energy center, your mind makes a leap in awareness by fusing these three in a spontaneous alchemical process. Your own spirit is purified and is one step closer to becoming centered in your body. It is important to know that these centers cannot be forced open, any more than a child can suddenly be forced to grow up. There are natural stages. That is why you must relax to entice the Tan Tiens to open; then you will experience a Valley Orgasm as a spontaneous gift, a sparkling jewel bestowed upon you by the Tao. This state has been described as one of profound clarity and serenity, but even these phrases are insufficient to convey its deep beauty and truth.

B. THE CULTIVATION OF DEEP RELAXATION

The more deeply you learn to relax during the Yin-Yang exchange, the more deeply you can surrender yourself to your lover, the more likely you are to reach the balance of polar forces needed to open each center. This process happens in a split second, but can take months or years of subtle fine tuning of energy between lovers. That is why a commitment is usually needed to get to the higher levels of Dual Cultivation—it requires a great deal of time to understand the play of subtle forces, and to refine your more gross physical and emotional energies.

C. THE DEVELOPMENT OF A STRONG NERVOUS SYSTEM

Your nervous system must also be strong enough to handle the increased flow of CHI experienced during a Valley Orgasm. Any Tai Chi, Yoga, Chi Kung or other purifying meditative work is invaluable in developing this kind of strength as it speeds up and clarifies the process.

D. MENTAL SPIRALING OF THE ENERGY

The Valley Orgasm can happen when both lovers have harmonized their will power and their breathing during the Yin-Yang exchange. The energy is flowing between the man and woman as they collectively focus their attentions on each center. It helps to mentally spiral the energy in a three-inch diameter circle (male clockwise, female counterclockwise) at a point about three inches inside the body near each center. You should experiment with the location of the point you focus on, as some people find the energy is more powerful a little closer to the spine.

The CHI energy likes to move in a spiraling motion; therefore, by mentally spiraling at key points, you may trigger the release of a far more powerful Valley Orgasm. This spiraling movement of the CHI itself is caused by the interaction of male and female energies. This can be seen geometrically in the symbol of the female—the circle, and that of the male—a straight line with an arrowhead. The fusion of these two signs is a spiral: a circular energy containing a linear energy moving toward the center of the circle. When a man and woman make love, the same thing occurs: the Yang CHI enters the circle of the Yin CHI. The CHI fuses, and the circle of energy expands and spirals upward through both bodies. The energy will naturally travel in a sequence, spiraling through the following centers.

(1) THE NAVEL CENTER, OR LOWER TAN TIEN

Many routes of the body join at the navel center, or lower Tan Tien. When the navel is open, all routes in the body will be joined. You will regain something of the terrific vitality of the newborn baby, for its energy has been fed to it by the mother through the navel.

(2) THE SOLAR PLEXUS

The solar plexus controls the digestive system, stomach, spleen and liver. This will greatly strengthen your health and will. At the solar plexus center the power is much stronger, purer and widespread. However, you must first open the navel for the power to flow up.

(3) THE HEART CENTER, OR MIDDLE TAN TIEN

Important to strengthening the heart, lungs and thymus gland and to amplify your power of love, sympathy and rejuvenation is your heart center. This is the center of the middle Tan Tien, and extends into the areas immediately above and below it.

(4) THE THROAT

The throat energy center is the thyroid gland and is the energy's doorway between man and Heaven. Since it controls speech, it is also known as the creative center.

(5) THE YIN-TANG, OR THIRD EYE

The Yin-Tang, or third eye, is located between the eyebrows, and controls the nervous system and soul. Its development calms the person and lessens the influence of stress and fear.

(6) THE PAI-HUI (CROWN) OR UPPER TAN TIEN

Finally, direct the power to the Pai-Hui, the crown, the center of spiritual knowledge, and the doorway to higher spiritual evolution.

6. Valley Orgasm SUMMARY

a. First make love actively, using three or six shallow strokes for each deep one, or nine shallow and one deep.

b. Stop thrusting when you feel you are approaching orgasm. Use the Orgasmic Upward Draw, or your male partner the Big Draw, to bring power up to the Pai- Hui (crown).

c. Embrace and synchronize the breathing. Place yourselves in comfortable positions without undue stress on the limbs.

d. Open the Microcosmic Orbit by directing your CHI around the circuit with the power of thought.

e. Exchange power by circulating your energy in and around your entwined bodies using meditation. Focus your attention on the polar balance of energy in your lower Tan Tien. When the power builds, move it upward in a wave toward your middle and upper Tan Tien.

f. When your energy has been transformed up, or you feel the loss of 50 percent of your arousal, start to thrust again if you wish and build up more energy, keeping the urogenital diaphragm closed, and stopping before ejaculation.

g. Exchange power several times. Each time try to bring the energy up to increasingly higher centers, meditating on each Tan Tien for as long as you feel comfortable.

The exchanging practice is a mental and spiritual operation. The higher energy in woman is different from man, a study that merits a complete undertaking and is projected for a later volume.

E. Helpful Hints

Many women who have partners will want to share the techniques learned here with their partners to enhance their mutual experiences. The following are some helpful hints in sharing the practice.

1. For Lesbian Couples

Women who share these techniques with their women partners will find it easy to communicate the information, since they both practice the same exercises. One area that the Taoists claim is important is the polarity of Yin and Yang. For Valley Orgasm to be experienced, the Taoists say that the polarity of Yin and Yang work together to produce a synthesis of their opposing qualities. If both partners are women, therefore Yin in nature, there may not be enough tension, or magnetic energy available to "lift off," as it were. One way to increase the polarization is for one partner to acquire more Yang energy. Since the most Yang source in our environment is the sun, one partner can take more sun, the absorption of which will increase her Yang energy. If possible, she can take the solar energy into her ovaries via the genitals, if she has the privacy to do this. Otherwise, she can sit in the sun and "think," or mentally direct, the energy into her ovaries.

2. In Teaching your Man

Once a woman masters these techniques, she can more easily share the information with her partner. The best way would be for him to carefully read the instructions in the companion volume, *Taoist Secrets Of Love: Cultivating Male Sexual Energy*. Short of that, a woman should know that when teaching a man, there are some essential differences that must be considered.

A. TESTICLE BREATHING

Testicle Breathing is performed similarly to Ovarian Breathing. A man has a visible testimony of his testicles lifting up with a contraction of the pubococcygeal muscle (PC Muscle). Also, temperature-wise, the energy for the man is cool or cold (remember, the ovarian energy during Ovarian Breathing is warm). Therefore, it is not necessary to emphasize bringing down this energy into the navel—the cool energy in his head will not harm the brain. He is welcome, of course, to bring the energy down to the navel and circulate it in the Microcosmic Orbit.

B. THE BIG DRAW FOR MEN

Having a partner who believes that withholding ejaculation is an acceptable idea removes one major obstacle. The will to want to try this method is already a step in the right direction, and you will soon have a partner with whom to practice and with whom to escalate the pleasure of sexual contact. Teaching the Big Draw to a man is a matter of great magnitude since men have a hard time controlling ejaculation. First of all, it will take a lot of solo practice before he feels comfortable with his control over his ejaculation. With you the additional excitement makes it more difficult to control. The role of coach and trainer, willing to guide him through the steps of the Big Draw, will serve you both best.

We have received varying reports from women students who have helped to cultivate the practice in their partners. One described her experience as if she were at a sporting event, rooting him on, which made her feel involved in his Big Draw and gave her something to do as she waited. Another women felt neglected, noting that all the emphasis was on his Big Draw. In her workshop training it was emphasized that the woman had to be patient for a time in order to help him. Therefore, attitude plays a large role in your success.

C. STOPPING EJACULATION

The Brauers, in their book *ESO: Extended Sexual Orgasm*, offer several techniques for delaying ejaculation and orgasm. One simple way is for both men and women to push down, as though having a bowel movement, and feel the genitals bulge. Holding the breath naturally accompanies this maneuver. It seems to work very temporarily, however: while you are actually bearing down the sexual sensations do not exist, then when you inhale and relax you are almost back where you started. It is, though, a chance to switch gears to a different kind of stimulation.

Another technique to delay ejaculation described in the Brauers' book is called the "scrotal pull." Its effectiveness is based on the fact that ejaculation will not occur when the testicles are low rather than being pressed against the body. You can both learn how to do this. The Bauers instruct the man to "grasp the scrotum between your testicles with the thumb and forefinger of your left hand. When you are near orgasm, pull firmly down." Another way is to "make a ring with your left thumb and forefinger between your testicles and body and pull downward."

The companion book for men, *Taoist Secrets of Love: Cultivating Male Sexual Energy*, describes other helpful techniques to delay ejaculation in men. The "Cold Water Skinny-Dip" is one method; that is, having a bowl of cold water by the bed for him to stick his penis in if he wishes to take a breather to get more control over himself. Another technique is the "Century Count," which is counting to 100 very slowly.

Sharing the techniques of the practice of Healing Love promotes kindness, understanding, selflessness, pleasure and happiness in you and your partner and is well worth the time spent in learning.

9. INTERVIEW WITH AN OVARIAN KUNG FU PRACTITIONER

The following interview with a 43-year-old Ovarian Kung Fu Practitioner and movement teacher was conducted by a Taoist teacher, Michael Winn.

Question: How long have you been practicing Ovarian Kung Fu?

Answer: For three years.

Question: Did you find the techniques difficult to learn?

Answer: I found them easy to learn, especially since from the very beginning the benefits were so immediately obvious. I was motivated to practice, but it did require a certain amount of time to completely embody them and make them a part of my life.

Question: Did you learn them alone or with a partner?

Answer: Initially I practiced alone having just ended a relationship. I immediately found they empowered me with control of my own sexual energy, and rediscovered sexuality as a resource for cultivating myself.

Question: What do you mean by resource?

Answer: In the sense that the Taoists speak of cultivating one's nature, refining energy for personal and spiritual development, with sexual energy being one raw material from which that refinement is accomplished. I actually had the experience of being able to direct my sexual energy within my body, and watch it transform my body and my emotions.

Question: Did you have a sense of sexual energy as a resource before you began Taoist practices?

Answer: No, not specifically as a resource. I felt confused after growing up in this Western culture which perpetuates a sense of separation of body and spirit. I am naturally a very sensuous person and totally enjoy the physical aspects of sex. I always had a sense of the mystical quality or spiritual communion possible in a sexually and emotionally intimate relationship. I longed for inner union and knew I would need to experience that union within myself before I would be able to experience it with a partner. This longing fueled my spiritual quest, leading me to meditation and eventually to the Taoist sexual practices.

Learning the Taoist sexual practices helped ground my meditations in my body and in my daily relationships. I was attracted to them because of the value placed on harmonizing heaven and earth, spirit and body. Sexual energy became for me a valuable resource as a fuel for my spiritual journey. I discovered I could enjoy sex and transform it into spiritual energy at the same time. The pleasure of sex actually became more intense and exquisite. Pleasure became ecstasy and ecstasy grew into bliss.

Question: Does this mean that sex is now something that you can have with yourself?

Answer: Yes. Almost like a twenty-four-hour-a-day experience of my being alive as a sexual being. That energy is now there and available to me constantly. Before I was stuck in a bit of a polarity: I was either blocking the sexual energy if I wasn't in a relationship in which I could express it, or feeling impelled to get involved in a relationship in order to experience it. Now I feel more sexually aroused and alive. I feel my energy is at its fullest potential, and am more "turned on" by life all the time. Now I don't feel that I always have to interact with a man in order to express it. Because my sexual energy flows in clearer channels, I can tolerate a higher level of energy without feeling an urgency to discharge it.

Question: What happens with the sexual energy when you are not interacting and making love?

Answer: When I first began doing Ovarian Breathing, I discovered immediately that I could move the sexual energy easily from my genitals throughout my whole body. It's very simple, but very powerful. I can increase my ability to be connected and present in life. Over time I have been able to refine it so that I can share more energy with other people in my work and daily relationships. It doesn't come across necessarily as purely sexual, but I know it is my sexual energy that I have transformed into healing and loving energy.

Question: Do you think that men are more attracted to you now that you do the Ovarian practice?

Answer: They seem to be.

Question: Has it changed the kind of men that you attract?

Answer: I would say that I seem to be more attractive to people in general. Although I seem to be more attractive to men, judging by the feedback that I get, I am attracting in a way that feels comfortable. I do not feel that men are leering at me. I used to feel that whenever I was strongly in touch with the full power of my sexual energy that I was somehow putting out a strong sexual message, inviting a kind of response that I really didn't want. Now I feel that people are interested in me as a whole person.

Question: Would you call this a personal magnetism?

Answer: Yes. A personal magnetism.

Question: Have you ever practiced Ovarian Kung Fu with a man?

Answer: Yes. I practiced by myself for about three months, and then I was very fortunate in attracting a man who had been doing the Taoist sexual practices for a period of time.

Question: During those first three months, did you see any changes in your menstrual period, or did you experience any other physical changes?

Answer: My periods had been healthy and trouble-free so I really didn't notice any change. But friends who have begun the practice who have had any kind of difficulty before have experienced dramatic improvement in terms of a relief of menstrual cramps, a shorter flow, and fewer pre-menstrual symptoms.

Question: What about emotions? Sexuality is supposed to be linked with emotions in many different ways. Once you began this practice, did it change your connection to your emotions?

Answer: Yes. Since at the time I began Ovarian Kung Fu I was already involved with other Taoist practices, it's difficult to differentiate which was having the effect on my emotions. I know that the Fusion of the Five Elements, Part I, had a profound effect on my emotional state since it involved recycling negative emotions into a purer form of energy. Combining that with the Taoist sexual practice, I gained a tremendous sense of personal responsibility, of being in charge of and able to direct both my sexual and emotional energy.

Question: Do you feel the Fusion and Ovarian Kung Fu practices go together?

Answer: Yes. It is wonderful to do the Taoist sexual practice with a partner, but it is extremely helpful to do the Fusion practice because it keeps the emotional energy so clear. It puts a relationship on a wholly different level without the normal kind of emotional confusion that often comes into a male-female relationship.

Question: Do you feel it is dangerous for someone to do just the sexual practice if it is not balanced by clearing out all the negative emotions?

Answer: I would say that really depends upon the person. If two people are very responsible about their emotions, acknowledging them so that they are able to let them go, then they will probably do well with just the sexual practices. But they would still benefit from doing the rest of the meditation practices as well. For couples who have any emotional confusion, I would say it is essential to do Fusion at the same time as the regular sexual practices.

Question: Do you know of anyone who is doing these practices who has had problems with them?

Answer: No, I don't. Everyone I know who has practiced them has been quite enthusiastic about the benefits.

Question: And there are no side effects?

Answer: I have never known anyone, male or female, who has had any side effects. This practice allows sexual energy to be transmuted and not just conserved. It also refines and spreads it throughout the body, revitalizing the whole body in mind and spirit. So the practice itself removes the negative side effects of sexual desire, which for most people appears as sexual frustration. Sexual frustration is simply blocked sexual energy.

Question: Once you became involved with your lover, did you find a big difference between the other lovers you've had who were not doing these practices?

Answer: Yes. It was quite dramatically and wonderfully different. This relationship, which continues happily, has all the elements that had been wonderful in my other relationships in terms of closeness and pleasure, but goes far beyond anything that I have ever experienced before. The whole quality of the relationship is very clear.

We experience very clear communication, a flow, and a true bonding on many, many levels that I hadn't experienced before. We are connected emotionally, mentally and psychically, and are often able to know what the other is thinking. We feel that even at long distances we are able to make love. We have a feeling of the spiritual connection that is very, very satisfying.

Question: What about women who learned the practices but who have been unable to find a man who would do these practices? Do you have any friends like that?

Answer: I think everyone I have known who has learned the practices has wanted to find a partner. It is interesting to me that people I speak with about the benefits of the practice are all initially cynical and suspicious. Most of us experience a lot of our greatest pleasure in life sexually, so we do not really want to give up the known for the unknown. Since this practice has spiritual benefits, most people think that it won't feel quite as good on the physical level. People are often a little reluctant initially to try. But everyone I know, once they learn the practices, wants to find a partner with whom to practice because they find the quality of their sexual experience far more pleasurable and satisfying, and they want to find someone with whom to share.

Question: What problems exist for the woman who does the practice, while her partner does not?

Answer: The quality of these relationships is probably better than previous relationships. Some of the refined sexual energy spills over, and the partner probably picks up on it on subconscious levels.

Question: Do you think there is danger of abuse, of someone drawing the energy out from the other person, something like "sexual vampirism"?

Answer: A method can always be abused. It is very important for anyone planning to do these practices with a partner to have a clear commitment to sharing fully to attain mutual spiritual growth.

Question: Can you describe your experience of orgasm with your partner?

Answer: The orgasm is a Valley Orgasm, rather than a Peak Orgasm. I experience a slow wave of energy rising within me. This actively stimulating phase rises to a prolonged peak of excitement, then I deeply relax in the "valley" for a period. I repeat this cycle two, three or more times. Each succeeding peak of excitement is higher and each valley is more deeply relaxing so that more and more of my whole body-mind-spirit is at the same time aroused and deeply surrendering.

The Valley Orgasm occurs spontaneously in the state of deep relaxation, and it is a very powerful experience which I feel in every cell, every particle of my being as an exquisite, ecstatic melting. The feeling of connection with my partner is profound. My whole being is shared with his, and his with mine, as one flow that knows no boundaries.

Sometimes our awareness expands to include the whole cosmos, and there is a powerful sense of being omnipresent and a part of all things. Sometimes the orgasm has felt like nuclear fission and fusion occurring simultaneously, as though I am both expanding infinitely and fusing into a point of nothingness. I have experienced a tremendous spectrum of sensations each time. In the beginning sometimes we spent the whole day making love and meditating with the energy we generated. I am always in awe of the tremendous power residing in male and female. We are all closer to being gods and goddesses than we think.

Question: Are you able to distinguish your energy from his during the cycling and sharing?

Answer: I definitely can distinguish his energy and can also feel the quality of the merging. I had been practicing the Microcosmic Orbit Meditation for about a year before I began doing the sexual practice, and had practiced the Single Cultivation of Ovarian Kung Fu for several months before actually being with my partner. Because my partner was also experienced in the practice, our merging was really spontaneous without any need to control it. I could feel from our first sharing the energy moving naturally into the Microcosmic, Belt and Thrusting Channels. If you meditate in these channels daily, your lovemaking energy will flow effortlessly into them.

Question: How long do you make love during this practice?

Answer: Several hours. Sometimes two hours, sometimes three or four. Quite frequently we experience the peaks and valleys all night, but with naps during some of the valleys. There is a saying that in love there is no sense of time. This really describes Taoist lovemaking. There is a sense of all the time in the world, of being in eternity, and of having more and more energy available. Now that we have created so many connections, we don't really need to spend as much time. Once we made love for only 30 seconds before experiencing a Valley Orgasm, but the polarity between us was so powerful that the Valley Orgasm lasted for hours. Now we are much more tuned to each other and feel that we are making love all the time.

Question: Are these cycles of the peaks and valleys determined by the male's erection?

Answer: I would say that the cycles of peaks and valleys is determined by both people. Both partners move to greater and greater excitement, and when a partner feels he or she is coming to the point of no return, then both partners pull the energy up to mingle it and share it in the quiet valley stage. It has always seemed spontaneous when another crest and wave begins, drawing both of us into it.

Question: During that resting period when you have reached the high peak of stimulation and have allowed that CHI energy to move up the body until the whole body feels tingling, warm and vibrant, is there a danger of feeling unconscious with this energy?

Answer: If I'm extremely fatigued there is a tendency to be more unconscious with it. My experience in general is of going into a totally altered state, finding a melting point with my partner in which I am very aware and yet very at ease. Then I can meditate and further refine our lovemaking.

Question: The technique of the Valley Orgasm as it is described requires you to meditate at different levels, or Tan Tiens. Did you find yourself able to meditate at specific centers with this energy?

Answer: It's very hard to generalize because every experience is unique. I found initially that the energy first moved in the Microcosmic Orbit, but I also started noticing that it would move through the whole body. It would tend with each valley to move up through another center. There would be times in the valleys when it would seem like a showering-up, sometimes more in the center or in the back, while at other times it would be like the rush of a rocket taking off, straight up.

Question: Does this feeling linger after lovemaking?

Answer: There is the sense of being a unique male and female each in our respective bodies, and yet being all man and all woman, god and goddess. I have clearly experienced this before in other sexual relationships, but in this relationship it exists all the time.

Question: After practicing in this relationship for almost three years, what has been the evolution of this practice?

Answer: I would say that one of the aspects of all the Taoist practices is the sense of active awareness of drawing energy in directly from the stars, the sun, the earth, and from one's sexual partner. What I feel is that I have been able to absorb, be nourished by, and bring into my own life some of the real masculine, Yang, qualities of my partner. With my partner's Yang energy as a resource available to me, I have been able to be more assertive, more creative, and more outspoken. The exchange with my partner of the whole essence of his being has enabled me to amplify my own personality and to include his qualities.

Question: How has the male energy you absorbed affected your daily meditations?

Answer: I want to be more integrated, including integrating the male and female energies within myself. Becoming more integrated and more balanced is one of the benefits of this practice. Being able to exchange with my partner has really enhanced my spiritual growth.

The same energy that could have been lost at times in emotional confusion or through miscommunication has become an energy resource that is available for my own growth. There is clarity that is illuminating in terms of my emotional and spiritual life. It is also more refined energy. My partner's energy is now available for my spiritual growth, and my energy is available for him.

Question: What do you feel is the highest level of this practice?

Answer: Refinement of one's own sexual, emotional, and mental energies into subtle spiritual energy and into a spiritual body that lives within the physical body, yet is free to move anywhere in time and space is the highest level. The sexual practice conserves and refines the fuel, but it is within the Kan and Li meditations that the real alchemy occurs. The essence of the Kan and Li practice is fire and water, male and female energies uniting creatively within each Tan Tien or center in the body.

Through the self-intercourse of Kan and Li, one impregnates oneself, nourishes the fetus, and finally gives birth to a spiritual child that dwells within. Then the challenge is to nourish the spiritual child with strong, refined energy and virtue through the ups and downs of daily living. And how does my partner fit into this? I enhance his self-generation as he helps me with mine.

Question: You can be both the mother and father of this spiritual child by having the additional help of outside masculine energy?

Answer: Yes. What I like so much about the Taoist practices is that in cultivating our own nature, we attain our fullest flowering and give birth to ourselves. With a partner in Dual Cultivation, there is obviously an added energy and mutual support in addition to joy and pleasure. I also know that I can cultivate my own sexual energy myself, and be creative with it.

Question: Do you feel the sexual cultivation practice is essential to your spiritual growth?

Answer: Yes, but it is not essential to have a partner. These practices can be done by a woman who has a commitment to celibacy as a way of utilizing her sexual energy for her own spiritual growth and directing the transformed energy toward service to others. For a woman who does want a partner eventually, Single Cultivation allows her to take her time to choose her partner well without rushing into a relationship purely to satisfy sexual needs. So I would say Single Cultivation is essential. Dual Cultivation is valuable, but optional.

There is something else that I feel is very important since we are talking about the benefits. From the beginning these practices were very transformative, enhancing my sense of being in control of my own energy and my own destiny. I have grown more responsible and able to use my energies creatively.

Question: Is the Tao all about controlling your emotions and energies? How does this figure in being effortless and flowing free?

Answer: I think about life as a river. Before I practiced Fusion and Ovarian Kung Fu, I felt in my emotional and sexual life as if I were a leaf on a current, and it was the current of circumstance that would sometimes direct me. Now, knowing these Taoist practices, I feel that I am more like a raft, and I can use the current for the purpose of following the river. When I look at my past and all the suffering that I went through in some of my emotional and sexual relationships, and I look at friends now, I see that the Taoist practices allow us to be in the river in a way that's harmonious and flowing without being knocked against the rocks. We are the navigators.

Question: Let's talk a little about the psychology of relationships. How do you feel this practice changes the psychology of the battle of the sexes?

Answer: I think it is essential for both partners to enter into a relationship with the intention of moving the energy up and fully sharing, because it is an exchange of energy designed to be redirected toward growth. This growth will naturally take its own direction, emotionally and spiritually. As the energy moves up during the practice, it takes care of itself. Everything else will flow naturally from that. The power struggle tends to dissolve. When things occur that must be clarified, the tools are available. It seems there is a harmony and a flow that is present that really extends far beyond the sexual act. There is also the other tremendous benefit of feeling attuned to the other person, wherever he might be.

Question: Why do you think this happens?

Answer: My experience is that as the energy moves up there are bondings, at the heart level, and at the mental and spiritual level, and those bondings are very profound.

Question: I have some specific questions about the actual technique. Do you really feel the energy flow up the spine in very direct pathways? It seems when you are making love these energies all get mixed together. This is a little confusing.

Answer: I think there is an interesting distinction between practicing on my own, if I am stimulating myself, than when my whole being is totally involved with another person. More of my whole body gets aroused when I am with my partner. So when the energies move up, they are more likely to expand and to fill my whole body. When I am alone I have a clearer sense of the energy going up my spine. If I'm with my partner I have a sense of the energy moving up through my whole body. Sometimes I have the sense of not only my own energy, but also of his, as one column or wave moving upward.

Question: Have you discovered any additional techniques to aid this sexual practice?

Answer: My lover and I have discovered certain things spontaneously. It requires a great deal more discipline for men to cultivate this practice than it does for women. For women, it is really control of the pelvic-floor muscles.

All I really need to do is contract my pelvic-floor muscles in the direction of my coccyx and tilt my pelvis slightly, and the energy will just begin to move up. Sometimes I will stroke up my partner's spine with my hand or he will stroke up my back as we are beginning to go into the resting phase. This gives us both the clear sense that we are directing the energy up. Sometimes we touch each other's heads on the crown, and this helps focus the energy there. The energy then begins to shower down. One of the most delicious and exquisite qualities of the Valley Orgasm is that the energy moves up the whole body and through the crown, sometimes moving out of the body, and then showers down like an exquisitely delicious nectar showering down through all the cells and all the atoms of the body.

Question: Have you found the practice has increased or decreased your sexual desire?

Answer: My sexual desire is about the same, but I feel much more satisfied. Also, my perception of sex and sexual relationships has continued to expand. I feel I am very slowly moving toward my goal of being totally alive, making love with the whole universe in every movement. I feel immensely grateful to have a partner with whom to practice loving.

We feel that we are always together, and whether we are physically together or apart, we can make love and share our energies. Our transformed sexual and emotional energies nourish our spirits and are shared with others as love.

BIBLIOGRAPHY

Anatomical Atlas of Chinese Acupuncture Points. Jinan, China: Shandong Medical College Cooperative Group, 1982.

Barbach, Lonnie. *For Yourself, Fulfillment of Female Sexuality*. New York, 1975.

Brauer, Alan P. et al. *Extended Sexual Orgasm: How You and Your Lover Can Give Each Other Hours of Extended Sexual Orgasm*. New York, 1983.

Britton, Bryce. *The Love Muscle: Everywoman's Guide to Intensifying Sexual Pleasure*. New York, 1983.

Chia, Mantak. *Awaken Healing Energy through the Tao*. New York: Aurora Press, 1983.

Chia, Mantak. *Chi Self-Massage: The Taoist Way of Rejuvenation*. New York: Healing Tao Books, 1986.

Chia, Mantak. *Iron Shirt Chi Kung I*. New York: Healing Tao Books, 1986.

Chia, Mantak. *Taoist Ways to Transform Stress into Vitality*. New York: Healing Tao Books, 1985.

Chia, Mantak, and Winn, Michael. *Taoist Secrets of Love: Cultivating Male Sexual Energy*. New York: Aurora Press, 1984.

De Smidt, Marc. *Chinese Eroticism*. New York, 1981.

Devi, Kamala. *The Eastern Way of Love: Tantric Sex and Erotic Mysticism*. New York, 1977.

Diagram Group. *Sex: A User's Manual*. New York, 1981.

Evans, Tom, and Evans, Mary Anne. *Shunga: The Art of Love in Japan*. New York, 1975.

Federation of Feminist Women's Health Centers. *A New View of a Woman's Body*. New York, 1981.

Grant, J. C. Boileau. *An Atlas of Anatomy*. Baltimore, 1972.

Gray, Henry. *Anatomy of the Human Body*. Philadelphia, 1954.

Hite, Shere. *The Hite Report*

Humana, Charles, and Wu, Wang. *The Chinese Way of Love*. Hong Kong, 1982.

Masters, W. J. and Johnson, Virginia. *Human Sexual Response*. Boston, 1966.

Nik, Douglas, and Slinger, Penny. *The Pillow Book*. New York, 1981.

Nik, Douglas, and Slinger, Penny. *Sexual Secrets*. New York, 1979.

Omura, Yoshiaki. *Acupuncture Medicine: Its Historical and Clinical Background*. Tokyo, 1982.

Shanshai College of Traditional Medicine. *Acupuncture: A Comprehensive Text*. Chicago, 1981.

Tortora, Gerard, and Anagnostakos, Nicholas P. *Principles of Anatomy and Physiology*. New York, 1981.

THE
INTERNATIONAL
HEALING TAO SYSTEM

The Goal of the Taoist Practice

The Healing Tao is a practical system of self-development that enables the individual to complete the harmonious evolution of the physical, mental, and spiritual planes the achievement of spiritual independence.

Through a series of ancient Chinese meditative and internal energy exercises, the practitioner learns to increase physical energy, release tension, improve health, practice self-defense, and gain the ability to heal oneself and others. In the process of creating a solid foundation of health and well-being in the physical body, the basis for developing one's spiritual independence is also created. While learning to tap the natural energies of the Sun, Moon, Earth, and Stars, a level of awareness is attained in which a solid spiritual body is developed and nurtured.

The ultimate goal of the Tao practice is the transcendence of physical boundaries through the development of the soul and the spirit within man.

International Healing Tao Course Offerings

There are now many International Healing Tao centers in the United States, Canada, Bermuda, Germany, Netherlands, Switzerland, Austria, France, Spain, India, Japan, and Australia offering personal instruction in various practices including the Microcosmic Orbit, the Healing Love Meditation, Tai Chi Chi Kung, Iron Shirt Chi Kung, and the Fusion Meditations.

Healing Tao Warm Current Meditation, as these practices are also known, awakens, circulates, directs, and preserves the generative life-force called Chi through the major acupuncture meridians of the body. Dedicated practice of this ancient, esoteric system eliminates stress and nervous tension, massages the internal organs, and restores health to damaged tissues.

Outline of the Complete System of The Healing Tao

Courses are taught at our various centers. Direct all written inquiries to one central address or call:

The Healing Tao Center
P.O. Box 578
Jim Thorpe, PA 18229

To place orders please call: (800) 497-1017
Or for overseas customers: (570) 325-9820
Fax: (570) 325-9821

www.healingtaocenter.com

INTRODUCTORY LEVEL I: Awaken Your Healing Light

Course 1: (1) Opening of the Microcosmic Channel; (2) The Inner Smile; (3) The Six Healing Sounds; and (4) Tao Rejuvenation—Chi Self-Massage.

INTRODUCTORY LEVEL II: Development of Internal Power

Course 2: Healing Love: Seminal and Ovarian Kung Fu.

Course 3: Iron Shirt Chi Kung; Organs Exercise and Preliminary Rooting Principle. The Iron Shirt practice is divided into three workshops: Iron Shirt I, II, and III.

Course 4: Fusion of the Five Elements, Cleansing and Purifying the Organs, and Opening of the Six Special Channels. The Fusion practice is divided into three workshops: Fusion I, II, and III.

Course 5: Tai Chi Chi Kung; the Foundation of Tai Chi Chuan. The Tai Chi practice is divided into seven workshops: (1) Original Thirteen Movements' Form (five directions, eight movements); (2) Fast Form of Discharging Energy; (3) Long Form (108 movements); (4) Tai Chi Sword; (5) Tai Chi Knife; (6) Tai Chi Short and Long Stick; (7) Self-Defense Applications and Mat Work.

Course 6: Taoist Five Element Nutrition; Taoist Healing Diet.

INTRODUCTORY LEVEL III: The Way of Radiant Health

Course 7: Healing Hands Kung Fu; Awaken the Healing Hand—Five Finger Kung Fu.

Course 8: Chi Nei Tsang; Organ Chi Transformation Massage. This practice is divided into three levels: Chi Nei Tsang I, II, and III.

Course 9: Space Dynamics; The Taoist Art of Energy Placement.

INTERMEDIATE LEVEL: Foundations of Spiritual Practice

Course 10:
Lesser Enlightenment Kan and Li: Opening of the Twelve Channels; Raising the Soul, and Developing the Energy Body.

Course 11: Greater Enlightenment Kan and Li: Raising the Spirit and Developing the Spiritual Body.

Course 12: Greatest Enlightenment: Educating the Spirit and the Soul; Space Travel.

ADVANCED LEVEL: The Immortal Tao (The Realm of Soul and Spirit)

Course 13: Sealing of the Five Senses.
Course 14: Congress of Heaven and Earth.
Course 15: Reunion of Heaven and Man.

Course Descriptions of The Healing Tao System

INTRODUCTORY LEVEL I: Awaken Your Healing Light
Course 1:

A. The first level of the Healing Tao system involves opening the Microcosmic Orbit within yourself. An open Microcosmic Orbit enables you to expand outward to connect with the Universal, Cosmic Particle, and Earth Forces. Their combined forces are considered by Taoists as the Light of Warm Current Meditation.

Through unique relaxation and concentration techniques, this practice awakens, circulates, directs, and preserves the generative life-force, or Chi, through the first two major acupuncture channels (or meridians) of the body: the Functional Channel which runs down the chest, and the Governor Channel which ascends the middle of the back.

Dedicated practice of this ancient, esoteric method eliminates stress and nervous tension, massages the internal organs, restores health to damaged tissues, increases the consciousness of being alive, and establishes a sense of well-being. Master Chia and certified instructors will assist students in opening the Microcosmic Orbit by passing energy through their hands or eyes into the students' energy channels.

B. The Inner Smile is a powerful relaxation technique that utilizes the expanding energy of happiness as a language with which to communicate with the internal organs of the body. By learning to smile inwardly to the organs and glands, the whole body will feel loved and appreciated. Stress and tension will be counteracted, and the flow of Chi increased. One feels the energy descend down the entire length of the body like a waterfall. The Inner Smile will help the student to counteract stress, and help to direct and increase the flow of Chi.

C. The Six Healing Sounds is a basic relaxation technique utilizing simple arm movements and special sounds to produce a cooling effect

Catalog-5

upon the internal organs. These special sounds vibrate specific organs, while the arm movements, combined with posture, guide heat and pressure out of the body. The results are improved digestion, reduced internal stress, reduced insomnia and headaches, and greater vitality as the Chi flow increases through the different organs.

The Six Healing Sounds method is beneficial to anyone practicing various forms of meditation, martial arts, or sports in which there is a tendency to build up excessive heat in the system.

D. Taoist Rejuvenation—Chi Self-Massage is a method of hands-on self-healing work using one's internal energy, or Chi, to strengthen and

rejuvenate the sense organs (eyes, ears, nose, tongue), teeth, skin, and inner organs. Using internal power (Chi) and gentle external stimulation, this simple, yet highly effective, self-massage technique enables one to dissolve some of the energy blocks and stress points responsible for

233

2233

33233

disease and the aging process. Taoist Rejuvenation dates back 5000 years to the Yellow Emperor's classic text on Taoist internal medicine.

Completion of the Microcosmic Orbit, the Inner Smile, the Six Healing Sounds, and Tao Rejuvenation techniques are prerequisites for any student who intends to study Introductory Level II of the Healing Tao practice.

INTRODUCTORY LEVEL II: Development of Internal Power

Course 2: *Healing Love: Seminal and Ovarian Kung Fu; Transforming Sexual Energy to Higher Centers, and the Art of Harmonious Relationships*

For more than five thousand years of Chinese history, the "no-outlet method" of retaining the seminal fluid during sexual union has remained a well-guarded secret. At first it was practiced exclusively by the Emperor and his innermost circle. Then, it passed from father to chosen son alone, excluding all female family members. Seminal and Ovarian Kung Fu practices teach men and women how to transform and circulate sexual energy through the Microcosmic Orbit. Rather than eliminating sexual intercourse, ancient Taoist yogis learned how to utilize sexual energy as a means of enhancing their internal practice.

The conservation and transformation of sexual energy during intercourse acts as a revitalizing factor in the physical and spiritual development of both men and women. The turning back and circulating of the generative force from the sexual organs to the higher energy centers of the body invigorates and rejuvenates all the vital functions. Mastering this practice produces a deep sense of respect for all forms of life.

In ordinary sexual union, the partners usually experience a type of orgasm which is limited to the genital area. Through special Taoist techniques, men and women learn to experience a total body orgasm without indiscriminate loss of vital energy. The conservation and transformation of sexual energy is essential for the work required in advanced Taoist practice.

Seminal and Ovarian Kung Fu is one of the five main branches of Taoist Esoteric Yoga.

Course 3: *Iron Shirt Chi Kung;*
Organs Exercises and
Preliminary Rooting
Principle

The Iron Shirt practice is divided into three parts: Iron Shirt I, II, and III.

The physical integrity of the body is sustained and protected through the accumulation and circulation of internal power (Chi) in the vital organs. The Chi energy that began to circulate freely through the Microcosmic Orbit and later the Fusion practices can be stored in the fasciae as well as in the vital organs. Fasciae are layers of connective tissues covering, supporting, or connecting the organs and muscles.

The purpose of storing Chi in the organs and muscles is to create a protective layer of interior power that enables the body to withstand unexpected injuries. Iron Shirt training roots the body to the Earth, strengthens the vital organs, changes the tendons, cleanses the bone marrow, and creates a reserve of pure Chi energy.

Iron Shirt Chi Kung is one of the foundations of spiritual practices since it provides a firm rooting for the ascension of the spirit body. The higher the spirit goes, the more solid its rooting to the Earth must be.

Iron Shirt Chi Kung I—Connective Tissues' and Organs' Exercise: On the first level of Iron Shirt, by using certain standing postures, muscle locks, and Iron Shirt Chi Kung breathing techniques, one learns how to draw and circulate energy from the ground. The standing postures teach how to connect the internal structure (bones, muscles, tendons, and fasciae) with the ground so that rooting power is developed. Through breathing techniques, internal power is directed to the organs, the twelve tendon channels, and the fasciae.

Over time, Iron Shirt strengthens the vital organs as well as the tendons, muscles, bones, and marrow. As the internal structure is strengthened through layers of Chi energy, the problems of poor posture and circulation of energy are corrected. The practitioner learns the importance of being physically and psychologically rooted in the Earth, a vital factor in the more advanced stages of Taoist practice.

Iron Shirt Chi Kung II—Tendons' Exercise: In the second level of Iron Shirt, one learns how to combine the mind, heart, bone structure, and Chi flow into one moving unit. The static forms learned in the first level of Iron Shirt evolve at this level into moving postures. The goal of Iron Shirt II is to develop rooting power and the ability to absorb and discharge energy through the tendons. A series of exercises allow the student to change, grow, and strengthen the tendons, to stimulate the vital organs, and to integrate the fasciae, tendons, bones, and muscles into one piece. The student also learns methods for releasing accumulated toxins in the muscles and joints of the body. Once energy flows freely through the organs, accumulated poisons can be discharged out of the body very efficiently without resorting to extreme fasts or special dietary aids.

Iron Shirt Chi Kung I is a prerequisite for this course.

Bone Marrow Nei Kung (Iron Shirt Chi Kung III)—Cleansing the Marrow: In the third level of Iron Shirt, one learns how to cleanse and

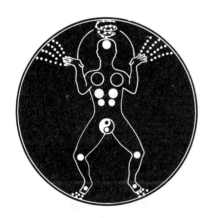

grow the bone marrow, regenerate sexual hormones and store them in the fasciae, tendons, and marrow, as well as how to direct the internal power to the higher energy centers.

This level of Iron Shirt works directly on the organs, bones, and tendons in order to strengthen the entire system beyond its ordinary capacity. An extremely efficient method of vibrating the internal organs allows the practitioner to shake toxic deposits out of the inner structure of each organ by enhancing Chi circulation. This once highly secret method of advanced Iron Shirt, also known as the Golden Bell System, draws the energy produced in the sexual organs into the higher energy centers to carry out advanced Taoist practices.

Iron Shirt Chi Kung is one of the five essential branches of Taoist Esoteric Practice.

Prior study of Iron Shirt Chi Kung I and Healing Love are prerequisites for this course.

Course 4: *Fusion of the Five Elements,*
Cleansing of the Organs, and
Opening of the Six Special Channels

Fusion of the Five Elements and Cleansing of the Organs I, II, and III is the second formula of the Taoist Yoga Meditation of Internal Alchemy. At this level, one learns how the five elements (Earth, Metal, Fire, Wood,

and Water), and their corresponding organs (spleen, lungs, heart, liver, and kidneys) interact with one another in three distinct ways: producing, combining, and strengthening. The Fusion practice combines the energies of the five elements and their corresponding emotions into one harmonious whole.

Fusion of the Five Elements I: In this practice of internal alchemy, the student learns to transform the negative emotions of worry, sadness, cruelty, anger, and fear into pure energy. This process is accomplished by identifying the source of the negative emotions within the five organs of the body. After the excessive energy of the emotions is filtered out of the organs, the state of psycho/physical balance is restored to the body. Freed of negative emotions, the pure energy of the five organs is crystallized into a radiant pearl or crystal ball. The pearl is circulated in the body and attracts to it energy from external sources—Universal Energy, Cosmic Particle Energy, and Earth Energy. The pearl plays a central role in the development and nourishment of the soul or energy body. The energy body then is nourished with the pure (virtue) energy of the five organs.

Fusion of the Five Elements II: The second level of Fusion practice teaches additional methods of circulating the pure energy of the five organs once they are freed of negative emotions. When the five organs are cleansed, the positive emotions of kindness, gentleness, respect, fairness, justice, and compassion rise as a natural expression of internal balance. The practitioner is able to monitor his state of balance by observing the quality of emotions arising spontaneously within.

The energy of the positive emotions is used to open the three channels running from the perineum, at the base of the sexual organs, to the top of the head. These channels collectively are known as the Thrusting Channels or Routes. In addition, a series of nine levels called the Belt Channel is opened, encircling the nine major energy centers of the body.

Fusion of Five Elements III: The third level of Fusion practice completes the cleansing of the energy channels in the body by opening the positive and negative leg and arm channels. The opening of the Microcosmic Orbit, the Thrusting Channels, the Belt Channel, the Great Regulator, and Great Bridge Channels makes the body extremely permeable to the circulation of vital energy. The unhindered circulation of energy is the foundation of perfect physical and emotional health.

The Fusion practice is one of the greatest achievements of the ancient Taoist masters, as it gives the individual a way of freeing the body of negative emotions, and, at the same time, allows the pure virtues to shine forth.

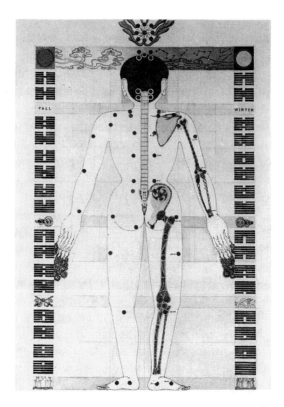

Course 5: *Tai Chi Chi Kung; The Foundation of Tai Chi Chuan*

The Tai Chi practice is divided into seven workshops: (1) the Original Thirteen Movements' Form (five directions, eight movements); (2) Fast Form of Discharging Energy; (3) Long Form (108 movements); (4) Tai Chi Sword; (5) Tai Chi Knife; (6) Tai Chi Short and Long Stick; (7) Self-Defense Applications and Mat Work.

Through Tai Chi Chuan the practitioner learns to move the body in one unit, utilizing Chi energy rather than muscle power. Without the circulation of Chi through the channels, muscles, and tendons, the Tai Chi Chuan movements are only physical exercises with little ef-

fect on the inner structure of the body. In the practice of Tai Chi Chi Kung, the increased energy flow developed through the Microcosmic Orbit, Fusion work, and Iron Shirt practice is integrated into ordinary movement, so that the body learns more efficient ways of utilizing energy in motion. Improper body movements restrict energy flow causing energy blockages, poor posture, and, in some cases, serious illness. Quite often, back problems are the result of improper posture, accumulated tension, weakened bone structure, and psychological stress.

Through Tai Chi one learns how to use one's own mass as a power to work along with the force of gravity rather than against it. A result of increased body awareness through movement is an increased awareness of one's environment and the potentials it contains. The Tai Chi practitioner may utilize the integrated movements of the body as a means of self-defense in negative situations. Since Tai Chi is a gentle way of exercising and keeping the body fit, it can be practiced well into advanced age because the movements do not strain one's physical capacity as some aerobic exercises do.

Before beginning to study the Tai Chi Chuan form, the student must complete: (1) Opening of the Microcosmic Orbit, (2) Seminal and Ovarian Kung Fu, (3) Iron Shirt Chi Kung I, and (4) Tai Chi Chi Kung.

Tai Chi Chi Kung is divided into seven levels.

Tai Chi Chi Kung I is comprised of four parts:
a. Mind: (1) How to use one's own mass together with the force of gravity; (2) how to use the bone structure to move the whole body with very little muscular effort; and (3) how to learn and master the thirteen movements so that the mind can concentrate on directing the Chi energy.
b. Mind and Chi: Use the mind to direct the Chi flow.
c. Mind, Chi, and Earth force: How to integrate the three forces into one unit moving unimpeded through the bone structure.
d. Learn applications of Tai Chi for self-defense.

Tai Chi Chi Kung II—Fast Form of Discharging Energy:
a. Learn how to move fast in the five directions.
b. Learn how to move the entire body structure as one piece.
c. Discharge the energy from the Earth through the body structure.

Tai Chi Chi Kung III—Long Form Tai Chi Chuan:
a. Learn the 108 movements form.
b. Learn how to bring Chi into each movement.
c. Learn the second level of self-defense.
d. Grow "Chi eyes."

Tai Chi Chi Kung IV—the Tai Chi Sword.
Tai Chi Chi Kung V—Tai Chi Knife.
Tai Chi Chi Kung VI—Tai Chi Short and Long Stick.
Tai Chi Chi Kung VII—Application of Self-Defense and Mat Work.

Tai Chi Chuan is one of the five essential branches of the Taoist practice.

Course 6: *Taoist Five Element Nutrition; Taoist Healing Diet*

Proper diet in tune with one's body needs, and an awareness of the seasons and the climate we live in are integral parts of the Healing Tao. It is not enough to eat healthy foods free of chemical pollutants to have good health. One has to learn the proper combination of foods according to the five tastes and the five element theory. By knowing one's predominant element, one can learn how to counteract imbalances inherent in one's nature. Also, as the seasons change, dietary needs vary. One must know how to adjust them to fit one's level of activity. Proper diet can become an instrument for maintaining health and cultivating increased levels of awareness.

INTRODUCTORY LEVEL III: The Way of Radiant Health

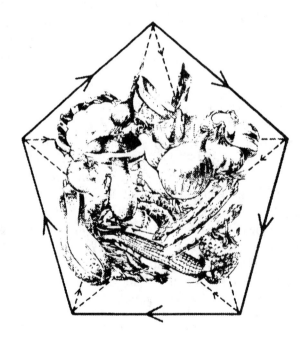

Course 7: *Healing Hands Kung Fu; Awaken the Healing Hand—Five Finger Kung Fu*

The ability to heal oneself and others is one of the five essential branches of the Healing Tao practice. Five Finger Kung Fu integrates both static and dynamic exercise forms in order to cultivate and nourish Chi which accumulates in the organs, penetrates the fasciae, tendons, and muscles, and is finally transferred out through the hands and fingers. Practitioners of body-centered therapies and various healing arts will benefit from this technique. Through the practice of Five Finger Kung Fu, you will learn how to expand your breathing capacity in order to further strengthen your internal organs, tone and stretch the lower back and abdominal muscles, regulate weight, and connect with Father Heaven and Mother Earth healing energy; and you will learn how to develop the ability to concentrate for self-healing.

Course 8: *Chi Nei Tsang; Organ Chi Transformation Massage*

The practice is divided into three levels: Chi Nei Tsang I, II, and III.

Chi Nei Tsang, or Organ Chi Transformation Massage, is an entire system of Chinese deep healing that works with the energy flow of the five major systems in the body: the vascular system, the lymphatic system, the nervous system, the tendon/muscle system, and the acupuncture meridian system.

In the Chi Nei Tsang practice, one is able to increase energy flow to specific organs through massaging a series of points in the navel area. In Taoist practice, it is believed that all the Chi energy and the organs, glands, brain, and nervous system are joined in the navel; therefore, energy blockages in the navel area often manifest as symptoms in other parts of the body. The abdominal cavity contains the large intestine, small intestine, liver, gall bladder, stomach, spleen, pancreas, bladder, and sex organs, as well as many lymph nodes. The aorta and vena cava divide into two branches at the navel area, descending into the legs.

Chi Nei Tsang works on the energy blockages in the navel and then follows the energy into the other parts of the body. Chi Nei Tsang is a very deep science of healing brought to the United States by Master Mantak Chia.

Course 9: *Space Dynamics; The Taoist Art of Placement*

Feng Shui has been used by Chinese people and emperors for five thousand years. It combines ancient Chinese Geomancy, Taoist Metaphysics, dynamic Psychology, and modern Geomagnetics to diagnose energy, power, and phenomena in nature, people, and buildings. The student will gain greater awareness of his own present situation, and see more choices for freedom and growth through the interaction of the Five Elements.

INTERMEDIATE LEVEL: Foundations of Spiritual Practice

Course 10: *Lesser Enlightenment (Kan and Li); Opening of the Twelve Channels; Raising the Soul andDeveloping theEnergy Body*

Lesser Enlightenment of Kan and Li (Yin and Yang Mixed): This formula is called *Siaow Kan Li* in Chinese, and involves a literal steaming of the sexual energy (Ching or creative) into life-force energy (Chi) in order to feed the soul or energy body. One might say that the transfer of the sexual energy power throughout the whole body and brain begins with the practice of Kan and Li. The crucial secret of this formula is to reverse the usual sites of Yin and Yang power, thereby provoking liberation of the sexual energy.

This formula includes the cultivation of the root (the Hui-Yin) and the heart center, and the transformation of sexual energy into pure Chi at the navel. This inversion places the heat of the bodily fire beneath the coolness of the bodily water. Unless this inversion takes place, the fire simply moves up and burns the body out. The water (the sexual fluid) has the tendency to flow downward and out. When it dries out, it is the end. This formula reverses normal wasting of energy by the highly advanced method of placing the water in a closed vessel (cauldron) in the body, and then cooking the sperm (sexual energy) with the fire beneath. If the water (sexual energy) is not sealed, it will flow directly into the fire and extinguish it or itself be consumed.

This formula preserves the integrity of both elements, thus allowing the steaming to go on for great periods of time. The essential formula is to never let the fire rise without having water to heat above it, and to never allow the water to spill into the fire. Thus, a warm, moist steam is produced containing tremendous energy and health benefits, to regrow all the glands, the nervous system, and the lymphatic system, and to increase pulsation.

The formula consists of:
1. Mixing the water (Yin) and fire (Yang), or male and female, to give birth to the soul;
2. Transforming the sexual power (creative force) into vital energy (Chi), gathering and purifying the Microcosmic outer alchemical agent;
3. Opening the twelve major channels;
4. Circulating the power in the solar orbit (cosmic orbit);
5. Turning back the flow of generative force to fortify the body and the brain, and restore it to its original condition before puberty;
6. Regrowing the thymus gland and lymphatic system;
7. Sublimation of the body and soul: self-intercourse. Giving birth to the immortal soul (energy body).

Course 11: *Greater Enlightenment (Kan and Li); Raising the Spirit and Developing the Spiritual Body*

This formula comprises the Taoist Dah Kan Li (Ta Kan Li) practice. It uses the same energy relationship of Yin and Yang inversion but increases to an extraordinary degree the amount of energy that may be

drawn up into the body. At this stage, the mixing, transforming, and harmonizing of energy takes place in the solar plexus. The increasing amplitude of power is due to the fact that the formula not only draws Yin and Yang energy from within the body, but also draws the power directly from Heaven and Earth or ground (Yang and Yin, respectively), and adds the elemental powers to those of one's own body. In fact, power can be drawn from any energy source, such as the Moon, wood, Earth, flowers, animals, light, etc.

The formula consists of:

1. Moving the stove and changing the cauldron;
2. Greater water and fire mixture (self-intercourse);
3. Greater transformation of sexual power into the higher level;
4. Gathering the outer and inner alchemical agents to restore the generative force and invigorate the brain;
5. Cultivating the body and soul;
6. Beginning the refining of the sexual power (generative force, vital force, Ching Chi);
7. Absorbing Mother Earth (Yin) power and Father Heaven (Yang) power. Mixing with sperm and ovary power (body), and soul;
8. Raising the soul;
9. Retaining the positive generative force (creative) force, and keeping it from draining away;
10. Gradually doing away with food, and depending on self sufficiency and universal energy;
11. Giving birth to the spirit, transferring good virtues and Chi energy channels into the spiritual body;
12. Practicing to overcome death;
13. Opening the crown;
14. Space travelling.

Course 12: *Greatest Enlightenment (Kan and Li)*

This formula is Yin and Yang power mixed at a higher energy center. It helps to reverse the aging process by re-establishing the thymus glands and increasing natural immunity. This means that healing energy is radiated from a more powerful point in the body, providing greater benefits to the physical and ethereal bodies.

The formula consists of:

1. Moving the stove and changing the cauldron to the higher center;
2. Absorbing the Solar and Lunar power;
3. Greatest mixing, transforming, steaming, and purifying of sexual

power (generative force), soul, Mother Earth, Father Heaven, Solar and Lunar power for gathering the Microcosmic inner alchemical agent;

4. Mixing the visual power with the vital power;
5. Mixing (sublimating) the body, soul and spirit.

ADVANCED LEVEL: The Immortal Tao
The Realm of Soul and Spirit
Course 13: *Sealing of the Five Senses*

This very high formula effects a literal transmutation of the warm current or Chi into mental energy or energy of the soul. To do this, we must seal the five senses, for each one is an open gate of energy loss. In other words, power flows out from each of the sense organs unless there is an esoteric sealing of these doors of energy movement. They must release energy only when specifically called upon to convey information.

Abuse of the senses leads to far more energy loss and degradation than people ordinarily realize. Examples of misuse of the senses are as follows: if you look too much, the seminal fluid is harmed; listen too much, and the mind is harmed; speak too much, and the salivary glands are harmed; cry too much, and the blood is harmed; have sexual intercourse too often, and the marrow is harmed, etc.

Each of the elements has a corresponding sense through which its elemental force may be gathered or spent. The eye corresponds to fire; the tongue to water; the left ear to metal; the right ear to wood; the nose to Earth.

The fifth formula consists of:

1. Sealing the five thieves: ears, eyes, nose, tongue, and body;
2. Controlling the heart, and seven emotions (pleasure, anger, sorrow, joy, love, hate, and desire);
3. Uniting and transmuting the inner alchemical agent into life-preserving true vitality;
4. Purifying the spirit;
5. Raising and educating the spirit; stopping the spirit from wandering outside in quest of sense data;
6. Eliminating decayed food, depending on the undecayed food, the universal energy is the True Breatharian.

Course 14: *Congress of Heaven and Earth*

This formula is difficult to describe in words. It involves the incarnation of a male and a female entity within the body of the adept. These two entities have sexual intercourse within the body. It involves the mixing of the Yin and Yang powers on and about the crown of the head, being totally open to receive energy from above, and the regrowth of the pineal gland to its fullest use. When the pineal gland has developed to its fullest potential, it will serve as a compass to tell us in which direction our aspirations can be found. Taoist Esotericism is a method of mastering the spirit, as described in Taoist Yoga. Without the body, the Tao cannot be attained, but with the body, truth can never be realized. The practitioner of Taoism should preserve his physical body with the same care as he would a precious diamond, because it can be used as a medium to achieve immortality. If, however, you do not abandon it when you reach your destination, you will not realize the truth.

This formula consists of:
1. Mingling (uniting) the body, soul, spirit, and the universe (cosmic orbit);
2. Fully developing the positive to eradicate the negative completely;
3. Returning the spirit to nothingness.

Course 15: *Reunion of Heaven and Man*

We compare the body to a ship, and the soul to the engine and propeller of a ship. This ship carries a very precious and very large diamond which it is assigned to transport to a very distant shore. If your ship is damaged (a sick and ill body), no matter how good the engine is, you are not going to get very far and may even sink. Thus, we advise against spiritual training unless all of the channels in the body have been properly opened, and have been made ready to receive the 10,000 or 100,000 volts of super power which will pour down into them. The Taoist approach, which has been passed down to us for over five thousand years, consists of many thousands of methods. The formulae and practices we describe in these books are based on such secret knowledge and the author's own experience during over twenty years of study and of successively teaching thousands of students.

The main goal of Taoists:
1. This level—overcoming reincarnation, and the fear of death through enlightenment;
2. Higher level—the immortal spirit and life after death;
3. Highest level—the immortal spirit in an immortal body. This body functions like a mobile home to the spirit and soul as it moves through the subtle planes, allowing greater power of manifestation.

HOW TO ORDER

Prices and Taxes:
Subject to change without notice. New York State residents please add 8.25% sales tax.

Payment:
Send personal check, money order, certified check, or bank cashier's check to:

The Healing Tao Center
P.O. Box 578
Jim Thorpe, PA 18229
To place orders please call: (800) 497-1017
or for overseas customers: (570) 325-9820
Fax: (570) 325-9821
All foreign checks must be drawn on a U.S. bank. Mastercard Visa, and American Express cards accepted.

Shipping
Domestic Shipping via UPS, requires a complete street address. Allow 3-4 weeks for delivery

✧ **Please call or write for additional information in your area** ✧

www.healingtaocenter.com

T.A.O. - Inc. (Transformational Assistance For Offenders)
James Cappellano, Executive Director
P.O. Box 471, Revere, MA 02151
E-mail: **taojching@msn.com**   Website: **www.tao-inc.org**

Teaching the Healing Tao to perpetrators of violence, many of who are drug and alcohol abusers, addresses the seed causes of crime and brutality. This invokes a deeper understanding of life resulting in personal transformation to a lifestyle of non-harming. It is an ideal self-help method to empower prisoners to help themselves within the confines of prison. Books and letters sent have an exponential effect with prisoners sharing the books and benefits of their practice with each other.

T.A.O. - Inc. is a non-profit organization and provides: an interactive newsletter for prisoners and instructors, a website pen-pal list, volunteer instructors and free books to inmates. The program is sustained through individual cash donations, office supplies and stamps (34¢, 55¢ & $1 are constantly needed). Contributions are tax-deductible. Please make checks payable to T.A.O., Inc. For a free copy of the newsletter please include a first-class stamp with your name and address.